Eating disorders and marital relationships

Anorexia and bulimia are on the increase in the Western world. They are now commonly recognized as disorders which affect not only teenage girls but older women as well. Most older women either do now or did once live with a partner, whether married or not, and much attention has been paid to these relationships in devising therapeutic regimes.

Eating Disorders and Marital Relationships takes a critical look at the evidence behind the assumptions of psychiatric illness in patients and their partners and comes up with some surprising results. Stephan Van den Broucke, Walter Vandereycken and Jan Norré take a scientist–practitioner perspective and look at issues such as marital satisfaction and intimacy, communication, conflict strategies, sexuality, pregnancy and parenthood. Findings in these areas then serve as a basis for the assessment and treatment of anorexic and bulimic patients.

This careful and well-balanced integration of theoretical views, empirical investigation and clinical implications makes this book important reading for practitioner and researcher alike.

Stephan Van den Broucke is a research psychologist at the Flemish Institute for Health Promotion and at the Catholic University of Leuven, Belgium. **Walter Vandereycken** is professor of psychiatry at the Catholic University of Leuven, clinical director of the Department of Behaviour Therapy at the Alexian Brothers Psychiatric Hospital in Tienen, and consultant psychiatrist at the Eating Disorders Unit at the University Centre St Jozef in Kortenberg, Belgium. **Jan Norré** is a clinical psychologist in private practice and consulting psychologist at the Centre for Fertility Research and Treatment, Leuven, Belgium. All have published widely in the field of eating disorders.

Eating disorders and marital relationships

Stephan Van den Broucke,
Walter Vandereycken
and Jan Norré

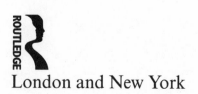

London and New York

First published 1997
by Routledge
11 New Fetter Lane, London EC4P 4EE

Simultaneously published in the USA and Canada
by Routledge
29 West 35th Street, New York, NY 10001

© 1997 Stephan Van den Broucke, Walter Vandereycken and Jan Norré

Typeset in Times by Routledge
Printed and bound in Great Britain by
T.J. International Ltd, Padstow, Cornwall

British Library Cataloguing in Publication Data
A catalogue record for this book is available from the British Library

Library of Congress Cataloguing in Publication Data
A catalogue record for this book has been requested

ISBN 0-415-13331-9 (hbk)
ISBN 0-415-14863-4 (pbk)

Contents

Illustrations

FIGURES

TABLES

Preface and acknowledgements

In recent decades, anorexia and bulimia nervosa have acquired a prominent position in psychopathology. This is largely due to the growing concern of mental health specialists with the epidemic-like proliferation of these disorders among young women, particularly in Western society. According to some surveys, approximately 10 to 20 per cent of the college-aged women in the US and in other industrialized countries are affected by an eating disorder. These figures are probably exaggerated, in the sense that they reflect the tendency for young women to be over-concerned about their weight rather than the actual incidence of the eating disorders as such. Nevertheless, it remains a fact that even if one uses more stringent diagnostic criteria, an estimated 5 per cent of the adolescent girls and young women between 16 and 25 suffer from a mild form of anorexia or bulimia nervosa, and 1 per cent from a serious form (Hoek, 1993).

At the same time, the age range of the patients presenting with these disorders appears to be expanding. Whereas until recently anorexia and bulimia nervosa were generally considered as typical disorders of adolescence, it is now commonly recognized that they may also be observed in adult women, either as a continuation of an eating disorder syndrome that originated during the patient's teens, or as one that developed *de novo* during her adulthood. Since many of these older patients are married or live together with a partner unmarried, the question can be raised of what impact an eating disorder has on the relationship with a partner, or alternatively, how the relationship with a partner influences the course of an eating disorder. This question has more than a purely theoretical relevance: if there is indeed a significant connection between the occurrence of an eating disorder and the properties of the patient's marriage, it is evident that the latter must be taken into consideration for the patient's treatment. In fact, a failure to do so would probably result in an incomplete or downright ineffective therapy. On the other hand, focusing on the marital relationship unjustly could slow down the therapy process, or reduce the patient's compliance with the treatment.

It is mainly these pragmatic considerations which have raised the interest of clinicians in the marital relationship properties of eating-disordered patients since the late 1970s. Indeed, with the proportion of married women presenting with anorexia or bulimia nervosa increasing progressively (at a certain point, one-third of the patients treated at our specialized eating disorder unit at the university hospital were married!), it was no longer justifiable to consider these patients simply as 'exceptional' cases and to follow the same treatment guidelines as for the unmarried patients. Instead, a more specific treatment approach for this patient group was in order. Hence, a number of clinical case studies about married anorexia or bulimia nervosa patients began to appear in the literature. Yet in spite of this increasing attention among clinical professionals, there remains a lack of reliable information about this patient group, and about the properties of their marital relationships in particular. Although most clinicians seem to agree that certain features of the patient's marriage play an important role in the onset, the development, the treatment and the prognosis of an eating disorder, there is no research-based evidence available to support this assumption. As a result, there is no consensus as to which particular aspects of the marital relationship are important, and how the relationship between these marital properties and the occurrence of an eating disorder must be conceived.

The apparent lack of empirical information regarding these questions is surprising in the light of two important themes which have pervaded the clinical literature in the past decades. The first one is the presumed role of family-related factors in the development and maintenance of eating disorders in adolescent patients. Ever since family therapists like Minuchin (Minuchin, Rosman and Baker, 1978) and Selvini-Palazzoli (1974) stressed the importance of such factors, anorexia and, to a lesser extent, bulimia nervosa have been promoted as *the* paradigmatic psychosomatic disorders, in which the dysfunction of the family is expressed by the child's symptomatology. Although some authors warn against an uncritical overreliance on family models which 'foster the naive conviction that by changing family interactions, a complex symptomatology as in the case of bulimia or anorexia nervosa will disappear all by itself' (Vandereycken, 1987, p. 464), there is an increasing amount of empirical evidence that family variables indeed contribute to the onset and perpetuation of an eating disorder (see Vandereycken, Kog and Vanderlinden, 1989). As a result, therapeutic work with the family has gained momentum as an indispensable component of a multidimensionally oriented approach to the treatment of eating disorders in adolescent patients.

The second theme appearing from the literature concerns the role of the marital relationship in the development and maintenance of other psychiatric disorders. Over the years, an impressive number of studies have been devoted to the marital relationships of patients suffering from disorders like depression or agoraphobia. Although many of these studies can be criticized on methodological grounds (Arrindell and Emmelkamp, 1985, 1986; Vandereycken, 1983), the impression remains that a poor marital quality contributes significantly to the occurrence of these disorders. Accordingly, the relationship with the marital partner is often considered an important focus for their treatment (Chambless and Goldstein, 1980; Hafner, 1986; Waring, 1988).

Both of the above themes fit in with an emerging trend in the social sciences, and in social psychology in particular, of paying more attention to the attributes and functions of personal relationships, as contrasted with the casual and short-lived relationships between strangers which dominated the field for decades (Hinde, 1978; Kelley, 1978). It is becoming increasingly clear that close personal relationships, like those between parents and their children or between husbands and wives, are the cornerstones of interpersonal behaviour and social contact, and as such determine the degree of well-being attained by the persons involved. To quote Jones and Perlman (1991), close relationships 'provide the context in which individual lives unfold, and the standard against which the quality of life is measured' (p. ix). The growing body of research findings demonstrating a connection between the quality of one's intimate relationships and the frequency, severity and prognosis of psychological and medical complaints is a case in point. It would appear, then, that a fuller understanding of the attributes and processes characterizing these personal relationships, as deriving from social psychological investigations, will help us explain their role in the onset and the maintenance of psychiatric disorders, and thus may guide us towards a more effective treatment.

In this book, we will rely on the emerging social psychological conceptualization of personal relationships and on the findings concerning the marital context of other psychiatric disorders to critically examine the attributes and processes which characterize the marital relationships of adult patients with anorexia or bulimia nervosa. Specifically, we will test the subjective impressions and unproven speculations about patients' marriages by looking at findings from empirical studies. Assuming a 'scientist–practitioner' perspective (Barlow, Hayes and Nelson, 1984), these findings may then serve as a sound basis for the assessment and subsequent treatment of patients according to the multimodal treatment of eating disorders proposed by many authors (e.g. Vanderlinden, Norré and Vandereycken, 1992).

The structure of the book is as follows. *Chapter 1* introduces the reader to the syndromes of anorexia and bulimia nervosa by way of summarizing their main clinical characteristics, diagnostic criteria and epidemiology. Given the focus of this book on married patients, this chapter also describes the incidence, clinical characteristics and prognosis for this particular patient group. *Chapter 2* reviews the predominant theoretical views and empirical findings with regard to the marital relationships of patients suffering from other psychiatric disorders, such as depression, alcoholism or anxiety disorders. As appears from this review, four recurrent themes seem to dominate the extensive literature on this subject: the correspondence between the patient and her spouse in terms of psychiatric illness, a lack of marital satisfaction and intimacy, a deficient communication style and inadequate conflict strategies. These four issues are further elaborated in *chapters 3 to 6*, where their presence in the marital relationships of anorectic or bulimic patients is critically examined by focusing both on the clinical and theoretical considerations and on their empirical substantiation. *Chapter 7* reviews the clinical and research-based findings regarding the sexual relationship of patients with an eating disorder, and also addresses the related issues of fertility, pregnancy and parenthood.

While all of the foregoing contributes to our understanding of these patients' marriages in relationship to their illness, the next three chapters focus on the practical implementation of this information. *Chapter 8* presents the main principles and guidelines for the clinical assessment and treatment of anorectic and bulimic patients, endorsing a research-based, goal-oriented approach based on the multidimensional process model of eating disorders. *Chapter 9* discusses how the therapist can apply the principle of empirically based practice by assessing the marital relationship of eating-disordered patients, pointing out the necessity of such an assessment as well as the possibilities and limitations of the different methods that may be used for that purpose. Finally, *chapter 10* focuses on the treatment of married patients with an eating disorder by way of discussing the possibilities of involving the husband in the treatment, and by reviewing the marital issues that must be considered during the treatment.

Taken as a whole, this book offers a blend of theoretical insight, empirical investigation and clinical experience. It is our hope that it will appeal both to researchers exploring the role of marital factors in the occurrence of anorexia and bulimia nervosa, and to clinicians involved in the treatment of these patients. But most of all, we hope that it will stimulate the exchange of ideas between those two groups, and that it will lead to a research-based practice as well as to practice-oriented research.

ACKNOWLEDGEMENTS

This book is based on a research programme at the Department of Psychology of the Catholic University of Leuven, in collaboration with the Eating Disorder Unit of the University Psychiatric Centre in Kortenberg. Neither the research nor the book would have been possible without the direct and indirect help of many people. We are specifically grateful to Hans Vertommen of the Department of Psychology in Leuven for his support and mentorship of the research programme, to Johan Vanderlinden and Ellie Van Vreckem of the University Psychiatric Centre in Kortenberg for their clinical expertise and collaboration, and to Cas Schaap of the University of Nijmegen, Kurt Hahlweg of the Technische Universität Braunschweig and Steve Duck of the University of Iowa for lending their expertise in the study of marital relationships to the studies that were at the base of this book. Finally, we thank all the couples who participated in our research programme or added to our clinical experience with this subject.

1 The nature of eating disorders in married patients

Over the past decades, eating disorders have become relatively well known both to health professionals and to the wider public. Yet in spite of this notoriety, many people have a wrong or incomplete idea of what an eating disorder actually represents. The popular view is that it stands for an 'eating problem', characterized either by overeating and being overweight or by restricted food consumption and emaciation, the latter usually affecting young teenage girls or women in their early adulthood. While this view certainly reflects the clinical features of *some* eating disorders, it also disregards their clinical complexity and diversity. The term 'eating disorders' is indeed a very broad one, which has reference to a variety of pathologies including obesity, binge eating, pica or self-induced vomiting. In many instances, however, it is used more restrictively to refer particularly to anorexia nervosa and bulimia nervosa, two syndromes which have gained prominence in the psychiatric literature of the past decades (see Vandereycken and Meermann, 1987; Vanderlinden, Norré and Vandereycken, 1992; Herzog, Deter and Vandereycken, 1992).

In this book, we will consider the eating disorders in the latter, more restrictive sense. To familiarize the reader with the syndromes of anorexia and bulimia nervosa, their main clinical characteristics and diagnosis will be summarized in the first part of this chapter. Because both syndromes occur predominantly in women, we shall refer only to female patients, noting that the characteristics and treatment of these disorders in males are essentially the same (Andersen, 1990; Vandereycken and Van den Broucke, 1984).

While it is true that the majority of patients with anorexia or bulimia nervosa are teenagers, it is increasingly recognized that these disorders occur in older women as well. In point of fact, the average age of onset in the population of diagnosed eating-disordered patients seems to be gradually increasing (Garfinkel and Garner, 1982;

Szmuckler, 1985). Many of these older patients live with a partner or did so previously, officially married or otherwise. Since these relationships are the focus of this book, the second part of this chapter will specifically address the incidence and clinical characteristics of the disorders as they occur in married women, as a preamble to the more in-depth analysis of the relationship characteristics and processes offered in the next chapters.

DEFINING ANOREXIA AND BULIMIA NERVOSA

Anorexia nervosa

Anorexia nervosa (AN) is probably the better-known type of eating disorder, and also the easier one to recognize. Its core characteristic is an irresistible urge to strive for thinness, as is eloquently expressed by the German term *Magersucht*. The term 'anorexia nervosa' itself is in fact a misnomer, for 'anorexia' means literally 'lack of appetite', whereas AN patients do not 'lack' appetite or hunger, but rather repress these feelings. In essence, their disorder is not a matter of being unable to eat, but of *not wanting* to eat, although most patients will frame this differently by referring to 'something that keeps them from eating normally and from achieving a normal body weight'.

The idea of a refusal to maintain a normal body weight is central to the diagnostic criteria for AN as proposed in DSM-IV (American Psychiatric Association, 1994) (see Table 1.1). As these criteria indicate, the root of the disorder is an all-dominating, abnormal attitude towards nutrition, body size and weight. AN patients are so preoccupied by these issues that they spend large parts of the day counting calories, thinking about food and weight, and preparing meals for others. Food is selected according to its caloric value and/or conceptions about its effect on weight, which implies that sweets and fatty foodstuffs are taboo. In addition, social situations in which one is expected to eat together with others are carefully avoided.

In association with the above symptoms, AN patients also suffer from a disturbed perception of their own body weight and shape. They typically perceive their normal weight for their age and height as 'much too fat', while their aspired weight level is far below the norm. To achieve and/or preserve an unusually low weight is considered as a form of self-mastery or self-control. However, the accomplishment of this goal yields only a temporary satisfaction: in spite of the attained weight loss the fear of growing fat remains, and the slightest weight increase is experienced as a terrifying sign of imminent loss of control.

Table 1.1   DSM-IV diagnostic criteria of anorexia nervosa

A. Refusal to maintain body weight over a minimal normal weight for age and height (e.g. weight loss leading to maintenance of body weight 15% below that expected; or failure to make expected weight gain during period of growth, leading to body weight 15% below that expected).

B. Intense fear of gaining weight or becoming fat, even though underweight.

C. Disturbance in the way in which one's body weight or shape is experienced, undue influence of body shape and weight on self-evaluation, or denial of the seriousness of current low body weight.

D. In females, absence of at least three consecutive menstrual cycles when otherwise expected to occur (primary or secondary amenorrhoea; a woman is considered to have amenorrhoea if her periods occur only following hormone administration, e.g. oestrogen).

Source: American Psychiatric Association (1994)

To avoid this, continued efforts are made to lose weight, and the subjective 'ideal' weight declines accordingly. Thus, the search for a slender figure becomes infinite.

Despite these emotional turmoils, AN patients try to keep up the appearance that they feel physically healthy and even in top condition for as long as they can. Many of them display hyperactivity and perform strongly in their studies, work or sports. Initially, they are mostly unaware of their problem, so that they do not often request help. Instead, they defend their eating behaviour and hyperactivity as 'normal' or 'healthy' and do not allow anyone to interfere with it.

To determine the seriousness of AN, the percentage of weight loss (as compared to the statistically normal weight according to age and length) is only a relative criterion. A more important aspect is the manner and speed of losing weight, along with the degree of preoccupation with body size. Patients with 'classic' or 'pure' AN, who slim only by restricting their food intake and through physical hyperactivity, appear to have a better prognosis than patients with a 'mixed' type, who also resort to self-induced vomiting and/or use of laxatives, often combined with binge eating. The latter symptoms resemble those of bulimia nervosa, which will be outlined below. However, in the case of a low body weight the diagnosis of AN must be given priority.

Bulimia nervosa

Bulimia nervosa (BN) is a relatively 'new' disorder, for it was only officially recognized as a separate diagnostic entity (simply referred to as bulimia) in DSM-III (American Psychiatric Association, 1980). *Bulimia* comes from the Greek words βουσ (*bous*, 'bovine') and λιμοσ (*limos*, 'hunger'), and means roughly 'gluttony'. Like anorexia, it is rather a misleading term, for the patient's tendency to consume large quantities of food is only one of the symptoms of BN, which occurs in a variety of other somatic and mental disorders as well. The extension 'nervosa' not only aims to differentiate between the syndrome and the symptom, but also underscores the relationship with AN. The correspondence between both disorders appears from the DSM-IV criteria for bulimia nervosa (Table 1.2).

Like AN patients, subjects suffering from BN are strongly preoccupied with their weight and afraid of growing fat. However, while the former manage to restrict their food intake in order to lose weight, BN patients surrender to frequent episodes of binge eating. To eliminate

Table 1.2   DSM-IV diagnostic criteria of bulimia nervosa

A. Recurrent episodes of binge eating, characterized by both of the following:

(1) eating, in a discrete period of time (e.g. within any 2 hour period), an amount of food that is definitely larger than most people would eat during a similar period of time in similar circumstances; and,

(2) a sense of lack of control over eating during the episode (e.g. a feeling that one cannot stop eating or control what or how much one is eating).

B. Recurrent inappropriate compensatory behaviour in order to prevent weight gain, such as: self-induced vomiting, use of laxatives, diuretics or other medications, fasting or excessive exercise.

C. A minimum average of two episodes of binge eating and inappropriate compensatory behaviours per week for at least three months.

D. Self-evaluation is unduly influenced by body shape and weight.

E. The disturbance does not occur during episodes of anorexia nervosa.

Source: American Psychiatric Association (1994)

the effect of these binges on their weight, they resort to compensatory behaviours such as vomiting (mostly self-induced), use of laxatives or diuretics, periods of fasting or rigorous dieting and excessive physical activity. These behaviours temporarily reduce the fear of weight increase, yet the preoccupation with nutrition, body size and weight persists. While initially the vomiting and purging are often experienced as signs of regained self-control after a binge, in the long run they result in an increasing *loss* of control, whereby the binges 'justify' the vomiting. This is expressed in the often-heard statement by patients that they 'are forced to vomit when they have eaten so much'. In this way, a vicious circle of self-destructive behaviour is installed.

BN patients usually have wrong conceptions of the effectiveness of these weight-reducing behavioural patterns (Mitchell, Specker and de Zwaan, 1991), and underestimate the health risks that are involved. The bingeing and purging can indeed lead to serious medical complications, such as laceration of the esophagus, swollen parotid glands and dental caries or damage to tooth enamel due to irritation by the acids emitted when vomiting. Excessive laxative abuse may lead to alternations between constipation and diarrhoea. Probably the most harmful effect of frequent vomiting and/or purging, however, is a disturbed electrolyte balance, in the form of a lack of body salt potassium (hypokalaemia), which may cause mortal heart rhythm disturbances.

Diagnosis of anorexia and bulimia nervosa

Although many clinicians will consider the possibility of AN on account of the patient's emaciated state, the diagnosis of AN should be based on the patient's behaviour rather than on her physical condition. When paying attention to the behavioural characteristics mentioned in DSM-IV (see Table 1.1), the diagnosis of AN is relatively easy to make, especially when not only the patient's but also the parents' or partner's story is attended to.

This does not imply, however, that physical symptoms are of no interest. Along with amenorrhoea (which the patients mostly do not experience as a problem) AN patients do have several *physical complaints*, such as constipation, sleeping disorders, cyanosis (blue discolouration of fingers and toes), coldness, hair loss and lanugo (downy body hair). All these symptoms are secondary to the patient's malnutrition and do not require separate treatment, although unfortunately enough this still happens. For example, laxatives are sometimes prescribed for constipation or hormones for amenorrhoea. An inexperienced physician may also be misled by certain somatic symptoms, such as a slow pulse rate (less than 60 per minute), low body temperature, anaemia, leucopenia (lack of white blood cells) and various disorders in hormonal functions, the most striking of which is the repression of the female hormones.

While a physical examination of the patient may not always be necessary to decide on the diagnosis, it does have its importance in evaluating the physiological state of malnutrition and in deciding on the need for hospitalization. Although the degree of emaciation is only a relative item in this regard, a weight loss of more than 20 per cent below the normal minimum should act as the alert for extreme caution. In this case, treatment should be entrusted to the hands of an experienced clinician. The need for medical attention applies even more strongly to AN patients of the 'mixed' type, who in addition to the low body weight present with extra risks for complications, comparable to those mentioned for BN. So, as a rule, a medical examination should precede therapy of AN patients regardless of the gravity or duration of the disorder.

Unlike AN, the diagnosis of BN is rather complex and often causes errors. Many clinicians, especially in the USA, apply the diagnosis too liberally, to include all sorts of disorders in which a form of binge eating is involved. To avoid overdiagnosis, a strict adherence to the DSM-IV criteria mentioned in Table 1.2 is required. An additional inspection may therefore be necessary, not only for diagnostic purposes but also to help the patient overcome the barrier of asking for medical assistance. Indeed, out of shame or guilt most bulimic patients will not spontaneously talk about their eating behaviour, but when direct and specific questions are asked they may feel that the interviewer is familiar with the problem and be more inclined to confide in him or her.

A first issue to investigate in this respect is whether the patient is actually suffering from bulimia. When someone claims 'to eat too much', it is often concluded without further ado (including by the patients themselves) that bulimia is involved, but this is not always the case. In order to find out the exact significance of the complaints, three important questions must be addressed: (1) Is the claim to 'eat too much' justified? (2) Did the overeating take place within a short period of time? (3) Did the patient experience a loss of control? (See Table 1.3.)

The first question concerns the *objectivity of the overeating*. To answer this question, one must get an idea of the exact quantities consumed, for example by asking the patient to monitor her food intake until the next session. Attention must be paid to the patient's

Table 1.3   Diagnosis of bulimia

Did the patient eat objectively too much?	Did she eat in a short time?	Did she suffer a loss of control?	Diagnosis
no	no	no	*subjective overeating*
yes	no	no	*objective overeating*
no	yes	yes	*subjective bingeing*
yes	yes	yes	*objective bingeing*

subjective norm, i.e. what she considers as 'normal'. In our society, where many women diet or adopt an anorectic attitude, the violation of self-imposed dieting rules may already be experienced as a form of 'overeating'. After inquiry, it often appears that what is reported as a binge is in fact an ordinary meal. This perceptual malformation is very typical for AN patients in particular.

When the amount of food eaten does appear to be exaggerated, the next question is whether the excess was consumed *in a short period of time*. A 'genuine' binge involves large quantities of food (e.g. 2,000 to 10,000 Kcal) eaten quickly (e.g. within 30 minutes to an hour). Very often, the so-called 'overeating' is the result of many small consumptions over an extended period of time, such as a whole day. In that case one should talk of 'objective overeating' or 'food addiction' rather than a binge. This is a pattern that is often found in obese people, whereas binges, or fits of gorging, imply a characteristic suddenness and a short period of time.

The third question concerns the feeling of *loss of control*. Bulimic subjects no longer experience conscious control over the eating behaviour, as expressed by the typical statement that 'once they start eating, they cannot stop'. This loss of control is very often triggered by particular foodstuffs, notably sweets.

If the above items apply, one may conclude that the patient suffers from objective binge eating. To decide on the diagnosis of BN, however, it must also be established that the patient wants to avoid weight increase and attempts to keep her weight under control (see Figure 1.1). Not all patients suffering from bulimia are concerned about their weight, as for example is the case in depression. On the other hand, bulimia may occur without compensating behaviour, in which case the patient's weight will increase after each binge and induce overweight. Some clinicians refer to this syndrome as the *binge eating disorder*, but this notion is still controversial. Only when compensatory behaviours such as vomiting, uses of laxatives or diuretics, fasting or excessive exercise occur is the diagnosis of BN in order.

Differential diagnosis

A difficult and still controversial issue in the diagnosis of eating disorders is the *co-morbidity* or co-existence of BN with other syndromes (Mitchell *et al.*, 1991). This issue is particularly relevant as it provides a pitfall for inexperienced clinicians: when 'diverted' by other characteristics associated with syndromes with which they are more familiar, clinicians who are inexperienced with eating disorders may 'forget' the bulimia or regard it merely as a secondary symptom. However, when BN appears together with another mental disorder, it is difficult to tell cause from effect, especially when the disorder is complex and chronic (two different but co-occurring issues). Even if the co-existing disorder is treated appropriately, its disappearance will not necessarily lead to the improvement of the BN, for the latter often leads an independent existence, fed by the vicious circle of self-destructive behaviours described above. Table 1.4 summarizes the relevant questions for the differential diagnosis between BN and co-existing disorders.

A frequently discussed topic, particularly in the American literature, is the connection between BN and *mood disorders*. When both occur simultaneously, the question arises of which one is primary. In our experience, the mood disturbance in BN is mostly secondary. This does not preclude the use of antidepressants as being useful in certain cases.

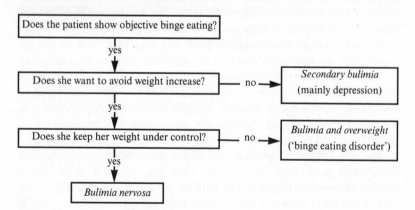

Figure 1.1   Diagnosis of bulimia nervosa

Table 1.4   Bulimia nervosa and co-morbidity

Specific questions
* Is there a mood disorder?
* Any symptoms of an anxiety disorder?
* Is there substance abuse?
* Any signs of impulsive behaviour?

General questions
* What is the relationship between bulimia nervosa and these
   phenomena (primary or secondary)?
* Do several disturbances occur in the same person?
* If they are linked to a negative self-image, consider:

   – borderline personality disorder and/or
   – history of (sexual) traumatization

However, if antidepressants are used in BN, this should always be done in combination with some form of psychotherapy (see Vanderlinden, Norré and Vandereycken, 1992). Furthermore, one should be aware of the possibility of a lack of therapy compliance, impulsive acts (including aggression and attempted suicide) and heart malfunctions. In the last case, an overdose of antidepressants (particularly the 'classical' tricyclic drugs) may be particularly life-threatening.

The combination of bulimia with *impulse control disorders* is not unusual. After their eating problems have been present for some time, many patients resort to stealing food or money to secure the food they require for their binges. This behaviour, which is mostly kept secret, is a direct function of their eating urge and not a sign of kleptomania. Sudden aggressive outbursts also frequently occur, both in the sense of hetero-aggression (outbursts of anger) or auto-aggression (self-mutilation).

In recent years, increasing attention has also been paid to the co-occurrence of eating disorders and *substance abuse*. In particular, bulimia frequently seems to concur with alcohol abuse, although the nature of the connection is still obscure. It is therefore important to inquire about the use of alcohol in bulimic patients. Alternatively, in women with a drinking problem the possibility of disturbed eating patterns should be checked for.

In many bulimic patients, several of the above behavioural disorders occur after some time. In this case they may reveal a more fundamental *personality disorder*, particularly of the borderline type. But even if the latter does not apply, one should always consider a possible history of *traumatization* (physical or sexual abuse), which seems to be the case in at least a quarter of the BN patients. Because of its particular relevance to the subject of this book, the issue of sexual abuse will be discussed in more detail in chapter 8. For the more general diagnostic, prognostic, theoretical and therapeutic aspects of this issue, the interested reader is referred to the comprehensive handbook by Brownell and Fairburn (1995).

EPIDEMIOLOGY OF ANOREXIA AND BULIMIA NERVOSA

When strict criteria are used for its diagnosis, the incidence of AN (i.e. the number of new cases in a given population) is estimated at approximately 1–4 per 100,000 inhabitants per year. If all cases, old and new, are added up at a certain point in time, a point prevalence of 1 per cent is attained for girls between 16 and 19 years old, and of 0.5–1 per cent for women aged 15 to 40 years. For BN, much higher prevalence rates have been reported (up to 5–19 per cent in female students aged 17 to 25 years in the US), but these 'epidemic-like' findings may probably be attributed to unjust diagnoses; more accurate studies yield a more realistic prevalence of BN of approximately 1 per cent (Hoek, 1993). The majority of AN patients are aged between 14 and 20 years, although there are cases in which the patient is under 10 years or older than 40. BN patients are generally a little older: 18–25 years for the majority of patients, with a variation between 12 and 50 years. Male subjects account for approximately 5 per cent of all eating disorder cases, with BN being the more prevalent type. The reason for this skewed sex distribution is as yet unknown, although it has been suggested that the differential social and cultural norms, putting more emphasis on slenderness in women than in men, are of influence. In any event, from a clinical point of view eating disorders are very similar in both sexes (Andersen, 1990; Vandereycken and Van den Broucke, 1984).

EATING DISORDERS IN MARRIED PATIENTS

Incidence

In the existing epidemiological studies of AN and BN, the marital status of the patients is seldom specifically addressed. The percentage of married women in the population of eating disorder patients can therefore only be estimated from the numbers of married patients involved in large-scale clinical studies. An elaborate study in this regard was done by Garfinkel and Garner (1982), who found that in their group of 193 anorectic patients, 33 (or 17 per cent) were married.

This rate is within the same range as the 21.2 per cent of married anorectics found in a series of 105 patients studied by Heavey *et al.* (1989).

While this suggests that approximately one in every five eating-disordered patients is married upon presentation, such an estimation may be inaccurate because the proportion of married subjects in a particular sample is often contaminated by other factors. Marriage is, for instance, more common among older patients. Dally and Gomez (1979) reported that of the older anorectic patients they treated, who developed the disorder at the age of 19 or more, 40 per cent were married. They also stated that women who develop AN when they are over forty are almost invariably married. Furthermore, the probability for a patient to be married and/or living with a partner is also greater among AN patients of the 'mixed' type and BN patients than among 'pure' anorectics. In the BN patient series described by Russell (1979), for example, about one-third of the subjects were married. Of the 112 BN patients contained in a study by Lacey (1992), 38 (34 per cent) were married or cohabiting whereas 73 patients (65 per cent) currently had a sexual partner. In Garfinkel and Garner's (1982) sample, the ratio of married bulimic patients versus married abstainers was almost two to one (i.e. 22.7 per cent of the bulimics and 11.5 per cent of the abstainers). In a same vein, Beumont, George and Smart (1976) reported that all the vomiters/purgers in their series of (anorectic) patients had regular boyfriends, as compared with only half of the abstainers.

Another interesting issue is the marital status of women who have suffered from an eating disorder in the past. In a follow-up study of 70 women who had previously been treated for AN, Sullivan (1996) found that after twelve years, 45.7 per cent of his sample (10 per cent of whom continued to meet the criteria for AN) had never been married, which is significantly more than the percentage attained by a control group of women selected at random from the same community (16.3 per cent never married).

Clinical characteristics

Information about the clinical characteristics of eating disorders in married patients must generally be inferred from descriptive case reports. An examination of the literature about this subject within the scope of a more extensive review (Van den Broucke and Vandereycken, 1988, 1989a) yielded more than sixty reports of married AN or BN patients. From these reports, it can be inferred that the presenting age of married eating disorder patients varies from as young as 22 to 60 years and older. The same age range is observed with regard to the onset of the disorder. When developed at a later age, the illness usually represents a relapse into an anorectic condition that previously existed subclinically, or is secondary to another pathological condition. In postmenopausal patients, for instance, it was found that the eating disorder developed as a sequel to depression.

In several cases, the disorder is triggered by a pregnancy or child-birth, hence the assumption that the fear of losing control over one's food intake and weight is induced by the changing body image and the typical cravings for food that are experienced during pregnancy – an assumption that has in the meantime inspired several authors to conduct further research into this issue (e.g. Brinch, Isager and Tolstrup, 1988; Lacey and Smith, 1987). Other precipitating factors include marital problems, separation from parents and difficulties with childrearing.

The physical and psychological symptoms of the eating disorders in married patients as reported in clinical case studies generally corre-spond with those of unmarried patients. For AN, behavioural symptoms such as dieting, secreting food, hyperactivity, laxative abuse, binge eating and self-induced vomiting are often described, in addition to symptoms constituting the DSM-IV criteria. In married BN patients, weight fluctuations and depressed mood episodes prevail in addition to the DSM-IV criteria of binge eating, compensatory behaviour such as self-induced vomiting, and preoccupation with body shape and weight. Although these symptoms are mostly severe, they often persist for a long period of time without being noticed, not even by the husband. Amenorrhoea, for instance, which is probably one of the most 'conspicuous' symptoms, is often disguised by the use of oral contraceptives.

The impression that the characteristics of AN or BN as presented by married patients are very similar to the ones observed in unmarried patients, except perhaps for the severity of the symptoms, is largely substantiated by the results of statistical comparisons between married and unmarried patients. When comparing 35 married patients to 102 single patients involved in an inpatient treatment programme, we found that for the married patients, who were mostly older than the unmarried ones, the duration of the illness was significantly longer, and the loss from their ideal weight (as a function of age and height) greater (Van den Broucke and Vandereycken, 1989b). Conversely, no differences were found between the two groups as regards their average presenting weight, weight loss (from their premorbid weight) or symptom pattern. In a similar vein, Heavey *et al.* (1989) concluded from the comparison between 39 married and 66 single patients, controlling for age of presentation and duration of illness, that the two groups were broadly similar in terms of the physical features of the illness and the degree of mental state abnormalities. There was a trend for more married patients to have habitually binged and vomited, but this trend did not reach significance.

An interesting finding in both our study and the one by Heavey and her collaborators was that the age difference between married and single patients was more significant at presentation than at the onset of the disorder. This suggests that for the married patients, and particularly for those with a postmarital onset, more time had elapsed between the beginning of the illness and its diagnosis.

Prognosis

The latter finding, as well as the longer duration of the illness in married subjects in general, suggests that having a relationship with a partner influences the course of an eating disorder. In view of this finding, it is hardly surprising that the prognosis of AN or BN in a married woman is generally deemed less favourable than when it occurs in an unmarried girl. As such, marriage is often mentioned among the factors which affect a poor outcome in an eating disorder (e.g. Crisp *et al.*, 1977).

CONCLUSIONS

In this chapter we have introduced the reader to the main characteristics and epidemiology of AN and BN, and reviewed the available information about the incidence and clinical characteristics of these eating disorders as they occur in married patients. The general impression deriving from the latter review is that AN and BN in married patients are clinically not very different from the disorders as observed in single patients, although the symptoms are usually more severe and the prognosis less favourable. Typically, eating disorders also last longer in married patients, which raises the question of the contribution of the marital relationship to the eating disorders and vice versa.

In the next chapters, we will further explore this issue by focusing on a number of marital relationship characteristics that are associated with the occurrence of an eating disorder. First, however, we will review the predominant views and empirical findings concerning the marital relationships of psychiatric patients as discussed in the literature.

2 The marital relationships of psychiatric patients

Although the majority of patients who seek psychiatric treatment present with individual diagnosable conditions, the relationship with a marital partner often represents a significant contextual variable for their psychological problems. Alternatively, spouses seeking marital therapy often present with individual psychiatric symptoms as well. It therefore seems reasonable to assume a connection between the occurrence of psychiatric disorders and marital functioning.

In recent years, attempts have been made to understand this connection by exploring the marital relationships of patients suffering from a variety of psychiatric disorders, including depression, alcoholism, psychosomatic disorders and anxiety disorders. As a result, several hypotheses have been proposed to explain the role of marital functioning in the onset or maintenance of a psychiatric disorder. Despite the considerable differences among these hypotheses in terms of their theoretical and empirical underpinnings, most of them revert to one of four basic issues: (1) a correspondence between the patient and the spouse with regard to psychiatric illness; (2) a lack of marital satisfaction and intimacy; (3) deficient communication; and (4) inadequate conflict strategies.

In this chapter, we will review the literature with regard to the marital relationships of psychiatric patients, using these four concepts as a structure for the discussion. As in most of the literature dealing with this topic, the discussion will be focused on 'neurotic' rather than psychotic disorders. Given the introductory purpose of the chapter, we will not review the extensive literature on marital therapy indication or outcome studies for different types of mental disorders. For that purpose, the interested reader is referred to the reviews by Beach, Whisman and O'Leary (1994), Emmelkamp and Gerlsma (1994), and O'Farrell (1994). Instead, we will critically examine the theoretical rationale which underlies these models as well as their empirical substantiation, before continuing our discussion of the marital relationships of eating-disordered patients in the chapters to follow.

THE SPOUSES OF PSYCHIATRIC PATIENTS

Interspouse similarity for psychiatric illness

A recurrent impression throughout the clinical literature is that marital partners of psychiatric patients are often afflicted with psychiatric symptoms themselves. This idea is strongly embedded within the literature about husband–wife similarities in general. Over the past fifty years, numerous studies have been conducted to investigate the similarity of spouses for all sorts of factors, including age, religion, education, socio-economic status, physical traits and psychological attributes.

With regard to the latter, the results generally support the idea of interspouse similarity for intelligence, attitudes and values, with mean husband–wife correlations for intelligence approximating 0.50, and those for attitudes and opinions ranging from 0.55 to 0.89 (Eysenck, 1974; Richardson, 1939). There is also some evidence of a similarity between husbands and wives for personality characteristics, although the mean within-couple correlation on personality scales generally does not exceed 0.21 (Vandenberg, 1972). Apparently, then, the popular wisdom that 'like marries like' seems to hold true, at least to some extent, for many important psychological and census-type variables.

In the light of these findings, the idea of a similarity between husbands and wives with regard to psychiatric illness does not seem far-fetched. Supporting this assumption, several correlational studies have revealed a significant interspouse accordance on variables indicative of psychopathology, such as neuroticism, sociopathy and hysteria (Cloninger, Reich and Guze, 1975; Kreitman, 1964; Ovenstone, 1973; Pond, Ryle and Hamilton, 1963). Others have found that when one partner shows psychiatric symptoms, the probability that the other will also evidence signs of psychopathology significantly exceeds chance level (Crago, 1972; Merikangas, 1982).

The latter idea has particularly gained acceptance with regard to agoraphobia and alcoholism. With respect to the former disorder, Lazarus (1966) noted that it is 'presumably impossible to become agoraphobic without the aid of someone who will submit to the inevitable demands imposed upon them' (p. 97). Partners of agoraphobic patients have been described as negativistic, anxious, compulsive, hostile and abnormally jealous (Fry, 1962; Hafner, 1977a,

1979). However, controlled studies generally contradict this view. Apart from one methodologically contestable study (Schaper, 1973), the general finding is that spouses of agoraphobic patients are not different from normal controls on measures of neuroticism (Agulnik, 1970; Arrindell and Emmelkamp, 1985; Buglass *et al.*, 1977).

Within the field of addiction research and treatment, the assumed illness of the 'healthy' partner has become known as *codependency* (Cermak, 1987; Hands and Dear, 1994). The core characteristics of this pathology are an impaired sense of self-worth, an excessive reliance on other people for approval, a compulsive sense of responsibility for others, and an urge to control other people's behaviour. Because of these characteristics, the codependent partner allegedly becomes excessively dependent or 'addicted' to the alcoholic partner, and therefore willing to engage in self-defeating behaviour so as to secure the relationship.

Despite the lack of consensus on its definition and validity, the codependency concept has become very popular among clinicians and within the self-help movement. Nevertheless, critical reviews have revealed a lack of empirical support for the presence of an underlying personality disorder in spouses of alcoholic patients (Haaken, 1990; Hands and Dear, 1994; Moos, Finney and Cronkite, 1990). In want of such an empirical substantiation, the alleged decrease of the psychological functioning of these spouses may just as well be considered a normal reaction to prolonged stress created by living with a problem drinker (Orford, 1990).

According to some scholars (e.g. Kreitman, 1964; Methorst, 1984), women are more likely to reflect the psychiatric illness of their spouses than men. This may be because their biological and/or psychological make-up makes them more susceptible to psychological disturbances (Dohrenwend and Dohrenwend, 1969), or because they experience more psychological distress due to their traditional role as a spouse, mother and housewife (Gove, 1984). Alternatively, the apparent greater 'vulnerability' of female spouses of male psychiatric patients may also be an artifact of response bias. It is possible, for example, that women are more capable of recognizing and expressing distress, or that admitting to emotional problems is more compatible with the traditional female role.

Assortative mating or pathogenic interaction?

In spite of the mixed results of the above studies, the idea of an increased incidence of mental illness in the spouses of psychiatric patients seems to be a recurrent theme in the psychiatric literature. To explain this phenomenon, several hypotheses have been advanced, two of which have become the subject of fierce scientific debate. The first one, which is referred to as the *assortative mating* theory, states that individuals tend to select a marital partner with similar or complementary personality traits, some of which may eventually produce symptoms in one or both spouses. The second one is the *pathogenic interaction* theory, which states that the interaction with a marital partner showing psychiatric symptoms 'infects' the emotional stability of the 'healthy' partner.

Proponents of the assortative mating theory base their views on the demonstrated homogamy for physical, social and demographic characteristics, and contend that marital interaction cannot explain the increased prevalence of mental disorders in the spouses' relatives. Proponents of the pathogenic interaction hypothesis, in contrast, argue that studies reporting a resemblance between spouses for personality traits have generally failed to disclose any specific traits that are associated with the development of mental illness, and that the incidence of mental disorders in the spouses of neurotic patients often increases with the duration of the marriage.

The debate concerning the two theories has important bearings on the prognosis for treatment. While the pathogenic interaction theory expects an improvement in the patient to result in an improvement of the spouse's condition as well, the assortative mating theory predicts the opposite: it assumes that the spouse will resist the patient's improvement in order to maintain the balance in the relationship. The latter was actually reported in a number of clinical studies indicating that a successful symptomatic treatment of phobic patients was related to a deterioration of the spouse's marital satisfaction and psychological well-being (Hafner, 1977b; Hand and Lamontagne, 1976; Milton and Hafner, 1979). However, better-controlled studies using more objective measures produced no evidence that phobia removal led to an exacerbation of problems in the non-phobic spouse, nor to an increase of marital difficulties (Bland and Hallam, 1981; Emmelkamp *et al.*, 1992; Monteiro, Marks and Ramm, 1985; Oatley and Hodgson, 1987). The same was found in other clinical populations. In obsessive-compulsive patients, for example, marital distress levels remained stable or even slightly improved following successful therapy (Emmelkamp, de Haan and Hoogduin, 1990; Riggs, Hiss and Foa, 1992).

MARITAL SATISFACTION AND INTIMACY

A process view on marital relationships

As appears from the above discussion, neither the assortative mating nor the pathogenic interaction model can explain the alleged husband–wife similarity for psychiatric illness. This may be because these models assume a reductionist view on marital interaction. By suggesting that the 'healthy' spouse is the 'architect' (as in the assortative mating theory) or, alternatively, the 'victim' of the patient's problems (as in the pathogenic interaction theory), both these models adhere to the single causality principle. Moreover, in both of them the partners' influence on each other is limited to negative effects. This is clearly at odds with the popular notion of social support (Hobfoll, 1988; Sarason and Sarason, 1985), which emphasizes the supportive nature of spouses' responses to each other, and suggests that these may decrease or even inhibit the occurrence of psychiatric symptoms.

In this regard, a more realistic view is offered by the more recent process models of marital relationships (e.g. Duck, 1990; Hahlweg and Jacobson, 1984). According to these models, marital partners influence each other's behaviour continuously, which makes it impossible to distinguish between causes and consequences. As such, the emergence of psychiatric symptoms represents only a single event in a continuous chain of mutually dependent behaviours: symptoms in one partner inevitably influence the other partner's functioning, regardless of his or her previous condition, and are in turn positively or negatively influenced by the spouse's behaviour. Thus, the question as to which came first, the patient's symptoms or the spouse's problems, boils down to a 'chicken-and-egg' issue.

Marital satisfaction

Instead of analysing the spouse's personality it therefore seems more fruitful to focus on the quality of the marital relationship itself. In fact, there is a growing body of research findings showing a strong concurrent relationship between measures of marital adjustment and psychopathology across many samples and types of disorders. For example, a large number of studies have demonstrated a connection between marital problems and alcoholism (O'Farrell and Birchler, 1987; Orford, 1990) and between marital dissatisfaction and depression (Beach and O'Leary, 1993; Birtchnell and Kennard, 1983; Brown and Harris, 1978; Coleman and Miller, 1975; Coyne *et al.*, 1987; Ineichen,

1976; Olin and Fenell, 1989; Weissman, 1987). For other psychiatric disorders the findings are less clear cut. With regard to anxiety disorders, for instance, Emmelkamp and Gerlsma (1994) concluded from a quantitative review that, with the exception of one study showing a substantially lower degree of marital adjustment in couples with an agoraphobic patient (Kleiner, Marshall and Spevack, 1987), the marital satisfaction of agoraphobics is generally not much different from that of normal controls. On the other hand, patients with an obsessive-compulsive disorder do report significantly higher degrees of marital distress (Emmelkamp *et al.*, 1990; Riggs *et al.*, 1992).

While it is likely that excessive drinking or the occurrence of phobic or depressive symptoms has a negative impact on marital quality, some researchers assume a reverse relationship, and argue that marital distress *contributes* to the occurrence of these problems. For example, Steinglass, Bennett, Wolin and Reis (1987) believe that marital problems stimulate excessive drinking as a means of facilitating the expression of emotion or regulating the distance between the partners. In addition, marital problems may also help to maintain alcohol problems once they have developed. In a different perspective, Goldstein and Chambless (1978) argue that phobic symptoms represent psychological avoidance behaviour in women who feel trapped in an unhappy relationship, from which they cannot escape because they are afraid of being alone. With regard to depression, Beach, Sandeen and O'Leary (1990) have proposed the 'marital discord model', which states that marital discord increases major stressors in the relationship and decreases the support available from one's partner. Individual vulnerability factors such as low self-esteem or chronic negative affectivity increase the risk of depressive episodes in response to negative marital events. As a result, marital distress and depression form a negative feedback loop for which women in particular appear to be vulnerable (Heim and Snyder, 1991; Thompson, Whiffen and Blain, 1995).

Marital intimacy

The above views underscore the importance of marital distress as a mediator in the development or maintenance of psychiatric illness in married subjects. However, while the notion of distress basically reflects the partners' overall appraisal of their relationship quality, attention should also be given to the factors which account for that quality. In this respect, the concept of marital intimacy appears to play a central role. Indeed, as a key qualitative characteristic of a relationship, intimacy has been empirically linked to marital satisfaction and distress (Schaefer and Olson, 1981; Waring, McElrath, Mitchell and Derry, 1981), while a failure to develop an intimate relationship with a partner has been associated with the experience of loneliness (Derlega and Margulis, 1982) and with physical illness (Reis *et al.*, 1985). With regard to psychiatric problems, a lack of marital intimacy has been correlated with depression (Basco *et al.*, 1992; Costello, 1982; Hickie *et al.*, 1990; Waring and Patton, 1984), psychosomatic illness (Waring, 1983) and sexual abuse (Marshall, 1989).

This does not mean that intimacy itself cannot have negative effects on psychological well-being. It has been noted, for example, that high prior levels of intimacy make coping with the ending of a relationship more painful (Perlman and Fehr, 1987). In addition, a number of authors (e.g. Hatfield, 1982) have identified the negative consequences of 'too much' intimacy, such as enmeshment, the inhibition of personal growth, fear of abandonment, and loss of control over one's destructive impulses. Since intimate partners are aware of each other's innermost feelings and needs, they know precisely how to exploit or injure each other. According to Fitzpatrick (1988) too much intimacy may be particularly harmful for those couples who define their rela-tionships as 'emotionally distant', and for whom intimate self-disclosure and open communication violate the partners' privacy and autonomy.

It can be questioned, however, whether these items should be regarded as negative effects of intimacy. Instead, it seems more plau-sible to consider those instances where partners violate each other's autonomy as a *failure* to achieve genuine intimacy. The consensus view is, then, that marital intimacy is generally beneficial to a person's well-being, whereas *not* achieving or maintaining intimacy in the relationship with one's partner may negatively influence one's physical, emotional or psychological well-being.

Several hypotheses have been advanced to explain these negative effects. They involve such diverse concepts and processes as the disrup-tion of complementary role behaviour in collusive relationships (Hafner, 1986), a discrepancy between the person's 'true' and 'false' self (Jourard, 1971), and a homeostatic reaction to an intolerably high or low distance between the partners (Byng-Hall, 1980). Notwithstanding their conceptual differences, these views are all based on the assump-tion that the emergence of symptom behaviour serves the purpose of avoiding something which the partners perceive as threatening their individuality or their relationship. In terms of the escape conditioning paradigm, it could thus be assumed that the emergence of psychiatric symptoms represents an avoidance reaction to situations that are perceived as threatening the patient's identity (e.g. the partner's attempts to achieve more intimacy), or alternatively the existence of the relationship itself (e.g. overt conflicts that arise as a result of the low level of intimacy).

The latter assumption underscores the importance of behavioural correlates of intimacy to account for its effects on well-being. In this regard, it is important to consider the role of marital communication as the medium that carries the behavioural expressions of intimacy and the vehicle through which intimacy is achieved and maintained.

MARITAL COMMUNICATION

Marital communication and well-being

Marital communication is probably one of the best-documented aspects of personal relationships. This may be due to the fact that a couple's way of communicating is strongly related to their marital satisfaction. Indeed, numerous studies, assuming a large variety of perspectives on communication, have demonstrated that the interactions of maritally distressed couples are characterized by disturbed communication patterns including: (1) the emittance of high rates of negative verbal and nonverbal communications; (2) direct reciprocity of negative interventions; (3) a high degree of predictability or rigidity; (4) the presence of cognitive distortions (i.e. the attribution of the spouse's negative behaviour to internal factors, and of his or her positive behaviour to external factors); and (5) the presence of a covert status struggle (for a review, see Schaap, 1984). In view of the observed relationship between marital distress and psychopathology reported previously, it is not surprising that these communication deficiencies have also been related to the occurrence or maintenance of psychiatric problems. For instance, Coyne's (1976) interactional model states that depression is maintained by negative interactional patterns, in that depressed people evoke negative moods in others and elicit negative responses such as rejection and avoidance. Similarly, Biglan *et al.* (1985) propose that depressive symptoms represent a functional set of behaviours that are likely to be reinforced in a relationship characterized by high levels of negative verbal behaviour.

Interaction in psychiatrically distressed couples

The above hypothesis has been tested in interaction process studies involving a number of psychiatric populations. For example, in a study of the communication between alcoholic patients and their spouses, Billings *et al.* (1979) found that alcoholic couples were more hostile than happily married couples, in the sense that they used more coercive statements and fewer friendly or cognitive acts. No differences were noted between alcoholic and maritally distressed couples. In the same vein, Jacob and Krahn (1988) observed that alcoholic couples were more critical and disagreeable than either nondistressed or depressed couples when they had been drinking. However, they were indistinguishable from the other couples when they had not been drinking.

With regard to depressed patients, several studies have indicated that the communication between the patients and their spouses is more negative and more disruptive than that between nondepressed persons (Biglan *et al.*, 1985; Gotlib and Whiffen, 1989; Hinchliffe *et al.*, 1975; Hickie *et al.*, 1990; Hooley and Hahlweg, 1986). When interacting with a stranger, however, depressed patients show more adaptive and reciprocal behaviour (Hautzinger, Linden and Hoffman, 1982). Linden *et al.* (1983) observed that the best discriminators between the communication of depressed and nondepressed couples were the depressed patient's negative verbal behaviour and the nondepressed spouse's positive self-centred and negative partner-centred statements, whereas nondepressed couples with marital problems evidenced more even and reciprocal communication patterns. In a similar vein, Hooley and Teasdale (1989) found high rates of negative comments in the spouses of depressed patients and demonstrated that this high rate of criticism predicted relapse. In other words, it may not be the disturbed marital interaction in itself which is associated with depression, but the asymmetrical nature of the interactions.

MARITAL CONFLICT

Marital conflict and well-being

Marital conflict influences the partners' well-being both directly and indirectly, through its association with marital satisfaction and communication. Whereas conflicts are likely to occur in any couple, the way conflicts are handled by the partners is indeed significantly related to their satisfaction with the relationship. It appears that a non-constructive way of dealing with a conflict causes great emotional distress which negatively influences the partners' satisfaction. In addition, conflict discussions often highlight the communication problems that are present in a relationship. Indeed, the fact that deficient communication patterns associated with marital distress become especially evident during conflict discussions is the main reason why couples are taught conflict resolution skills in marital therapy (e.g. Hahlweg *et al.*, 1984a; Jacobson and Margolin, 1979). Similarly, disturbed behaviours such as depressive or phobic reactions are also most likely to appear in the context of (potentially) conflictual discussions (Biglan *et al.*, 1985; Goldstein and Chambless, 1978). For that reason, a large number of the interaction studies involving maritally and psychiatrically distressed couples explicitly focus on the couple's communication when dealing with conflicts.

Apart from their connection with marital satisfaction and communication, however, conflicts may also be more directly related to the occurrence of psychiatric problems. In this regard, two pertinent issues are the underlying structure of the conflict and the strategy that is used to handle conflicts.

Conflict structure

Couples may argue about all kinds of things, many of which can be solved relatively easily by way of compromising. However, as argued by systems and communication theorists (e.g. Watzlawick, Beavin and Jackson, 1967), the real conflict of interest is often not the actual topic of the argument but the question of who is in command. This issue in turn influences the way the conflict is handled. In *symmetrical* relationships, where the partners strive towards maintaining an egalitarian power distribution, conflicts typically entail an escalation process, whereby both partners openly reject each other's point of view. This is often seen in the escalating conflicts of maritally distressed couples. In contrast, conflicts in rigidly *complementary* relationships, where one of the partners occupies a 'one-up' and the other a 'one-down' position, are characterized by an ignoring of the other partner's position, which may have more serious psychological consequences.

The latter also applies in the use of conflict as a means of regulating the distance in the relationship. According to some systems theorists (e.g. Byng-Hall, 1980; Feldman, 1979) conflicts are triggered when one of the partners perceives the level of intimacy as too high. This would explain the repetitive cycles of nonproductive conflicts that are observed in the marriages of psychologically distressed people.

Conflict strategies

Since marital partners are usually unaware of the above patterns and/or unable to state explicitly what their predicaments are with regard to a particular disagreement, the structure of a conflict is often difficult to pinpoint. This explains the lack of empirical research on this subject. In contrast, more empirical studies have been conducted with regard to overt conflict strategies in married couples. From these studies, it appears that a *distributive* strategy, involving tactics such as threatening, insulting or demanding unilateral change from the partner, is typical for maritally distressed couples, whereas an *integrative* strategy, making use of such tactics as seeking agreement, negotiating and expressing trust, is more prevalent in nondistressed couples. Furthermore, a *conflict avoidance* strategy, which is aimed at minimizing explicit discussions of conflict by denying the presence of disagreements, shifting the focus of the conversation or communicating indirectly or ambiguously, appears to be modestly associated with relationship dissatisfaction (Canary and Cupach, 1988; Peterson, 1983; Sillars *et al.*, 1982).

The latter pattern is also assumedly connected with the onset or maintenance of psychiatric distress, whereby an escape conditioning process can be assumed. Specifically, psychiatric symptoms can be conceived as a means of avoiding the aversive emotional stimuli provoked by marital conflicts. This view has been particularly articulated with regard to depression and agoraphobia. Concerning the former, several authors (e.g. Biglan *et al.*, 1985; Hinchliffe *et al.*, 1975) have pointed out that depressive behaviour such as self-derogation, complaining and displaying negative affect is most likely to appear in a context of potential conflict with the partner. With regard to agoraphobia, Goldstein and Chambless (1978) hypothesize that agoraphobic patients have learned not to recognize negative affects such as anger, and tend to mislabel the emotional distress that is caused by marital conflicts as diffuse anxiety. Since these negative feelings decrease upon termination of the anxiety-producing conflicts, the use of conflict-avoidance strategies is negatively reinforced. At the same time, however, this increases the patient's feelings of helplessness and dependency on the spouse.

These views highlight the possible role of conflict resolution strategies in the occurrence of psychological disorders. However, their applicability to other psychiatric disorders, including eating disorders, needs to be substantiated by further research.

CONCLUSIONS

In this chapter, we have summarized the main views expressed in the literature with regard to four conceptual issues that are often considered of interest to the marriages of psychiatric patients: the psychiatric profile of the spouse, marital satisfaction and intimacy, communication and conflict resolution. As appears from this outline, the occurrence of a psychiatric disorder in a married person is often accompanied by an increased level of psychiatric distress in the spouse, and may be related to high levels of marital dissatisfaction, a low level of marital intimacy and to deficient patterns of marital communication. The latter may become particularly apparent during conflict discussions. A major assumption is, then, that the emergence of psychiatric symptoms represents a conditioned and negatively reinforced avoidance reaction to emotionally aversive situations, such as the partner's attempts to achieve more intimacy than the patient can tolerate on account of his or her level of identity achievement, or the emotional distress caused by negatively escalating marital conflicts. While the patient's symptoms may also invoke emotional distress in the spouse, the latter's emotional instability will probably interfere with his capability to respond constructively to the patient's problems, and thus add to the complexity of the problems.

In the chapters to follow, we will elaborate on these concepts as they manifest themselves in the marital relationships of patients suffering from an eating disorder. For the sake of clarity, each topic will be discussed in a separate chapter focusing both on the clinical and theoretical considerations and on their empirical substantiation. The main conclusions will then be translated into clinical implications that will be discussed in the final chapters.

3 The husbands of eating-disordered patients

Being the spouse, lover or fiancé of a woman with an eating disorder is probably a very uncomfortable position. Not only has one to deal with the agony and distress which normally results from living with a psychiatrically ill partner; in addition, the marital and sexual relationships of anorectic or bulimic patients are reportedly very distant and emotionally barren. Hence, it comes as no surprise that clinicians are puzzled by the characteristics and motives of the men who choose to live with these patients (for the sake of simplicity, we will use the terms 'husband' and 'spouse' for all the heterosexual partners throughout this book, even if they are not officially married). Some regard these men as near-saints, who generously devote their lives to caring for their ill spouse; others regard them as weak and immature persons, who suffer from psychological difficulties themselves, and whose personalities represent an important factor in the development or perpetuation of their wives' eating disorders (Woodside *et al.*, 1993).

The latter assumption is obviously inspired by the similarity between patients and spouses that is reported with regard to various psychiatric disorders, as documented in the previous chapter. As applied to the spouses of eating-disordered patients, however, this assumption remains speculative as long as it is not substantiated that the incidence of psychiatric problems in the marital partners of eating-disordered patients is higher than in nondistressed subjects, and that the patient–spouse correspondence that has been reported with regard to other psychiatric disorders is also observed in couples with an eating-disordered patient.

These issues are the focus of the present chapter. First, we will review the main impressions of the spouses of eating-disordered patients deriving from case reports and clinical observations, and critically discuss them by referring to the literature on partners of psychiatric patients in general. Next, we will counterbalance the existing 'clinical' bias by presenting data from studies in which the psychiatric profiles of the husbands of eating-disordered patients were empirically assessed and compared to those of control subjects.

CLINICAL VIEWS OF THE HUSBAND'S PERSONALITY

General impressions

Authors who describe the occurrence of AN or BN in married patients often distinguish between cases with a premarital and a postmarital onset. Depending on the timing of the illness, different assumptions are made with regard to the spouse's role in the development of the disorder.

If the patient was already anorectic *before* her marriage, the dynamics of the partner choice are considered a pivotal issue. While the patient is believed to settle for a partner 'whom she would not marry if she were not ill because she feels she doesn't deserve anyone better' (Andersen, 1985, p. 142), the spouse's 'choice' to marry an anorectic or bulimic woman is mostly explained in terms of unrealistic rescue phantasies, or by the fact that he has identity problems of his own and is therefore attracted to a person who possesses about the same level of identity confusion. Either way, according to Crisp (1980), the relationship is embedded in the strong neurotic needs of both partners. Although this may at first have a mutually sustaining aspect (hence the opposition to treatment that is often seen in spouses of anorectics), dissatisfaction with the relationship usually arises when the husband senses that his efforts to rescue his ill wife have failed. When this becomes apparent, overt conflicts may arise and act as an incentive to seek treatment.

When the eating disorder develops *after* the marriage, a strong collusive bond between two immature partners is assumed, in which the spouses take up the complementary roles of the 'sick' patient and the 'caretaker', respectively. A remarkable example of such an extreme collusion was reported by Love *et al.* (1971): one of their patients managed to persuade her husband to help her smuggle her stools out of the hospital and to replace them by his, in order to deceive the medical staff who wanted to inspect her faeces for signs of laxative abuse!

This collusion between the patient and her husband is allegedly rooted in unresolved developmental conflicts, typically involving separation–individuation issues, that are displaced to and enacted within the context of the marital relationship (Dally and Gomez, 1979; Foster, 1986). According to Dally and Gomez (1979),

[The patient] has transferred her adolescent conflicts and problems onto her husband and has, in a sense, put some distance between herself and her family. The husband is expected to be a superman: strong, protective, understanding, loving and undemanding, thinking always of his wife and her needs. Since the type of man these immature girls choose to marry is usually himself sexually immature, wanting a woman he can look after and who does not threaten his frail masculinity, it is obvious that problems are likely sooner or later to arise.

(Dally and Gomez, 1979, p. 124)

In a similar vein, Foster (1986) states that

While the identified patient displays inattention to her own needs most strikingly in the medically dangerous symptomatic behavior, both spouses exhibit a developmental deficit with regard to identifying, articulating, and engaging in constructive behavior regarding their own thoughts and feelings.

(Foster, 1986, p. 579)

In other words, eating-disordered patients appear to shift between asserting autonomy and submitting to the perceived needs of the spouse, while the lack of ego strength in both partners is masked by an identification with stereotyped sex roles that prevents them from expressing their true feelings. As a result, they accept each other's false presentation of self, and expect one another to be strong, loving, protective and undemanding. Any event which is not in keeping with this 'perfect' image of the spouse (e.g. a marital conflict) or which upsets the fragile balance in the relationship (e.g. a pregnancy or childbirth) may trigger the disorder. The symptoms then serve the purpose of protecting the partners' pseudo-identity and the marital unit itself (Fishman, 1979; Foster 1986).

Clinical studies

As appears from the above, the general impression of clinicians is that the husbands of AN or BN patients are usually immature and neurotic persons, whose own psychological problems provide a basis for a problematic or pathological partner choice which eventually leads to the establishment of a 'collusive bond' with the patient. This impression is confirmed by the results of two clinical studies that were specifically aimed at investigating this issue.

In the first study, Dally (1984) examined the backgrounds and personalities of 50 anorectic patients and their spouses, using data collated from ongoing information recorded on index cards or extracted *post hoc* from medical records. Most of the spouses were described as 'immature men, who doubted their ability to satisfy and retain the affection of their wives' and 'whose expectations of marriage were unrealistic', in the sense that they 'saw their wives through idealistic eyes; sweet, kind, understanding and forgiving' (p. 425). Dally distinguishes between three general patterns of husband behaviour. In more than half of the cases the husband's behaviour was described as:

> emotionally and sexually passive. He loathes quarrelling with his wife and goes to considerable lengths to avoid open confrontation. He wants to be close, accepted and loved, but he makes this increasingly impossible by continuing to expect her to behave as someone she is not. Part of him welcomes her retreat into anorexia [nervosa]. He understands that she is ill. Now he can look after her and she will depend on him. Sooner or later he comes to rely on his wife being ill to maintain the security of his marriage. There is now mutual collusion and dependence.
>
> (Dally, 1984, p. 426)

The husbands belonging to the second category, about a third of the sample, were more capable of growth and change. This type of husband:

> does not passively accept his wife's anorectic behaviour. He resents her refusal to eat normally with him, and becomes increasingly angry. If she fails to change he may decide to abandon the marriage, usually by involving himself with another woman. Alternatively he may detach himself emotionally from his wife and put all his energies into his work.
>
> (p. 426)

The husbands in the third and smallest category were mainly older men, who established a firm power imbalance in the relationship by forcing their wives into a childlike dependency. They are described as:

> kind and loving, only as long as his wife does as he expects. She can have no life of her own. Everything she is and does must be an extension of her husband if they are to live in harmony.
>
> (p. 426)

Dally's conclusion is that, although not all of the relationships fit the same pattern, in most cases the relationship between an anorectic patient and her husband represents a collusive bond which is essential for the development and maintenance of the disorder. Specifically, he believes that the weak and passive character of the husbands, who had mostly been chosen for their kindness and tolerance, establishes a strong neurotic centre to the marriage, and thus represents an important prognostic factor (Dally, 1984).

While the above concerns the spouses of anorectic patients, Lacey (1992) examined the sexual partners of BN patients. His study involved 73 subjects, each of whom received a mailed questionnaire asking for psychiatric and family histories. If they showed signs of psychopathology, an invitation to a clinical interview followed. Of all the partners thus contacted, a quarter (18 cases) appeared to have had an emotional or psychiatric disorder warranting treatment. Four partners had suffered from anxiety-phobic disorders, and four were diagnosed as having a personality disorder. Twenty partners (27.4 per cent) reported eating or weight problems, including overweight (15 cases), obesity (4 cases), bingeing (2 cases), AN (1 case) and bizarre food fads linked to sexual perversity (1 case). Many of the partners used alcohol excessively, with 29 (40 per cent) who reported drinking over 36 units of alcohol per week, and 10 (14 per cent) who had received treatment or consulted a doctor for alcohol-related problems. Twenty men came from families with psychiatric or emotional problems which had warranted medical treatment.

While these data reveal a level of psychiatric disorder in spouses of bulimic patients that is high by any standards, Lacey (1992) concludes that his findings suggest a process of homogamy or assortative mating. The latter idea is fuelled by the author's previous clinical findings that spouses of bulimics tend to illness after the patients have given up their symptoms.

Critical appraisal

As appears from the overview presented above, and from the last study in particular, many clinicians implicitly adhere to the 'assortative mating' hypothesis by assuming a similarity between eating-disordered patients and their spouses, based on a pathological partner choice. As pointed out in the previous chapter, however, it must be borne in mind that an increased prevalence of psychiatric distress in the spouses of psychiatric patients, if indeed there is any, need not necessarily refer to a process of homogamy, but may also be explained as the result of a pathogenic interaction. To the extent that one partner's deviant behaviour may 'infect' the other's emotional stability, this implies that the husbands of eating-disordered patients may well be the 'victims' rather than the 'architects' of their wives' eating problems.

A more fundamental concern, however, is that the idea of a patho-logical partner choice (and, for that matter, of a pathogenic interaction) to explain the husbands' pathology entails a limited conceptualization of relationships. As discussed earlier, marital rela-tionships are in essence dynamic processes, in which both partners influence each other's behaviour continuously. Thus it is conceivable that a husband develops symptoms of psychiatric distress as a reaction to his wife's eating problem, and that these reactions in turn influence the further exacerbation of the wife's difficulties. In other words, a husband may be both the 'victim' *and* the 'architect' of his wife's eating disorder. On the other hand, it is also possible that spousal responses to the patient's problems are supportive and help slow down or inhibit the illness rather than exacerbate it. Finally, it can be argued that both the patient's *and* the husband's psychiatric distress result from the couple's marital difficulties. Indeed, a failure to achieve marital satisfaction has been repeatedly identified as a major cause of psychiatric illness (Brown and Harris, 1978; Costello, 1982; Stewart and Salt, 1981).

This does not mean, of course, that the psychiatric distress in the husbands of eating-disordered patients does not deserve any attention in its own right. On the contrary: regardless of his condition before the patient's illness, the spouse's emotional instability at the time of referral will most probably influence his ability to deal constructively with his wife's eating problems. Thus it is important to take the spouse's current psychiatric status into account. A pivotal question, then, is whether the marital partners of AN and BN patients *are* psychiatrically distressed. While the available clinical data strongly suggest so, they should be considered with some caution, given their lack of reliability and the absence of control samples. So, in order to really understand the role of the spouse's psychiatric condition in the development of an eating disorder, we should rely on empirical data indicating whether the incidence of psychiatric problems among the marital partners of eating-disordered patients is indeed higher than that among nondistressed subjects, and whether there is a correspon-dence between eating-disordered patients and their spouses in terms of psychological make-up. These issues are now addressed.

EMPIRICAL FINDINGS REGARDING THE SPOUSE'S PERSONALITY

Comparison with neurotic patients

Empirical data which shed light on the above assumptions were supplied by two studies of our own. For the first one (Van den Broucke and Vandereycken, 1989c) 25 married couples were investigated, in 12 of which the female partner had developed an eating disorder (5 AN and 7 BN). In the remaining 13 couples one of the partners (6 females and 7 males) suffered from a non-phobic neurotic disorder (i.e. an anxiety disorder or obsessive-compulsive disorder in 7 cases, and a depressive disorder in 5 cases). All subjects were asked to complete a series of self-report inventories measuring the quality of their marital relationship. In addition, the spouses' psychological profile was assessed using a Dutch adaptation of Derogatis' (1977) Symptom Checklist (SCL-90) by Arrindell and Ettema (1986). This self-report questionnaire yields scores on eight primary symptom dimensions (agoraphobia, anxiety, depression, somatization, cognitive performance difficulty or insufficiency, interpersonal sensitivity and paranoid ideation, anger-hostility and sleep disturbances), as well as a global 'psychoneuroticism' score.

The analysis of the data revealed that the scores of the husbands in both groups did not differ markedly, whereas the husbands of the eating-disordered patients scored significantly higher than the norm scores of nondistressed males for a number of symptoms, including depression, sleep disturbance and, particularly, insufficiency. As such, these findings seem to support the assumption of psychological distress in the spouses of eating-disordered patients. However, they must be treated with caution given the small subject sample, the different sex ratios and the lack of a properly matched group of nondistressed couples.

Comparison with nondistressed and maritally distressed men

The latter issue was included in the second study (Van den Broucke, Vandereycken and Vertommen, 1994), which was specifically aimed at testing two hypotheses. First, we wanted to verify whether husbands of eating-disordered patients evidence significantly *more* symptoms of psychological distress than nondistressed or maritally distressed male subjects. Second, we tested the assumption of a *correspondence* between the psychiatric distress symptoms reported by eating-disordered patients and their husbands, as predicted by the hypothesis of patient–spouse concordance for psychiatric illness. Because of the relevance of the findings for the topic addressed in this chapter, plus the fact that the sample will also be returned to in future chapters, the general outline of the study will now be discussed in more detail.

To investigate the above questions, a group of 21 eating-disordered (ED) patients and their spouses were compared to two control groups as regards their psychiatric distress. The ED patients were recruited from the three types of clinical settings in which patients with an eating disorder may seek treatment: the inpatient eating-disorder unit of a university psychiatric centre, an outpatient therapy practice and a self-help organization. Nine patients fulfilled the criteria for BN specified in DSM-IV, and 12 those of AN (American Psychiatric Association, 1994). Of the latter, 9 patients suffered from 'pure' AN, and 3 showed a mixed binge/purge symptomatology. The duration of the patients' illness varied between 1.5 and 18 years, with an average of 5 years at the date of investigation. In 8 cases (38 per cent of the sample) the eating disorder had preceded the beginning of the relationship with the spouse. Seventeen patients (81 per cent) were married, and the other 4 were cohabiting with their partner. Further information with regard to the clinical characteristics of the three subgroups is presented in Table 3.1.

The two control groups were composed of maritally distressed and maritally and psychologically nondistressed couples, respectively. The couples in the 'marital distress' (MD) condition (n = 21) were recruited via a marital consultation service, where they had applied for marital therapy. The presence of marital distress was verified by their scores on a marital questionnaire. The couples in the 'nondistressed' (ND) sample (n = 21) were volunteers, recruited through the intermediary of a community social service. The absence of psychological and marital distress was checked by means of a symptom checklist (SCL-90) and a marital satisfaction questionnaire, respectively.

Both control groups were matched to the ED group with regard to age, duration of the relationship, marital status, number of children and social class (see Table 3.2). Except for the higher number of children in the MD couples, the groups did not differ significantly with regard to any of these variables.

The husbands' psychiatric distress

Psychological distress in the spouses was assessed by the Dutch adaptation of Derogatis' (1977) Symptom Checklist (SCL-90). Preliminary

Table 3.1   Characteristics of the eating disorder subgroups

	AN				BN (n=9)	
	Abstaining (n=9)		Binge/purge (n=3)			
	M	SD	M	SD	M	SD
Age	28.0	4.81	29.6	4.17	29.7	9.46
Height (cm)	162.0	5.28	166.7	6.35	161.3	11.03
Average weight (kg)	40.4	3.79	45.0	2.90	52.4	6.70
Weight fluctuation[a]	6.2	2.95	5.0	2.45	5.8	3.56
Per cent fluctuation[b]	14.4	6.46	10.0	5.13	11.3	5.95
Duration (yrs)	6.0	4.75	6.5	1.50	6.4	6.34
Cohabitation (yrs)[c]	4.7	3.39	7.3	3.94	7.3	6.55

[a] During the 6-month period prior to assessment
[b] As a percentage of the highest reported body weight
[c] Number of unmarried couples: 1, 1 and 2 respectively; number of couples without children: 2, 0 and 5 years respectively
Source: Van den Broucke *et al.* (1994)

analyses revealed no significant differences in psychological distress between husbands of patients with abstaining AN, binge/purge AN or BN, nor between husbands of patients whose illness had begun before or after the marriage, indicating that the couples in the ED group could be treated as one sample.

To determine whether the levels of psychological distress reported by the husbands differed significantly across the three groups, their scores on the scales of the symptom checklist (excluding the overall psychoneuroticism scale, which is a linear transformation of the other scales) were entered into a MANOVA, yielding a significant multivariate group effect (Wilks' lambda = 0.616, approx. $F(16,106)$ = 1.816, p = 0.038). To interpret this effect, univariate analyses were performed for each scale separately. Table 3.3 lists the univariate effects of interest, as well as the mean scores and standard deviations of the husbands in each group. As this table indicates, significant intergroup differences were observed for interpersonal sensitivity and hostility. An inspection of the group means of interest, however, indicated that these effects must be attributed to the elevated scores of the MD husbands, and not to those of the husbands of the ED patients as

Table 3.2   Demographic characteristics of the three groups

	ED (n=21)		MD (n=21)		ND (n=21)		F	p
	M	SD	M	SD	M	SD		
Husbands' age	31.2	7.2	33.6	7.2	28.8	8.7	1.998	0.15
Wives' age	28.9	5.7	31.9	7.7	27.7	7.6	1.945	0.15
Cohabitation (months)	74.1	53.9	114.7	81.8	62.8	92.7	2.581	0.08
No. of children	0.7	1.1	1.6	1.2	0.9	1.2	3.240	0.05
	N		N		N		X^2	p
Unmarried	4		4		5		0.194 (df=2)	0.91
Social class[a]							4.719 (df=6)	0.58
higher	3		4		6			
middle	9		11		8			
lower	9		6		7			

[a] According to the husband's occupation
ED = eating-disordered couples, MD = maritally distressed couples,
ND = nondistressed couples
Source: Van den Broucke *et al.* (1994)

expected. In fact, *a posteriori* Scheffé tests revealed no significant differences in scores by ED husbands and ND husbands on any of the symptom scales, yet indicated lower scores than the MD husbands for interpersonal sensitivity and hostility. In other words, husbands of patients with an eating disorder do not evidence more complaints of psychological distress than ND husbands, and actually report less distress than MD husbands.

This conclusion was further substantiated by the results of a discriminant analysis on the husbands' symptom scores, producing one significant discriminant function (explaining 92.4 per cent of the variance) which mainly discriminated between the MD husbands on the one hand and the ED and ND husbands on the other, but not between the latter two groups. Specifically, the discrimination mainly referred to the MD husbands' higher levels of hostility, interpersonal sensitivity and insufficiency in their relationship with others. The ED husbands, on the other hand, could not be discriminated from the ND husbands on the basis of their psychological distress scores.

Table 3.3   Husbands' psychiatric distress scores (SCL-90)

	ED (n=21)		ND (n=21)		MD (n=21)		
	M	SD	M	SD	M	SD	F
Anxiety	14.3	5.1	12.9	3.3	15.2	6.4	1.128
Agoraphobia	8.1	3.1	7.7	1.1	8.9	4.3	0.737
Depression	24.6	8.3	21.7	6.6	26.1	9.1	1.663
Somatization	16.6	4.0	15.3	3.0	17.7	7.6	1.129
Insufficiency	14.0	3.5	14.1	3.6	16.1	5.6	1.628
Sensitivity	25.1	6.9	24.3	4.8	31.5	11.2	4.966*
Hostility	7.8	1.8	7.5	1.4	10.3	3.7	7.798**
Sleep disturbance	5.2	2.9	4.8	2.0	4.9	2.4	0.203

* $p < 0.01$; ** $p < 0.001$
Source: Van den Broucke *et al.* (1994)

Husband–wife correspondence

Whereas the findings discussed in the previous section referred to the levels of psychiatric distress experienced by the husbands in the different conditions *across* relationships (between-group comparisons), another question concerns the correspondence between the partners *within* each relationship as regards their psychiatric symptoms. Indeed, the husbands' symptoms may well resemble those of the patients even if their levels of psychological distress are lower. To verify this assumption, a further analysis was performed on the data of the aforementioned study by computing within-couple correlations between the patients' and their husbands' symptom scores.

As shown in Table 3.4, a number of these correlations appear to be quite high (up to 0.39). However, none of them were statistically significant. Moreover, the median within-couple correlation across the eight symptom subscales was very low for all three groups and approximated zero for the ED couples. The same applies to the correlations regarding the overall psychoneuroticism scale, which can be considered as an overall measure of psychiatric illness: only in the MD couples was the correspondence between the partners' scores on the psychoneuroticism scale somewhat more elevated ($r = 0.24$, $p = 0.289$).

While these results lend very little support to the assumed husband–wife correspondence for psychiatric distress, another way of looking at the data is to consider the *relative* correspondence between the partners' distress symptoms. It is indeed possible that the husbands exhibit the same kind of symptoms as the patients, but that there is no actual covariation with respect to the levels in which the various symptoms apply, as is implied by Pearson's correlation coefficient. In other

Table 3.4   Within-couple correlations on the scales of the SCL-90

	ED (n=21)	ND (n=21)	MD (n=21)
Anxiety	0.31	-0.17	0.14
Agoraphobia	-0.13	0.15	0.20
Depression	-0.17	0.01	0.14
Somatization	0.01	0.10	0.20
Insufficiency	-0.03	-0.16	0.28
Sensitivity	0.20	-0.17	0.30
Hostility	0.17	0.39	0.14
Sleep disturbance	-0.05	-0.16	-0.26
Psychoneuroticism	-0.06	-0.02	0.24
Median[a]	-0.01	-0.08	0.17

[a] For all except the overall psychoneuroticism scale
Source: Van den Broucke *et al.* (1994)

words, it could be that there is only a qualitative correspondence between the patients' and the spouses' symptoms, yet not a marked quantitative one.

To investigate the latter possibility, the mean item scores on the eight SCL-90 scales were computed for the husbands and the wives in the three groups, and then rank ordered to obtain an idea of the relative importance of each symptom. As a result, the mean rank order of the symptoms reported by ED patients and their husbands appeared to be very similar, with depression, sleep disturbance and insufficiency ranking highest, and somatization, hostility and agoraphobia lowest. However, the relative correspondence of the symptoms *within* the couples, as measured by Spearman's rank-order correlation, was not significant (median $\rho = 0.41$, $p = 0.297$). The same was also observed for the ND husbands and wives, where again no significance was attained for the relative within-couple correspondence (median $\rho = 0.24$, $p = 0.540$). Also, the difference between the median rank-order correlations of ED and ND couples was not significant ($p = 0.382$). The lowest median within-couple rank-order correlation was observed for MD couples ($\rho = 0.13$, $p = 0.750$), where the husbands obtained comparatively higher scores on the interpersonal sensitivity and hostility scales. Again, the difference between the median rank-order correlations of ED and MD couples was not significant ($p = 0.316$).

In sum, these findings suggest that although there may be a qualitative correspondence between symptom scores of ED patients and of their husbands across couples, there is no systematic correspondence with respect to the relative importance of the partners' distress symptoms within the couples. In this regard, ED couples are actually quite comparable to ND ones: not only is the mean rank order of the scores for the husbands and the wives of both groups (across couples) almost identical, but there also appears to be no significant difference between the median within-couple rank-order correlations of both groups. As such, the clinical assumption that the husband–wife correspondence with regard to psychological distress represents a distinct characteristic of ED patients' marriages can hardly be sustained.

CONCLUSIONS

Despite the lack of reliable research data on this topic, the psychiatric profile of the spouse is one of the major issues discussed in the clinical literature about AN and BN in married patients. Many theorists and practitioners assume a correspondence between the patients and their husbands as regards their neurotic tendencies, and consider the emotional instability of the partner as playing an important role in the development of a patient's eating disorder. In this chapter we have challenged these clinical impressions, relying both on theoretical considerations and on the findings from an empirical study. First, we have expressed our concerns about the theoretical underpinnings of these views, arguing that they are based on a constrained conceptualization of relationships. We have asserted that since marital relationships are essentially dynamic processes in which it is impossible to distinguish causes from consequences, it is trivial whether the husband's psychiatric distress occurred before or after the patient's eating disorder. The important issue is that the spouse's distress influences his capability to constructively respond to the patient's problem.

More fundamentally, however, we have supplied empirical data indicating that husbands of eating-disordered patients do not evidence significantly more symptoms of distress than nondistressed men, and in fact reported a lower degree of psychological distress than men presenting with marital distress. Furthermore, within-couple analyses of psychiatric distress scores indicated that there is neither a significant quantitative nor a systematic qualitative correspondence between the psychopathological profiles of eating-disordered patients and those of their husbands, which contradicts the hypothesis that the latter reveal a symptom pattern closely resembling that of their ill partners.

In this respect, the findings presented in this chapter are in close agreement with those reported on husbands of agoraphobic females. Arrindell and Emmelkamp (1985), for example, found no evidence for a concordance between the neurotic symptoms of agoraphobics and of their partners, whereas such a concordance is commonly assumed in the clinical literature. Thus it appears that the alleged correspondence between eating-disordered patients and their husbands in terms of their psychopathological condition, like that in agoraphobics' relationships, is probably a 'self-perpetuating myth, with clinicians seeing in their own patients only what has been reported by other clinicians' (Hafner, 1982, quoted by Arrindell and Emmelkamp, 1985).

4   Marital satisfaction and intimacy

Marital relationships are more than simply the sum of the husbands' and the wives' individual characteristics. In order to investigate the marital context of anorexia and bulimia nervosa, it is therefore not enough to study the personalities of the spouses: one must also pay attention to the qualities and processes that characterize the relationship between the patients and their husbands. In this regard, the intimacy that is attained in their marriages deserves specific attention. As pointed out in the second chapter, intimacy represents a key topic in current social psychological theories about personal relationships, and is considered an important determinant of a person's psychological well-being. As such, intimacy problems are considered an important feature of the marital relationships of psychiatric patients.

In this chapter, we will elaborate on this issue by examining the nature of intimacy in the marriages of patients with an eating disorder. Because the term 'intimacy' is sometimes used rather carelessly to designate a variety of different relationship qualities, we will begin the chapter with an introductory paragraph about the meaning of the intimacy construct as proposed in the social psychological literature. Next, the main clinical impressions about intimacy in eating-disordered patients' marriages will be discussed. Finally, these impressions will be substantiated by the findings of empirical studies focusing on this subject.

THEORETICAL VIEWS ON MARITAL INTIMACY

Conceptual definitions of marital intimacy

Over the past two decades, the concept of intimacy as a relational characteristic or process has become an important research focus in social psychology and related disciplines. This is probably due to the emergent cross-disciplinary interest in close or 'personal' relationships (Hinde, 1978; Duck *et al*., 1984; Duck and Perlman, 1985) or relationships in which the persons involved are not interchangeable, as opposed to the casual meetings among strangers which for a long time were the main subject of studies of interpersonal behaviour. As a qualitative attribute of such personal relationships, intimacy has become a key construct in relationship studies. Its importance is reflected in the large number of publications that are concerned with intimacy or intimacy-related issues, either as dependent or independent variables, or as the focus of theoretical analysis (for a review, see Van den Broucke *et al*., 1995a).

With this emergent interest, earlier definitions of the concept have been expanded and refined. For a long time, most investigators of close relationships relied on Altman and Taylor's (1973) *social penetration theory* to define intimacy as the disclosure of personally relevant thoughts and feelings to another person (e.g. Derlega and Chaikin, 1975; Hinde, 1978). More recent conceptualizations suggest that the self-disclosure process alone is insufficient to capture the essence of intimacy. Chelune, Robison and Kommor (1984), for example, propose that intimacy should also entail an aspect of shared, reciprocal understanding, arising from the appraisal of revealed information. In the same vein, Acitelli and Duck (1987) stress the importance of a meta-perspective or 'relationship awareness', involving a conscious yet not always verbally communicated acknowledgement of the behavioural, cognitive and affective interaction patterns between the partners, in maintaining intimacy in a personal relationship.

In addition to these cognitive aspects, some theorists have argued for the inclusion of emotional components in the definition of intimacy. Reis and Shaver (1988), for instance, point out that significant self-disclosure seems unlikely if the listener is perceived as uninterested or uncaring. Accordingly, they consider the discloser's feelings of being understood, validated and cared for as fundamental characteristics of intimacy. This view is shared by others including Sternberg (1988), who considers intimacy as the emotional component of love, referring to feelings of warmth, support and commitment to the relationship; and Levinger (1988), who defines intimacy as a combination of affective and behavioural interdependence of two partners.

The above views suggest that intimacy must be thought of as a multicomponent phenomenon that includes such diverse aspects as the disclosure of personally relevant facts and feelings, reciprocal understanding, self-validation, affection and caring. Intimacy may accordingly be defined as a process – that is, a characteristic way of relating which develops over time (Clark and Reis, 1988) – or as a state – that is, a relatively stable structural quality of the relationship that emerges from this process (Acitelli and Duck, 1987). In the latter sense, the term 'intimate' must be reserved for relationships that fulfil the conditions of these intimacy processes, as exemplified by the fact that the behavioural expressions of intimacy can be observed in the partners' overt interactions.

Components of marital intimacy

In accordance with the above conceptualization, Waring and his associates (Waring, 1988; Waring *et al.*, 1981) have developed a working definition of marital intimacy containing eight dimensions: (1) *affection* is the degree to which feelings of emotional closeness are expressed by the spouses; (2) *expressiveness* is the degree to which thoughts, beliefs, attitudes and feelings are communicated within the marriage; (3) *compatibility* indicates the degree to which the couple are able to work and play together comfortably; (4) *cohesion* refers to the degree of commitment to the marriage; (5) *sexuality* indicates the degree to which sexual needs are communicated and fulfilled; (6) *conflict resolution* refers to the ease with which differences of opinion are resolved; (7) *autonomy* refers to the couple's degree of positive connectedness to family and friends; (8) *identity* indicates the couple's level of self-esteem and self-confidence.

This definition is based on lay conceptualizations of intimacy rather than on existing psychological theories of interpersonal relationships, and as such does not distinguish between experiential and behavioural variables or between dimensions referring to individual, relational or systemic phenomena. In addition, some of the elements contained in this model (e.g. sexuality) could be viewed as possible manifestations of intimacy rather than components of the construct itself. By including these aspects in the definition of intimacy, the term more or less becomes a synonym for marital quality in general.

Using a different approach, we have proposed an alternative model of marital intimacy (Van den Broucke *et al.*, 1995a), which is based on existing social psychological views regarding 'intimate' relationships, and incorporates the systemic principle that relational phenomena must be considered in relation to elements at other – individual and situational – system levels (Hinde, 1978; Cromwell and Peterson, 1983). In this model, components of marital intimacy are distinguished on three distinct levels:

1 on the dyadic level, intimacy refers to the *affective, cognitive and behavioural interdependence* between two partners, as reflected in the couple's emotional closeness, the validation of each other's ideas and values and the implicit or explicit consensus about the rules which guide their interactions;
2 on the individual level it includes *authenticity*, or the ability to 'be oneself' in the relationship with the partner, and *openness*, or the readiness to share ideas and feelings with the partner;
3 on the social group or network level it entails an aspect of dyadic identity or *exclusiveness* that is related to long-term commitment and revealed by the partners' use of private expressions or their reference to the relationship in dyadic terms (i.e. 'us' or 'we' instead of 'me' or 'I'). The six intimacy dimensions of interest are summarized in Table 4.1.

An empirical validation of this model is documented by Van den Broucke *et al.* (1995e). Moreover, the components of our model show a strong resemblance to other operational definitions of marital intimacy that have been arrived at on different conceptual and evidential grounds (e.g. L'Abate, 1986). Hence, we believe that this model may serve as a useful basis for investigating intimacy in the marital relationships of patients with an eating disorder.

Table 4.1　　Components of marital intimacy

Individual level	
Authenticity	The ability to 'be oneself' in the relationship with the partner
Openness	The readiness to share ideas and feelings with the partner
Dyadic level	
Affective interdependence	The degree of emotional closeness experienced by the partners
Cognitive interdependence	The degree to which the partners validate each other's ideas and values
Instrumental interdependence	The degree of implicit or explicit consensus about the rules which regulate the partners' interactions
Social group or network level	
Exclusiveness	The degree to which dyadic privacy is maintained in the relationship with others (e.g. friends, family, etc.)

Source: Van den Broucke *et al.* (1995a)

CLINICAL VIEWS OF INTIMACY IN EATING-DISORDERED COUPLES

General impressions

Although the above discussion suggests that an integrated and agreed-upon model of marital intimacy is not yet fully established, there appears to be a remarkable consensus among clinicians about the fact that eating-disordered patients and their husbands often fail to develop genuine intimacy in their marital relationships. Apparently, clinicians rely mostly on the layperson's implicit understanding of intimacy when they use this term to designate such issues as the subjects' inability to communicate their deeper feelings to their partners (Dally and Gomez, 1979; Foster, 1986), their lack of mutual warmth and understanding (Dally, 1984), their lack of honesty and mutual respect (Boskind-White and White, 1983), the barrenness of their sexual relationships (Crisp, 1980) and their avoidance of open confrontations (Dally, 1984; Foster, 1986).

Dally and Gomez (1979), for example, state that both the anorectic patient and her partner show a tendency to identify with stereotyped sex roles, which prevents them from expressing their true feelings and attaining genuine intimacy. In a similar vein, Foster (1986) notes that the patient's 'false self' – that is, her failure to identify and express her own feelings, thoughts and wishes – is often complemented by the spouse's tacit acceptance of the former's self-presentation. This concurs with Dally's (1984) observations in his sample of 50 AN couples (see also chapter 3), noting that the patients 'tried to draw closer but felt continually rebuffed. Husbands became worried by what seemed to be unreasonable possessiveness and attention-seeking behavior. Yet it was rare for any of them to express their feelings openly' (Dally, 1984, p. 426).

In another example, Dally notes that some of the patients in his sample 'were aware of and resented the lack of mutual warmth and understanding in their marriages, [yet apparently they were] unable to face, let alone express their turbulent emotions' (p. 426).

This lack of intimacy is reportedly compounded by a continuing, frequent and intensive 'close' relationship with the family of origin (Foster, 1986; Barrett and Schwartz, 1987), which not only compromises the boundary between the marital dyad and the family, but also impairs whatever ability the couple may have to distinguish their own perceptions of their relationship issues from those of extended family members.

A similar lack of intimacy is also reported with regard to the relationships of BN patients. While it is a well-known fact that bulimics often manage to keep their bingeing and purging a secret from their husbands (Andersen, 1985; Hall, 1982), the open expression of feelings is reportedly poor, especially at the beginning of the illness. With regard to emotional closeness, the relationships between bulimic patients and their partners are found to be either rigidly overinvolved (i.e. pseudo-intimate) or rigidly distant (Root *et al.*, 1986). According to Barrett and Schwartz (1987), the bulimic symptoms actually serve the purpose of regulating proximity and distance in the relationship: the bulimia is the catalyst that allows the couple to regain closeness after a period of distance. Responding to the bulimia, the couple dare to discuss sensitive topics or engage in sexual intimacy. They are protected from too much closeness by the patient's distraught behaviour and the spouse's focus on her as the problem. When the conversation or sexual proximity becomes too intimate, however, either party can withdraw. This constant shift provides the couple with periods of both intense closeness and prolonged withdrawal.

Critical appraisal

In view of the conformity between these observations reported by different authors, it seems reasonable to believe that there is probably some truth in the assumption that the marriages of AN and BN patients are characterized by a low level of intimacy. However, since these observations are neither objective nor independent from one another, it is also possible that this consensus of views simply reflects a self-perpetuating myth based on the reporters' bias. More specifically, it is plausible that a false impression of conformity is created by the fact that the term 'intimacy' is used to designate a whole range of marital properties and behaviours. Clinicians thus may *think* they observed similar characteristics in their patients' marriages, while in truth they may be referring to different aspects. Or, alternatively, they may simply be using a different name to designate the patients' or their partners' feelings of unhappiness with their marital relationships.

Another important point is that the deficient intimacy level of these couples is often implicitly regarded as the *cause* of the eating disorder. In fact, however, the relationship between the marital problems that are referred to above and the occurrence and/or development of an eating disorder may well be a circular one, with the marital relationship both being influenced by the presence of the disorder and in turn influencing the further course of the disorder. This does not imply that a deficiency in the couple's intimacy would by any means be less important: regardless of whether or not it precedes the eating disorder, a lack of intimacy in the relationship with her partner most probably represents an additional source of distress rather than support for the patient.

So whatever the causal connection with the occurrence of an eating disorder, the alleged presence of intimacy problems remains an important focus. It is therefore necessary to evaluate the tentative clinical impressions regarding intimacy in the relationships of eating-disordered patients by way of systematic research, based on clear and theoretically sound conceptualizations and operationalizations of intimacy. With this, it must be substantiated that what appears to be a lack of intimacy to most clinicians is something other than the subjects' dissatisfaction with their relationship. In the next section, we will present the results of the few studies that have specifically addressed this issue.

EMPIRICAL FINDINGS REGARDING INTIMACY IN EATING-DISORDERED COUPLES

Level of intimacy

As part of a larger study investigating the nature of marital relationships in eating disorders, Woodside *et al.* (1993) measured the level of marital intimacy in 20 married anorectic or bulimic patients and their spouses. Assessments of intimacy were done at the time of the patient's admission to a day hospital programme, using the Waring Intimacy Questionnaire (WIQ; see chapter 9). This self-report questionnaire yields scores on the eight intimacy dimensions contained in Waring's (1988) model (i.e. affection, expressiveness, compatibility, cohesion, sexuality, conflict resolution, autonomy and identity), as well as on a total intimacy and social desirability scale. In 15 of the couples, intimacy was also assessed at the time of discharge from the programme, which lasted 10 to 12 weeks. Because of the relatively small number of subjects involved in this part of the study, no distinction was made between subgroups of patients according to the diagnostic condition (i.e. AN versus BN).

The results of this study revealed that at admission the patients' intimacy was generally low, with very low scores on total intimacy and identity, whereas the husbands attained higher scores than their wives on all the intimacy dimensions. After the treatment, an improvement was attained for most aspects of intimacy, although for some of the dimensions (the patients' cohesion and autonomy, and the spouses' affection and expressivity) the post-treatment scores were lower. The differences within couples were diminished but still reached significance. It was also noticed that patients with a poor clinical outcome (as measured at discharge) tended to rate their marital intimacy as higher than other patients and higher than the spouses at admission.

Woodside and his co-workers conclude that patients who suffer from an eating disorder experience a serious degree of marital discord, and particularly report very low degrees of affection (i.e. nonsexual expression of caring) and cohesion (i.e. commitment to the relationship) in addition to a low self-esteem. While the patients' views are not entirely shared by their spouses, the authors do not infer from this that one view is correct and the other incorrect. On the contrary: the very existence of discrepancies is considered an indication of a lack of intimacy. Further, it is noted that the removal of the patients' symptoms induces an increase of the congruence between the partners, since the patients' intimacy scores significantly improve over the course of hospitalization while the spouses' ratings remain fairly consistent over time.

The findings from this study generally corroborate those of two earlier ones. In the first, Van Buren and Williamson (1988) compared 12 bulimic couples with 14 maritally distressed and 15 normal control couples on self-report measures of relationship satisfaction and beliefs about intimate relationships. The bulimic patients were found to experience a degree of relationship dissatisfaction comparable to that of maritally distressed women. They also resembled that group in their irrational belief that neither their partners nor the quality of their relationship could be changed. The spouses of the bulimics were more dissatisfied with their marriages than the normal control spouses, but not as dissatisfied as the male partners in the distressed group. They also did not differ from either group with regard to their beliefs about the relationship.

In the second study (Van den Broucke and Vandereycken, 1989c), a series of self-report measures assessing marital quality were completed by 12 AN patients and their spouses and 13 couples with one partner suffering from a non-phobic neurotic disorder (see also chapter 3). The results revealed that the eating-disordered patients and their spouses, like the neurotic patients in the control group, experienced marital distress. However, whereas the husbands reported severe dissatisfaction with the marital relationship itself, the patients focused more on the maladjustment of their social and work relationships. Further, the husbands considered their partners' attitude towards them, and to a lesser extent their own attitudes towards their wives, as unfriendly. In contrast, the patients themselves considered both their own and their spouses' affective attitudes towards each other as only moderately negative. So, apparently, eating-disordered patients and their partners differ with regard to their appreciation of the relationship's affective quality, and especially of the patients' attitudes towards their husbands. This discrepancy could not be attributed to an inaccurate assessment of the partners' attitude, as was revealed by comparisons between each partner's reported attitude towards the relationship and the other partner's construal of this attitude. Rather, the lack of correspondence between the partners' opinion about their relationship should be regarded as a reflection of a low marital intimacy.

Marital intimacy and distress

Taken together, the findings from the above studies seem to confirm the clinical impression that the marriages of patients with an eating disorder are characterized by low levels of intimacy. However, they do not establish whether this low intimacy reflects more than a mere dissatisfaction with their relationship. This issue was addressed in our own research project (Van den Broucke *et al.*, 1995b), using the same samples as the ones described in chapter 3: a group of 21 eating-disordered patients and their spouses, and two control groups of 21 maritally distressed and nondistressed couples, respectively. To investigate these couples' intimacy, the patients and their husbands each completed the *Marital Intimacy Questionnaire* (MIQ; see chapter 9 and Appendix 1), which measures five factors reflecting the dimensions of our multidimensional intimacy model: (1) *intimacy problems* measures a lack of intimacy; (2) *consensus* measures the cognitive and instrumental aspects of intimacy; (3) *openness* measures openness and to a lesser extent authenticity (i.e. the individual components of intimacy); (4) *affection* measures the affective component of intimacy; and (5) *commitment* measures the degree of commitment and privacy of the relationship (i.e. the situational component of intimacy).

Since preliminary analyses revealed no differences between relevant subgroups of subjects as defined according to the type of the patient's disorder ('pure' or abstaining AN, 'mixed' or binge/purge AN, or BN) or the timing of onset (premarital or postmarital), the eating-disordered (ED) couples were treated as a homogeneous sample. Unlike the data in the study by Woodside *et al.* (1993), the within-couple differences were nonsignificant on all the MIQ subscales, whereas within-couple correlations were highly significant (rs 0.55 or higher, all ps < 0.001). Consequently, it was concluded that the preferred unit of analysis would be the husbands' and wives' summed scores.

The mean intimacy scores for the couples in the three groups are presented in Table 4.2. As this table indicates, the nondistressed (ND) couples attain the highest scores and the maritally distressed (MD) couples the lowest on all the scales except intimacy problems, where the pattern is reversed. The ED couples' scores are always situated between those of the two comparison groups. To test the significance of the observed differences, a one-way MANOVA was performed on the MIQ scores, with the number of children included as a covariate (since the groups differed significantly with regard to this variable). This analysis produced a highly significant multivariate effect for group membership ($p < 0.001$), while the results of univariate tests revealed significant differences between the three groups for all five of the scales of the MIQ. Subsequent pairwise MANOVAs indicated that the differences between the ED and ND couples ($p < 0.001$) and between the ED and MD couples ($p = 0.003$) were significant.

These data again confirm that the level of intimacy of ED couples is lower than that of ND couples, albeit higher than that of couples presenting with overt marital difficulties. However, the possibility must be ruled out that these differences simply reflect the different marital satisfaction levels of the three groups, which could be asserted on account of the strong relationship between marital intimacy and marital satisfaction (which in this study was indicated by the very significant correlations between the scales of the MIQ and the Maudsley Marital Questionnaire). Therefore, the couples' MIQ scores were entered into a multiple group discriminant analysis to break down the between-groups effect into several uncorrelated discriminant

Table 4.2   Mean intimacy scores for eating-disordered couples and comparison groups (MIQ)

	ED (n=21)		ND (n=21)		MD (n=21)		
	M	SD	M	SD	M	SD	F^{a}
Intimacy							
problems	41.2	24.2	19.5	8.5	51.6	15.3	17.428
Consensus	64.8	19.1	81.8	7.8	43.0	17.5	29.378
Openness	60.6	15.7	80.6	7.6	53.2	14.2	24.206
Affection	48.1	9.6	57.5	5.2	40.1	11.6	16.428
Commitment	58.3	12.3	65.7	7.7	50.1	9.1	12.272

[a] all $ps < 0.001$
Multivariate effect of group: Wilks' lambda = 0.357, appr. F (10,108) = 7.274, $p < 0.001$
Source: Van den Broucke *et al.* (1995b)

functions. After removing a first significant function (which was similar to the between-groups effect reported above), the residual also reached significance ($p = 0.002$), implying that in addition to the effect of marital satisfaction a second discrimination could be made between the groups. This second function mainly discriminated between the ED couples on the one hand and the MD and ND couples on the other, and most strongly correlated with the 'openness' and 'intimacy problems' subscales (absolute *r*s of 0.45 and 0.31, respectively). In other words, when the effects of marital distress were singled out, ED couples could be discriminated from the comparison groups on account of their relatively low level of openness and high level of intimacy problems. In general, this seems to confirm the clinical impression that an intimacy deficiency, and particularly a lack of openness, is a major characteristic of the marriages of anorexia or bulimia nervosa patients.

CONCLUSIONS

Marital intimacy is an issue that seems to evoke mixed reactions among clinicians and social researchers alike. To some, it represents one of the most central features of marital relationships, the achievement of which is essential to the spouses' mental and physical well-being (Birtchnell, 1986; Feldman, 1979; Waring, 1988). To others, the recent concern with intimacy by investigators of personal relationships merely represents an idealization of egalitarian middle-class models of marriage, which should not be raised to a universal norm (Carpenter, 1986; Gadlin, 1977). At all events, it is difficult to disregard the current fascination with the subject, both among lay people and within the psychological community (Chelune and Waring, 1984; Fisher and Stricker, 1982; Kantor and Okun, 1989; Perlman and Fehr, 1987; Reis, 1990).

Given the general appeal of the intimacy construct, it is not surprising to see that the notion has also emerged in the clinical literature on married eating-disordered patients, if only to serve as a common denominator for the aspects which are presumed as 'missing' in these patients' marriages. The predominant clinical impression is indeed that the relationships between eating-disordered patients and their husbands are characterized by low degrees of mutual warmth, understanding, honesty and respect, which could all be considered as indicators of the couples' failure to achieve marital intimacy.

In this chapter we have tried to substantiate these impressions, first by looking at the conceptual definitions and models of marital intimacy as discussed in the personal relationships literature, and then by critically examining the existing clinical impressions against the backdrop of these models. Next, we have looked at the results of two studies in which the intimacy of eating-disordered couples was empirically assessed using operationalizations of intimacy based on theoretically sound models.

Although the results of these empirical studies are not completely comparable, they both largely confirm the assumption that eating-disordered patients, and to a lesser extent their spouses, report lower levels of intimacy than nondistressed couples at the time of referral. On the other hand, it was also demonstrated that this low intimacy must not be attributed simply to the couples' dissatisfaction with their relationship. Specifically, eating-disordered couples can be discriminated from both nondistressed and maritally distressed couples on the basis of their lower levels of openness and higher levels of intimacy problems. This means that eating-disordered and control couples not only differ with respect to the *level* of marital intimacy that is achieved, but also with regard to the *nature* of their intimacy.

The identification of a lack of open communication in these couples as an aspect of their poor intimacy is in keeping not only with the clinical impressions of married eating-disordered patients, but also with the more general findings regarding the relationship between intimacy and self-disclosure. It has indeed been demonstrated that a large share of the variance in a couple's level of intimacy can be explained by their self-disclosing behaviours (Waring and Chelune, 1983). In the light of these findings, the lack of openness in the eating-disordered patients' marriages may be considered as a serious relational deficiency, which may represent an important obstacle for the growth and enhancement of their marital intimacy and, in the end, become an additional source of distress rather than support for the patient.

5   Communication

The idea that the communication between marital partners to a great extent determines the quality of their relationship is largely supported by theoretical reflections and empirical findings. From a theoretical point of view, marital communication is the medium through which intimacy, as a key qualitative characteristic of a relationship, is both achieved and maintained. From an empirical angle, it has been demonstrated that the interactions of maritally distressed couples are characterized by disturbed communication patterns such as high negativism, negative reciprocity, rigidity, negative attributions and the presence of a covert status struggle (Schaap, 1984).

Apart from their impact on marital quality, however, deficiencies in the communication between partners have also been related to the occurrence and maintenance of psychiatric problems, as we have pointed out in chapter 2. This is particularly the case for depression and alcoholism, but it may also apply to eating disorders. In point of fact, communication problems are among the prevailing issues mentioned in the clinical literature about married AN and BN patients, although empirical research data are seldom provided to support this.

In this chapter, we will clarify the role of communication by looking at the communication process between eating-disordered patients and their husbands. As in the previous chapter, we will start with a review of the main theoretical models of marital communication to arrive at a workable definition of the subject of interest. Next, we will discuss the predominant clinical impressions about communication in the marriages of patients with an eating disorder, and then present data from an empirical study about this subject.

THEORETICAL VIEWS ON MARITAL COMMUNICATION

Definitions of marital communication

The fact that communication plays a pervasive role in intimate relationships is most convincingly expressed by the well-known axiom of orthodox communication theorists that 'all behaviour is a potential form of communication, and becomes communication when it is assigned a meaning by another person' (Watzlawick *et al.*, 1967). The great value of this view lies in its emphasis on the impossibility of *not* communicating in an interpersonal setting. However, as a definition of communication it is evidently too broad to allow for a systematic study of the processes involved. To that effect, a more specific working definition is required. Given that most contemporary definitions of communication include a minimum requirement of non-randomness or constraint (Penman, 1980), marital communication may for the purpose of this outline be defined as the multi-faceted, patterned, verbal and nonverbal interaction process through which marital relationships are established, maintained and changed.

This definition still allows for a variety of ways to study communication in marital relationships. Fitzpatrick (1988) in this regard distinguishes between three different theoretical approaches to marital communication. In the *typological approach*, marriages which share the same communication patterns are placed in the same categories, to summarize the diversity of phenomena that characterize marital interaction. An example of this approach is Lederer and Jackson's (1968) distinction between symmetrical, complementary and parallel relationships. The second approach, which is referred to as the *co-orientation* approach, is more concerned with the outcomes of communication. Important qualities in this regard are the agreement between spouses (i.e. the sharing of opinions), the accuracy of the communication (i.e. the partners' ability to interpret each other's messages as they were intended) and the awareness of the communication (i.e. the partners' knowledge of whether or not their communication is accurate). These properties are investigated by exploring the ways in which messages are encoded and decoded by the persons who communicate. Finally, the *interaction approach* focuses on the exchanges that lead to a particular outcome. This may involve paying attention to the contents of the exchange as well as to the communication patterns, the intensity of the interactions, the level of physiological arousal during conversations and the cognitions which transform the partners' messages.

An important asset of the latter approach is that it captures the complexity of the communication process by focusing directly on the exchange of verbal and nonverbal messages between the spouses. As such, it helps to explain *why* couples communicate effectively or ineffectively, rather than simply stating *if* they do. In the next section, we will discuss the most important interactional models that have been proposed to explain the communication processes characterizing successful and unsuccessful marriages.

Interaction models of communication

Borrowing from the reviews by Fitzpatrick (1988) and Schaap, Buunk and Kerkstra (1987), we may distinguish between several models of marital interaction, each of which focuses on different aspects of the communication between partners.

The *physiological model* starts from the premise that men are more easily physiologically aroused in tense situations than women, and are slower to calm down afterwards (Gottman and Levenson, 1987). This effect is stronger for unhappily married than happily married husbands. Consequently, husbands, unhappily married ones in particular, experience greater distress during marital confrontations than their wives, which explains why they more often withdraw from conflicts. This model accounts for some of the gender differences that have been reported with regard to marital communication, such as the fact that unhappily married husbands are more insensitive to subtle nonverbal displays of (negative) feelings than their wives. Because of the heavy emphasis on biologically determined processes, however, the behavioural and structural components of marital interaction may be oversimplified.

The *relational control model* has mainly been advanced by 'communication theorists' (e.g. Watzlawick *et al.*, 1967) and focuses on the distinction between the content level of communications (i.e. what people say to each other) and the command level (i.e. the speaker's view on who is in command of the relationship). Couples may agree or disagree with the content of each other's messages as well as with the command aspect. In complementary relationships, one partner's messages are intended to assert control and the other's to relinquish control; in symmetrical relationships both partners want to assert control. The distinction between these two levels of communication may account for a number of communication problems in relationships. Couples may, for instance, confuse both levels and fight about content issues while their problems concern the command level. Other problems arise from discrepancies between the content and command levels, which often take the form of a discordance between verbal and nonverbal messages. Finally, problems may also result from the disqualification of messages or from interpunction differences. These communication problems can usually be resolved by way of metacommunication, yet it appears that nondistressed couples are better able to switch back and forth between communication and metacommunication than distressed ones (Raush *et al.*, 1974).

The *social learning and behaviour exchange model* draws from social learning theory (Stuart, 1969) and social exchange theory (Thibaut and Kelley, 1959) to explain the role of social reinforcement in marital interactions (Jacobson and Margolin, 1979). Reinforcement is 'social' when it consists of a spouse's feedback. Positive reinforcement occurs when one spouse administers a pleasant stimulus (e.g. giving attention or approval) following a specific behaviour of the partner; negative reinforcement occurs when an aversive stimulus is removed after the behaviour has been performed (e.g. giving in to the spouse's nagging). Interactions in which the behaviour of one spouse is controlled by aversive stimulation and the behaviour of the other spouse by positive reinforcement are called coercive (Patterson and Reid, 1970). This type of interaction is typical for distressed relationships, whereas nondistressed couples rely more on positive reinforcement strategies to influence the spouse's behaviour (Birchler, Weiss, and Vincent, 1975; Raush *et al.*, 1974). The model also holds that spouses evaluate their relationships in terms of the balance between the costs (inputs) and the rewards deriving from the mutual exchange of positive and negative behaviours in marital interaction (Stuart, 1969). In order to obtain rewards for themselves, spouses are compelled to provide rewards to the partner and to reciprocate the rewards obtained from the partner, yet a direct reciprocity, particularly of negative behaviours, is characteristic of distressed relationships (Gottmann, 1979). In nondistressed marriages rewards are exchanged on a less contingent basis, probably because the history of high reward rates renders immediate reciprocity unnecessary to maintain behaviour (Robinson and Jacobson, 1987).

The *structural model* (Gottman, 1979) is based on a combination of behavioural and systems principles, and focuses on the structure and patterning of the interactions in marriages. Its main premises are that unhappily married couples are more rigid and inflexible in their communication patterns than happily married couples; that they express significantly more negativity both verbally and nonverbally; that they are more likely to reciprocate negative messages; and that in unhappy marriages one spouse dominates the other spouse. These views have been largely supported by empirical studies (e.g. Margolin and Wampold, 1981; Revenstorf *et al.*, 1980), indicating that negative reciprocity is the better discriminator between distressed and nondistressed couples. In contrast, it is not clear whether or not positive reciprocity discriminates between happily and unhappily married couples.

The *cognitive-behavioural model* emphasizes the mediating role of cognitive and perceptual processes to account for marital satisfaction or distress. The general assumption is that marital distress is related to cognitive distortions and dysfunctional perceptions of the spouse's behaviour. For instance, Weiss (1980) uses the concepts of 'sentiment override' and 'efficacy expectations' to describe processes where spouses evaluate each other's behaviour on the basis of affective-cognitive representations of each other and affective belief systems about the outcomes of their interactions, rather than relying on the actual behaviours. From an attribution theoretical perspective, nondistressed couples are believed to attribute their spouse's negative behaviour primarily to external or situational factors (e.g. 'He is probably preoccupied with his work right now'), and their positive behaviour to internal and stable factors (e.g. 'She really is a nice person to say this to me'). Distressed couples tend to do the opposite (Jacobson *et al.*, 1985; Newman and Langer, 1981). It is probable that these attributions negatively affect the spouses' subsequent behaviour towards each other, and thus mediate the behaviour exchange processes (Fincham and Bradbury, 1988).

The *interdependence model* emphasizes the role of emotions in communication. Its central premise is that positive or negative emotions are caused by interruptions in the completion of organized behavioural sequences (Berscheid, 1983), of which two types are distinguished: 'intrachain' sequences are the spouses' individual goal-directed activities, and 'interchain' sequences require the co-operation of the other spouse in order to achieve a successful completion (e.g. having a conversation, or lovemaking). The greater the range and diversity of interchain sequences in a marriage, the more interdependent are the spouses (Kelley *et al.*, 1983). However, interchain sequences may interrupt the completion of the spouses' intrachain sequences and trigger a physiological arousal producing the experience of emotion, which is negative when the interruption is seen as interfering with the accomplishment of the individual goal. By emphasizing the role of emotions in interaction, this model explains some of the apparent contradictions of marital relationships. For instance, some couples may be very intimate and yet experience very little emotion, because their interactions are so well-meshed that they do not interrupt each other's behaviour sequences. On the other hand, couples may also be very distant without there being any negative feelings, when the spouses have very few common goals and do not interfere with each other's attempts to accomplish their goals.

Finally, the *communication competency model* posits that the capability to communicate effectively can be conceived of as a social skill (Guerney, 1977; Hahlweg *et al.*, 1984a; Jacobson and Margolin, 1979). Couples can be differentiated on the basis of their competence to apply these skills and to communicate effectively with each other. This includes the appropriate use of speaker skills (e.g. expressing feelings towards each other, describing specific situations and behaviours and avoiding generalizations and side-tracking) as well as listener skills (e.g. listening attentively, paraphrasing, using open-ended questions, giving positive feedback and disclosing one's own feelings when hurt by the partner). A lack of adequate communication skills does not necessarily affect a couple's marital satisfaction immediately, but may predict unhappiness with the marriage several years later (Markman, 1984). It may be noted that this model in fact borrows views from other models, but rephrases them in terms of communication 'skills'. The use of this term does not imply that the individual partners do not have the necessary behaviours in their repertoire; in fact, it has been demonstrated that maritally distressed persons are able to communicate in a constructive manner when interacting with strangers (Birchler *et al.*, 1975; Vincent *et al.*, 1975). So it seems that distressed husbands and wives possess the proper skills, but do not use them when interacting with each other. In terms of the learning theoretical paradigm, one could say that each partner represents an inhibitory stimulus for the other to apply the skills.

The categorization of marital problems as a manifestation of deficient communication skills is not only pragmatic but also very hopeful, for it implies that couples can learn how to communicate more effectively. Furthermore, it allows for a more positive (i.e. less stable) re-attribution of marital problems by the couples themselves. It is not surprising, then, that this model has been widely adopted by marital therapists working from a cognitive-behavioural perspective, and that it has served as a basis for applied clinical research. In this way, it also provides an interesting framework for investigating the communication between eating-disordered patients and their spouses.

CLINICAL VIEWS ON COMMUNICATION IN EATING-DISORDERED COUPLES

General impressions

Despite the fact that communication deficits are frequently mentioned in the clinical literature on married AN or BN patients, specific and objective information about this subject is very scarce. Except for our own empirical study to be presented further on in this chapter, no systematic investigation of this topic has been performed, which means that information is usually obtained from clinical observations. The predominant view among clinicians seems to be that the communication between eating-disordered patients and their husbands is 'superficial', or that it is 'blocked' by the partners' inability to disclose their feelings. Foster (1986), for example, refers to an inability of eating-disordered patients, restricting AN patients in particular, to identify and express their feelings, thoughts and wishes. This deficit is complemented by the spouse's tacit acceptance of the patient's presentation of false self. In the author's opinion, 'In such marital relationships there is little ability to engage constructively in well-directed metacommunication about relationship issues' (p. 578). She adds that the same dysfunctional interaction processes are also present during therapy, for example when the spouses address comments exclusively to the therapist rather than to each other, or compete for the therapist's attention by interruptions and disqualifications of the partner's reactions. In a similar vein, Andersen (1985) mentions communication problems as an area which often requires treatment in married eating-disordered patients, and also stresses these couples' inability to express feelings in particular. In his view, the latter is related to the problem of alexithymia, the long-standing difficulty of anorectic patients to identify and express feelings.

Other authors take a broader look at communication, and include general interactional patterns as well. Barrett and Schwartz (1987), for instance, state that interactions in bulimic couples are characterized by rigidity and repetition, in the sense that the partners respond to one another with a set of emotional sequences that seldom allow individuation, flexibility or independent alternatives. Endorsing a communication theoretical perspective, these authors consider the bulimic symptoms themselves as an indirect method of communication: through bingeing and purging, the patient voices her displeasure with the world, her marriage and herself. At the same time, the bulimia also helps her to gain a more powerful position within the relationship, for it is a behaviour that no one else – including the husband – can control. As such, an extremely complementary interaction pattern is maintained within the couple.

In sum, most clinical sources regard the communication between anorectic or bulimic patients and their husbands as inadequate. Except for the deficient expression of feelings and the rigid complementarity of the interactions, they remain rather unspecific as to the particular deficiencies which characterize these communication processes.

Critical appraisal

While emphasizing the importance of communication in the relationships of married eating-disorder patients, the clinical impressions presented above can be criticized on several grounds. First of all, as already mentioned, they are too vague to allow for an identification of the specific communication deficiencies involved, and thus for an appraisal of the role of communication in the onset and/or maintenance of an eating disorder. Second, since the observations are generally not based on existing models of communication, they often show a considerable overlap with other concepts. For example, the apparent difficulty of the couples to express their feelings to each other may be regarded as an aspect of their poor intimacy, as discussed in the previous chapter, rather than a communication deficit. Although there is obviously a conceptual relationship between intimacy and communication, a clear distinction should be made between particular interactive behaviours such as self-disclosure (i.e. the process of making oneself known to another person by revealing personal information; Jourard, 1971) and the dimensions of intimacy as 'higher-order' relationship qualities, which emerge from these interactions. As such, self-disclosure represents an important determinant of intimacy, but should not be confused with it (Van den Broucke *et al.*, 1995a; Waring and Chelune, 1983).

A third and probably most important consideration regarding the above clinical impressions is that they lack empirical substantiation. In order to really understand the role of communication in the development or maintenance of an eating disorder, one should rely on findings from empirical research rather than on clinical conjecture. Specifically, it must be demonstrated whether and in what respects the communication between eating-disordered patients and their marital partners differs from that of other (nondistressed) couples. Preferably, this substantiation should be based on a theory-based definition of communication, and be directed at testing specific hypotheses. The latter, however, is somewhat problematic, given the lack of specificity of the clinical observations on communication in eating-disordered couples. More useful information may therefore be obtained from research findings relating to communication in other clinical groups, such as maritally distressed spouses or couples with a depressed or alcoholic partner. As pointed out earlier in this chapter, maritally distressed couples have repeatedly been found to emit higher rates of negative and lower rates of positive verbal and nonverbal messages than happily married partners, and to reciprocate negative messages. Similarly, studies of communication in alcoholic and depressed couples have shown them to be more critical and disagreeable and to use more coercive statements than nondistressed couples, which in the case of depressed couples is mainly due to the depressed partner's negative self-focused statements (see chapter 2). So, apart from its higher negativity, the communication in couples with a depressed patient also entails an asymmetry. While evidently the generalizability of these findings to other clinical groups remains to be proven, they do provide an interesting framework for the empirical study of the communication in eating-disordered couples.

EMPIRICAL FINDINGS REGARDING THE COMMUNICATION IN EATING-DISORDERED COUPLES

Observation of marital communication

To investigate a couple's communication, researchers may use self-report questionnaires which measure relevant aspects of communication. A number of such questionnaires will be described in more detail in chapter 9. A problem with these questionnaires, however, is that they assess the partners' *subjective* appraisal of their communication rather than their actual interactions. This makes them very vulnerable to response styles and 'fake good' tendencies – a problem that is particularly relevant in eating-disordered patients. Moreover, most self-report measures fail to capture the dynamic and dyadic nature of communication. Because of this, many investigators of marital communication (e.g. Cromwell, Olson and Fournier, 1976; Notarius and Markman, 1989) prefer to use observational methods, which allow for a more objective and precise assessment of the communication processes.

Observational data on the communication of patients with an eating disorder have been reported in two instances. In the first, Grissett and Norvell (1992) used a combination of self-report and direct observation to assess the quality of the interpersonal interactions of 21 bulimic patients and a matched control group of nondistressed women. Since this study was focused on the interaction with members of the patients' social network rather than with their marital partners, it is less relevant for the present discussion, although its results do confirm that bulimic women interacting with confederates have a higher occurrence of negative interventions and appear less socially competent than normal controls. The second study, which was part of our own research programme (Van den Broucke *et al.*, 1995c), was specifically concerned with the communication between eating-disordered patients and their husbands. It will therefore be presented in more detail.

On the analogy of studies involving maritally distressed couples and clinically depressed patients and their spouses, our study was focused on four aspects of the couples' communication: the presence of effective *speaker and listener skills* in their verbal interaction, the positivity or negativity of their *nonverbal communication*, the *symmetry* of the patients' and spouses' interactions, and the *reciprocity* of the interactions. To investigate these issues, the communication processes were examined in the sample of 21 eating-disordered (ED) couples and the two control groups of maritally distressed (MD) and nondistressed (ND) couples described earlier (see chapter 3). Each couple's interactions during a low-conflict and high-conflict discussion were videotaped and subsequently analysed using an existing interaction coding system: the *Kategoriensystem für Partnerschaftliche Interaktion* (KPI; Hahlweg *et al.*, 1984b). This coding procedure basically implies that each intervention with a more or less homogeneous content, regardless of its duration or syntactic structure, received one of the twelve pre-defined verbal codes specified in Table 5.1, as well as one nonverbal code (positive, neutral, or negative behaviour). This way, the stream of interactions was converted into series, or 'strings', of verbal and nonverbal codes, which served as the basis for further analyses. To verify the reliability of the coding process, inter- and intra-observer agreement was computed, revealing a sufficient degree of reliability (i.e. Cohen's kappas well above 0.80). For more information about this reliability study, the reader is referred to Van den Broucke *et al.* (1995c).

Verbal and nonverbal communications

Parallel to the findings regarding the marital interactions in other clinical groups, one may assume that the communication between ED patients and their husbands reflects a lack of effective speaker and

Table 5.1 Verbal codes of the KPI

Codes	Description
Self-disclosure	Direct expression of feelings, of wishes and needs or of attitudes, opinions and behaviour
Positive solution	Constructive proposal or compromise
Acceptance	Paraphrasing; asking open questions; giving positive feedback; expressing understanding for the partner
Agreement	Direct expression of agreement, of accepting responsibility, or of assent
Problem description	Neutral description of a problem; neutral question
Metacommunication	Suggestion or remark related to the topic; request for clarification
Criticism	Disapproval of partner's behaviour; global accusation, insult or charge
Negative solution	Unacceptable suggestions for change; demand for unilateral change
Justification	Excuse or denial of own responsibility
Disagreement	Direct expression of disagreement; short disagreeing objection; interruption; 'yes, but' statement
Rest category	Inaudible or unintelligible intervention
Listening	(is coded for the listener when the speaker's intervention receives a double code)

Source: Adapted from Hahlweg *et al.* (1984b)

listener skills. Given their low level of intimacy, such deficits are particularly expected in the area of disclosing personal feelings and thoughts. Furthermore, their nonverbal interactions, like those of maritally distressed spouses, are likely to be more negative and less positive than in normal couples.

To investigate these aspects, the relative frequencies of the ED couples' verbal and nonverbal interaction codes mentioned in the previous section were compared with those obtained by the MD and ND couples. Since preliminary analyses had indicated that neither the subtype of eating disorder (abstaining AN, binge/purge AN or BN) nor the timing of its onset (before or after the marriage) was related to differences in marital interaction, the ED sample was treated as one group. Because the linear dependency of the data precluded multivariate analyses, the significance of the differences between the groups was tested by means of univariate analyses of variance, using the Bonferroni procedure (Grove and Andreasen, 1982) to control for the large number of tests and the increased risk for capitalizing on chance. Simply stated, this technique implies that an overall error risk (α) is chosen for the total group of tests, to be divided by the number of tests (k) in order to obtain individual significance levels (α_i) for each test separately. In this case, the overall α was 0.20, yielding α_is of 0.015 for each F-test.

Table 5.2 shows the results of these comparisons, revealing that the communication in the three groups differs significantly in several ways. On the one hand, the ED couples emitted less criticism, justification and disagreement than MD couples; on the other hand, they used fewer neutral problem descriptions and metacommunications and more negative solution requests than ND couples. So, although they seem less destructive in their interactions than couples with overt marital problems, they do reflect a relative lack of speaker and listener skills, in the sense that they appear less capable than nondistressed husbands and wives to describe situations and behaviours in a neutral, nonblaming manner, and are more inclined to demand unilateral change from the partner. Unexpectedly, however, the ED couples also displayed more self-disclosure than both control groups. This could mean that they are better able to express personal thoughts and feelings to one another than is usually assumed. On the other hand, it is also conceivable that they simply *need* to disclose more often because they experience more relational or personal distress than other people. As such, their comparatively high levels of self-disclosure may well obscure a larger discrepancy between their subjective need to discuss personal feelings and thoughts and their actual self-disclosing behaviour. Moreover, it is also likely that many of the self-disclosures are about negative feelings, and therefore do not represent true instances of constructive communication.

With respect to the nonverbal channel, the ED couples emitted significantly fewer positive and more neutral cues than the nondistressed couples, but also significantly fewer negative and more neutral cues than the MD ones. The similarity of the findings regarding the couples' verbal communication is clear: in both cases, the interactions of the ED couples were not as negative or destructive as those of the MD spouses, yet were also less constructive than those of the ND ones. In other words, it seems as if the ED patients and/or their husbands manage to 'edit out' most of the negative messages during their conversations, but fail to leave in sufficient degrees of positive interventions, thus making their interactions less rewarding for each other.

Table 5.2   Relative frequencies for the verbal and nonverbal interactions

	Means and standard deviations			Group effects	Pairwise tests	
	ED (n=21)	ND (n=21)	MD (n=21)	F	ED/ND t	ED/MD t
Verbal[a]						
SD	8.6 (+4.8)	5.1 (+3.7)	6.5 (+2.3)	4.71*	3.05**	1.85
PS	0.8 (+1.5)	0.8 (+1.0)	0.6 (+0.8)	0.10	-0.14	0.30
AC	2.8 (+1.8)	2.1 (+2.0)	2.0 (+1.7)	1.30	1.34	1.45
AG	12.8 (+5.1)	14.1 (+5.3)	10.4 (+5.1)	2.82	-0.84	1.51
PD	28.8 (+7.6)	34.2 (+5.7)	25.5 (+6.6)	8.95*	-2.61*	1.58
MC	3.7 (+2.1)	5.5 (+3.0)	4.9 (+3.2)	2.24	-2.09*	-1.36
CR	4.6 (+3.2)	3.4 (+2.6)	7.4 (+4.0)	7.88*	1.15	-2.71**
NS	1.8 (+1.4)	0.8 (+0.7)	1.5 (+1.5)	3.27	2.49*	0.74
JU	2.2 (+1.8)	1.6 (+1.3)	3.4 (+1.8)	6.16*	1.22	-2.24*
DG	10.5 (+5.6)	9.9 (+5.1)	17.2 (+8.5)	7.90*	0.33	-3.26**
Nonverbal						
Neg	11.8 (+9.4)	5.4 (+6.9)	27.8 (+21.3)	14.23*	1.48	-3.70***
Neu	76.2 (+10.3)	63.6 (+11.4)	63.1 (+18.5)	5.98*	2.94**	3.05**
Pos	12.0 (+10.1)	31.0 (+13.2)	9.1 (+10.5)	23.23*	-5.45***	0.82

[a]See Table 5.1. Data for rest category and listening code are omitted
*$p < 0.015$ (overall $\alpha = 0.20$) for F-test and $p < 0.05$ for pairwise t-tests;
**$p < 0.01$; ***$p < 0.001$
Source: Re-analysis of the data of Van den Broucke *et al.* (1995c)

Communications of patients and spouses

Since the communication in eating-disorder couples shows a number of deficiencies, a further question arises: who contributes to this more significantly, the patient or her partner? In accordance with research findings obtained in psychiatrically depressed patients, one may indeed assume that patients with an eating disorder emit higher rates of negative cues than their husbands. This issue was investigated by computing relative frequencies separately for the husbands' and wives' interventions, and comparing these between the three groups using a series of 2 x 3 (gender by group) ANOVAs, with gender included as a repeated measure (as recommended by most authors in the field; see Schaap, 1984). As in the previous analysis, the risk of capitalizing on chance was controlled by means of the Bonferroni procedure.

As a result of these analyses, significant gender effects were observed for self-disclosure, criticism, negative and neutral nonverbal communication (see Table 5.3). More particularly, the wives tended to self-disclose more often than the husbands but also emitted higher rates of criticism, while their nonverbal behaviour was more negative and less neutral than that of their husbands. These findings are comparable with the sex differences reported by other investigators (e.g. Hahlweg *et al.*, 1984b; Notarius and Johnson, 1982; Raush *et al.*, 1974), and suggest that there is in fact a certain degree of asymmetry in the communication of *all* couples, regardless of the group they belong to. However, no significant gender by group interaction effects were found, which implies that the asymmetry of the ED couples' communication is *not* greater than that of either the ND or the MD couples. So, it appears, the asymmetry which characterizes the marital communication of clinically depressed couples does not apply to the same extent to the interaction of patients with an eating disorder.

Positive and negative reciprocity

The concept of reciprocity as used in marital interaction literature can be defined as the tendency of a partner to respond to his or her spouse's positive or negative interventions with similar behaviours (Patterson and Reid, 1970; Jacobson and Moore, 1981). Positive reciprocity occurs in both distressed and nondistressed couples,

Table 5.3   Relative frequencies of the husbands' and wives' interventions

	Group means						*Gender*	*Gender x group*
	ED (n=21)		*ND (n=21)*		*MD (n=21)*			
	H	W	H	W	H	W	F	F
Verbal[a]								
SD	6.4	10.3	4.1	6.4	5.3	7.4	20.11*	0.94
PS	0.7	0.7	0.8	0.8	0.7	0.6	0.05	0.01
AC	2.6	2.9	1.9	2.4	1.8	2.1	0.69	0.04
AG	14.3	11.2	15.1	13.3	10.3	10.6	1.64	0.70
PD	30.7	27.2	32.3	36.1	23.9	27.8	0.87	2.71
MC	3.8	3.2	5.1	5.3	4.8	4.6	0.20	0.24
CR	3.5	6.2	2.7	4.1	6.2	8.5	8.46*	0.32
NS	2.1	1.5	0.7	0.9	1.5	1.6	0.08	0.70
JU	2.6	2.1	1.6	1.6	3.6	3.1	0.88	0.16
DG	10.9	10.9	9.5	10.3	17.0	17.6	0.75	0.21
Nonverbal								
Neg	10.1	15.2	4.3	6.9	24.2	31.8	11.24*	0.93
Neu	77.5	73.9	66.4	60.9	67.6	58.6	17.00*	1.19
Pos	12.5	11.0	29.3	32.2	8.2	10.0	0.85	1.61

[a]The listener and rest category codes are omitted
* $p < 0.015$ (overall $\alpha = 0.20$)
Source: Van den Broucke *et al.* (1995c)

whereas negative reciprocity is more typical for maritally distressed couples (Gottman, 1979; Margolin and Wampold, 1981). Hence, it may be hypothesized that eating-disordered couples exhibit less positive reciprocity than either nondistressed or maritally distressed couples, and less negative reciprocity than maritally distressed couples.

To measure reciprocity, two distinct approaches have been proposed (Mettetal and Gottman, 1980; Schaap, 1984). The first is based on the *baserates* of the couple's positive or negative interventions. If these baserates are approximately the same for the two partners, one could say that the couple's interaction is reciprocal on a long-term basis (that is, for the total duration of their discussion). This similarity can be determined by computing within-couple correlations between the rates of positive and negative interventions emitted by each of the partners. Following this approach for the interaction data described in the previous section, we were able to assess the reciprocity of the couples' interactions during their low-conflict and high-conflict discussions, finding a moderate degree of positive and a high degree of negative verbal reciprocity as well as a high degree of positive nonverbal reciprocity for the couples in all three groups. During the high-conflict discussion, all couples tended to exhibit more negative and less positive verbal reciprocity. However, when comparing the data for the ED, ND and MD couples, we only found evidence for the predicted lower degree of positive reciprocity on the part of the ED couples (compared to the ND group) during the high-conflict discussion ($p = 0.10$, one-tailed, for the nonverbal positive reciprocity). On the other hand, a lower degree of negative verbal and nonverbal reciprocity for the ED couples compared to the MD ones was found during the low-conflict discussion (only $p = 0.054$ and 0.057, respectively). In other words, the degree to which the predictions of the reciprocity of each couple's communication could be confirmed largely depended on the topic of the discussion.

A similar conclusion was obtained when the second approach to operationalize reciprocity was used. This focuses on the *contingencies* between the spouses' interventions (Gottman, 1979; Revenstorf *et al.*, 1984). Contingency-based reciprocity is assessed by computing the conditional probabilities of one partner's positive or negative interventions following a similar intervention by the other partner, and converting these probabilities into binomial z-scores to control for the different baserates (Bakeman and Gottman, 1986). This computation was performed on the couples' low- and high-conflict discussions, collapsing the verbal codes into summary codes by considering self-disclosure, positive solution, acceptance and agreement as positive;

problem description and metacommunication as neutral; and criticism, negative solution, justification and disagreement as negative. To compare the reciprocity data of the three groups, the z-scores were entered into one-way analyses of variance (ANOVAs).

The results of these analyses are presented in Table 5.4. First, it can be established whether there *is* actually any reciprocity in the interactions by looking at the values of the z-scores: an absolute value of z higher than 1.96 means that the conditional probability of interest is significantly different from the baserate (at $p < 0.05$, two-tailed), with the sign indicating whether the transitional probability is higher (+) or lower (-). Thus, one will notice that, on the average, all three groups display a significant degree of positive nonverbal reciprocity during the low-conflict discussion. This means that in all couples a positive nonverbal intervention during this discussion increases the probability of a positive nonverbal response by the partner. This is not the case for the verbal or the negative nonverbal interactions. For the high-conflict discussion the results are mostly similar, except for the lack of significant positive nonverbal reciprocity in the ED group (as opposed to both control groups).

While the latter finding suggests that the ED couples display a low

Table 5.4   Reciprocity of the couples' interactions

	Mean z-scores			F	p
	ED (n=21)	ND (n=21)	MD (n=21)		
Low conflict					
Verbal codes					
positive	-0.386	-0.578	-0.245	0.680	0.510
negative	0.798	0.958	1.787	3.667	0.032
Nonverbal codes					
positive	2.371	2.735	2.605	0.191	0.826
negative	0.256	0.625	0.527	0.275	0.760
High conflict					
Verbal codes					
positive	-0.079	-0.454	-0.110	0.902	0.411
negative	1.364	1.017	1.542	1.015	0.369
Nonverbal codes					
positive	1.672	3.125	1.964	2.510	0.090
negative	0.409	0.519	1.124	1.649	0.201

Source: Van den Broucke *et al.* (1995c)

degree of (positive and negative) reciprocity, a direct test of this prediction requires a comparison between the scores obtained by the couples in the different samples. When looking at the mean z-scores listed in Table 5.4, it appears that in most instances the scores for the ED couples are indeed lower than those for the comparison groups, but that these differences are not significant, except for the negative verbal reciprocity during the low-conflict discussion. This effect, however, is mainly due to the higher scores of the MD couples, who attain significantly higher levels of negative verbal reciprocity than the ED couples ($p < 0.05$) but not than the ND couples. In sum, we may conclude that there is indeed a *tendency* for the ED couples' communication to be less reciprocal than that of other couples, but that this tendency is not strong enough to yield significant differences.

CONCLUSIONS

Whereas most clinical sources regard the communication between ED patients and their husbands as inadequate, clinical observations with regard to this issue are usually not very informative about the particular communication deficiencies that are involved. This lack of information precludes a proper understanding of the role marital communication plays in the occurrence or maintenance of an eating disorder. In an effort to provide more specific and objective information about this topic, the present chapter has clarified the characteristics of the communication between eating-disordered patients and their husbands, starting from a theory-based definition of communication, and providing data from empirical research endorsing an observational approach.

The conclusions of this research can be summarized as follows. First, eating-disordered patients and their partners were seen to lack certain skills in communicating effectively with one another: compared to nondistressed couples they use less metacommunication and neutral problem description, and they demand more unilateral change from their partner as a way of solving the issue. Similarly, their nonverbal interactions are less constructive or rewarding than those of nondistressed couples, in that they emit fewer positive and more negative interventions. On the other hand, they manage to avoid the destructive communication style of maritally distressed couples, which is characterized by criticism, justification, disagreement and high rates of negative nonverbal behaviour. Also, contrary to most clinical impressions, eating-disordered couples do not evidence an incapacity to disclose personal topics: in fact they use even more self-disclosure than other couples, but this may be due to their greater need to self-disclose because of the seriousness of their problems.

Unlike clinically depressed patients, patients with AN or BN do not emit higher rates of negative verbal and nonverbal messages than their husbands, at least not more so than other couples. On the other hand, it does appear that it is usually the patient who makes an appeal to her partner and who is coercive, while it is the husband who takes care of 'editing out' the negative messages, and who makes sure that the negative affect does not escalate. In this way, these couples' communication is suggestive of the 'traditional' role complementarity that is reportedly characteristic of most other couples (Raush *et al.*, 1974). Finally, eating-disordered patients and their husbands seem less inclined than nondistressed couples to reciprocate positive interventions with positive responses, and display less negative reciprocity than maritally distressed couples, although the differences between the groups seldom reach significance. This relative lack of both positive *and* negative reciprocity may explain why the communication between these patients and their partners often gives the impression of being 'cold' or 'distant'.

It should again be emphasized that the above characteristics do not imply that a deficient communication style is the *cause* of the eating disorder, as is sometimes assumed. In fact, it is more plausible that the relationship between these communication problems and the occurrence of an eating disorder is a circular one, with the marital communication both being influenced by the presence of the disorder and in turn influencing the further course of the disorder. In any event, however, regardless of the causal relationship it is likely that a deficient communication with the marital partner represents an additional source of distress for the patient rather than a source of support.

6 Marital conflicts

Few aspects in marriage influence the spouses' satisfaction with their relationship and their sense of psychological well-being more rigorously than their ability to resolve their conflicts successfully. This may be because on a covert level marital conflicts are often concerned with issues that define the nature of the relationship itself, such as the question of who is in command or how much intimacy is desired. When the spouses' positions with regard to such issues are incompatible, conflicts not only occur more frequently, but are also perceived as more threatening to the relationship. Also, during conflicts the communication between the spouses is usually more aversive than in normal circumstances. Sometimes couples try to avoid this aversion by shunning confrontations about issues that may generate conflict. This strategy may temporarily relieve the tensions between the partners, but it is obvious that in the long run it also prevents them from finding suitable solutions for their conflicts.

The latter strategy is often mentioned in connection with the way married eating-disordered patients and their husbands handle conflicts. The main assumption is that unresolved marital conflicts inhibit the growth of the relationship and contribute to the development of an eating disorder. In this chapter, we will examine this assumption by considering three relevant aspects of the conflicts between married AN and BN patients and their spouses: the conflict topics, the underlying balance of power and the communication process during conflict. First, however, we will clarify these aspects by presenting a theoretical model of marital conflicts.

THEORETICAL VIEWS ON MARITAL CONFLICT

A marital conflict model

In order to understand marital conflicts in all their complexity, it is necessary to obtain information on at least three different aspects: the subject about which the partners disagree, the unspoken issues which occasion the conflict, and the behaviour of the partners during the conflict. In the marital conflict model proposed by Christensen (1987), which is based on Gottman's (1979) structural model of marital interaction (see chapter 5), these aspects are labelled as the conflict topic, structure and interaction, respectively.

The overt *topic* of a marital conflict can be virtually anything, including the behaviour or characteristics of the partner, the relationship with third parties or the marital relationship itself. These topics may well be different for maritally distressed and nondistressed couples. Hahlweg *et al.* (1980) found that couples who are dissatisfied with their relationship often endorse the issues of sexuality, attention from the partner, trust in each other and personal freedom in the relationship as conflict-generating areas. In contrast, happily married couples more often argue about trivial issues, such as their use of free time or unpleasant habits of one partner. Yet the main difference between the conflicts of maritally distressed and nondistressed couples is probably the frequency with which they occur: whereas nondistressed couples *sometimes* argue about certain topics, distressed spouses repeatedly have conflicts about the same topics (Kerkstra, 1985). This suggests that their conflicts often remain unresolved.

While the topic of a marital conflict may be of secondary importance, its *structure* is what the conflict is really about. The distinction between the topic and the structure of a conflict parallels that between the content and command levels of interpersonal communication (Watzlawick *et al.*, 1967). Couples may argue about topics that would otherwise be relatively easy to solve by way of compromise (e.g. the way in which the children should be raised), but the real conflict of interest is often about the different goals the spouses have set for themselves and for their partner, and about who sets the rules in achieving these goals. In this regard, a distinction is often made between symmetrical relationships, where the partners strive towards maintaining an egalitarian power distribution, and complementary relationships, where one of the partners takes on a 'one-up' position, and the other a 'one-down' position (Haley, 1964; Watzlawick *et al.*, 1967). The conflicts deriving from the former type typically entail an escalation process, in which both partners openly reject each other's viewpoints. Conversely, in rigidly complementary relationships the partners tend to ignore each other's standpoint, which may have more serious psychological consequences. In terms of social learning theory, the dominance of one partner over the other entails a coercive control over the latter's interactions, which has been associated with psychopathology (Patterson and Reid, 1970).

While both the content and the structure of a conflict are essential parameters, most theorists and practitioners will agree that the important issue of marital conflicts is not what the arguments are about, but how the partners try to resolve them. A number of investigators have therefore tried to identify the *interaction processes* which characterize the conflicts between marital partners. Despite the variety of methods they use, two major approaches prevail. The first one uses a molar level of analysis to distinguish between different strategies couples use to resolve their conflicts; the second assumes a molecular level of analysis, and focuses on the communication patterns which characterize marital conflict discussions. In the next two sections, both approaches will be discussed in more detail.

Conflict resolution strategies

People may respond to their environment in three basic ways: by moving towards it, moving against it or moving away from it. Accordingly, conflict theorists (e.g. Canary and Cupach, 1988; Peterson, 1983; Sillars *et al.*, 1982) have arrived at a threefold typology of conflict resolution strategies in personal relationships.

The *integrative* or co-operative strategy involves a mutual orientation towards the relationship, and includes such tactics as seeking areas of agreement, negotiating and expressing trust in the partner. It can be considered a prosocial strategy (Roloff, 1976).

The *distributive* or confrontation strategy reflects the primacy of individual over relational goals, and entails competitive tactics such as threatening, insulting and demanding unilateral change from the partner. This strategy is clearly antisocial.

Finally, the *avoidance* strategy is aimed at minimizing explicit discussions of conflict, and involves tactics such as denying the presence of disagreements, shifting the focus of the conversation and communicating about conflicts indirectly or ambiguously. This strategy may be either prosocial or antisocial, depending on the topic of the conflict, the timing of the conversation and the specific communication tactics (Fitzpatrick, 1988). A prosocial use of avoidance would for instance occur when a couple postpone the discussion of a serious conflict until they have time to handle it, or when they channel an essentially unresolvable issue into a more agreeable topic.

Canary and Cupach (1988) have demonstrated that the use of an integrative strategy is positively associated with relational intimacy and satisfaction, perceived communicator competence, effectiveness and attractiveness. In contrast, distributive tactics are negatively correlated with these same issues. Finally, conflict-avoidance tactics are modestly associated with satisfaction with the communication and with the partner. For traditional couples, who have settled in clearly differentiated roles and who value interdependence between partners, conflict avoidance may represent a pragmatically benign strategy to maintain positive affect in their relationship (Fitzpatrick, 1988). On the other hand, it inhibits the growth and development of a relationship, and limits a couple's capability to deal effectively with changes that are imposed upon them by external sources.

In general, dominant partners seem less likely to avoid conflicts than those with less power: by engaging in the conflict, they may re-establish the superior position which the conflict threatened to upset (Peterson, 1983). However, even a dependent partner may be willing to endure whatever punishment the conflict entails and, by the act of engagement itself, gain greater influence over future interactions. So, once the weaker partner 'stands up and fights', the dominant one must reckon with the cost of active conflict in pursuing personal aims at the expense of the other. On the other hand, if both partners perceive the risk of open conflict to be greater than the uncertain gains that can be achieved through active dispute, conflict is likely to be avoided.

Communication patterns during marital conflict

While the above strategies reflect a couple's global mode of dealing with conflicts, an alternative approach is to consider the communication patterns that emerge during conflict discussions. As pointed out in chapter 5, conflicts usually bring out the deficits which characterize the communication in maritally or psychologically distressed couples. In addition, however, typical problem-solving sequences have been identified for maritally distressed and nondistressed couples. More particularly, nondistressed couples have been found to exhibit the following sequences (Gottman, 1979; Fitzpatrick, 1988): (1) *validation* implies that one spouse gives a problem description, which is then responded to by the other spouse with an agreement or assent; (2) *contracting* involves a problem-solving suggestion by one spouse, followed by the other spouse's agreement; (3) *counterproposal* is one spouse's problem-solving proposal, followed by a problem-solving proposal by the other spouse; and (4) *metacommunication* is when the spouses metacommunicate briefly, and then return to the topic of conflict.

Sequences that are characteristic of distressed couples include: (1) *cross-complaining*, i.e. one spouse's expression of feelings about the problem, followed by the other spouse's expression of feelings; (2) *non-acceptance*, i.e. the expression of feelings by one spouse, followed by the other spouse's disagreement; (3) *'pulling and leaning back'*, i.e. one partner asking for information, and the other giving very little information; (4) *'no deal'*, i.e. one spouse's problem-solving proposal followed by the partner's disagreement; (5) *disagreement* or *squabbling*, i.e. one spouse's expression of disagreement followed by the other spouse's disagreement; (6) *ignoring*, i.e. mindreading followed by disagreement or interruption; (7) *non-involvement*, i.e. one partner's negative statement followed by the other's agreement; and (8) *struggle for power*, i.e. one spouse's disagreements or interruptions followed by the other spouse's same behaviour as before (Gottman, 1979; Fitzpatrick, 1988; Kerkstra, 1985).

The above sequences illustrate the importance of communication patterns in solving marital conflicts. However, as they are concerned with one partner's reaction to the other one's behaviour, they refer only to very short pieces of interaction. In order to capture the relevant communication patterns in conflict discussions, it is necessary to also consider longer interaction sequences. Revenstorf *et al.* (1984) distinguish between four such sequences: (1) *acceptance* refers to an alternation of (neutral) problem descriptions and positive responses; (2) *attraction* is an alternation of positive responses; (3) *distancing* is basically an alternation of negative responses; and (4) *problem escalation* is an alternation of problem descriptions and negative responses. Revenstorf and his collaborators (1984) could demonstrate that, as compared to nondistressed couples, maritally distressed couples show a higher tendency to engage in escalation processes during problem discussions. Furthermore, the problem-escalation sequences of distressed couples last longer, whereas their attraction sequences are likely to break down earlier. As such, their interactions are reflective of a distributive rather than an integrative conflict strategy.

CLINICAL VIEWS ON CONFLICT INTERACTION IN EATING-DISORDERED COUPLES

General impressions

Like many other aspects of their marital relationships, the way eating-disordered patients and their spouses deal with conflicts has been the subject of various clinical speculations. The predominant impression is that these couples tend to avoid open conflicts, and that this avoidance is related to the occurrence of the eating disorder. For example, Fishman (1979) refers to the family systems principle of homeostasis to conclude that anorectic symptoms serve the purpose of protecting the marital unit when it is threatened by conflict: by focusing on the patient's symptoms, the tension between the partners is released. In a similar vein, Foster (1986) notes that in couples with a restricting anorectic the degree of conflict avoidance may range from moderate to markedly severe. In her terms, the couple may

> rigidly deny any area of conflict; admit to difficulties in relatively trivial content areas but without significant emotional tone; describe areas of conflict but only with difficulty articulate their own positions; or show periods of identifying affects and cognitions followed by relatively 'blank' exchanges.
>
> (Foster, 1986, p. 579)

Compared with those of anorectic patients, the conflicts of bulimics are sometimes more overtly hostile and chaotic. As such, they range between 'a sense of conflict and hostility that is only occasionally stated openly by either partner; repetitive cross-complaining; or open and direct expressions of anger and attack accompanied by threats of separation or divorce' (Foster, 1986, p. 579). Nevertheless, avoidance of open conflicts seems to be the preferred tactic in bulimic patients as well. Barrett and Schwartz (1987) even consider the continued avoidance of conflict as one of the main functions of BN in couples. In their view, the dysfunctional patterns of interaction in the patient's family of origin, including a lack of conflict resolution, are duplicated in the marriage because the patient has not learned the skills to resolve conflicts. By becoming enmeshed in their focus on the bulimic symptoms, the couple manage to avoid conflicts. However, the longer the bulimia protects them from the struggles of their married life, the more necessary it becomes. In other words, the avoidance of conflict not only 'may function to maintain the symptom, but conversely the symptom may function to maintain the interaction of the couple' (Barrett and Schwartz, 1987, p. 26).

At the same time, the binge–purge cycle also helps to regulate the balance of power in the relationship in a way that is comparable to that of alcoholic couples. Like the nondrinker, the nonbulimic is dedicated to being competent and helpful, and assumes an over-responsible position with regard to the under-responsible bulimic partner. This brings the latter into a position which is at the same time powerful and powerless: power is derived from the fact that the world revolves around her, with her spouse meeting her demands and protecting her; powerlessness, on the other hand, results from the fact that her weak position allows others to take control (Barrett and Schwartz, 1987).

The idea that the bulimic symptoms provide an interpersonal gain to the patient has also served as a basis for therapeutic strategies. The basic assumption is that the symptoms will disappear if the patient can replace the bulimia by another means of getting back at the husband for dominating her (e.g. Madanes, 1981).

Critical appraisal

As can be inferred from the previous section, most clinical authors who report on the conflicts between eating-disordered patients and their husbands focus on the structural issues which underlie these conflicts, and rely on strategic or family systems concepts to clarify the role of conflicts in the development of the anorectic or bulimic symptoms. This narrow focus on structural issues may explain why there are so few empirical data about this subject. Indeed, the structure of a conflict is not easy to assess, since the partners don't usually state explicitly what their predicaments are with regard to a specific area of disagreement. Moreover, people are seldom aware of their goals and behaviours during conflict. So, unlike the conflict topic, which is manifest (but often considered unimportant by therapists), the structure of a conflict must usually be inferred from the couple's interaction. Because of this difficulty, theorists and therapists often refrain from systematic assessment, and rely on clinical hermeneutic methods to acquire information about a couple's conflict tactics. It is evident, however, that in order to achieve more precise and objective data the use of more quantifiable and objective measures is a prerequisite. Moreover, one should not only concentrate on the covert structure of a conflict, but also pay attention to the overt issues, including the conflict topics and processes. Whereas the measurement of these conflict characteristics may be an elusive task, it need not necessarily be an impossible one. In the next section, we will demonstrate this point by verifying the available clinical impressions about the conflict characteristics of eating-disordered couples against empirical data, focusing on conflict topics, structure and interactions, respectively.

EMPIRICAL FINDINGS REGARDING CONFLICT MANAGEMENT IN EATING-DISORDERED COUPLES

Conflict topics

To understand the conflict tactics of eating-disordered patients and their husbands, it is important to know more about the discriminative stimuli which elicit conflict or conflict avoidance. In this regard, two questions must be addressed: the *number* of topics that provoke conflict, and the *content* of these topics. With regard to the first issue, it is likely that eating-disordered patients and their spouses disagree about more issues than nondistressed couples, given their low degree of marital intimacy (see chapter 4). Thus their range of potential conflict areas is probably greater than that of the latter group. With regard to the second aspect, one may assume that as in maritally distressed couples, the conflicts of eating-disordered couples are concerned with more 'serious' topics, which call for more emotional involvement by the spouses and are more difficult to deal with constructively (for example: the causes and/or the symptoms of the eating disorder, or their sexual relationship).

Both aspects were investigated in our own research project (Van den Broucke *et al.*, 1995d), using the samples described in chapter 3: 21 couples where the wife suffered from an eating disorder (ED), 21 maritally distressed couples (MD) and 21 nondistressed couples (ND). The number and content of the couples' conflict topics were assessed by means of the *Problem List* (PL; Hahlweg *et al.*, 1980), which is a 17-item inventory of common problem areas in marriage to be rated on a four-point scale (0 = no problems; 1 = problems, but we can usually solve them; 2 = problems which are difficult to solve and which we often quarrel about; 3 = problems we don't even discuss any more, since we cannot find any solutions for them). An overall 'conflict score' is obtained by summing the items with a score of 2 or 3 for each partner separately.

The mean *number of conflict-generating topics* (as measured by the conflict scores) obtained by the husbands and wives in each group is shown in Table 6.1, along with the corresponding standard deviations. There is clearly a substantial difference between the three groups, in that the MD spouses marked the highest number of conflict-provoking topics and the ND spouses the lowest, while the ED spouses took up an intermediate position. A two-way (group x gender) analysis of variance indicated that these differences were highly significant (F(2,60) = 20.68, $p < 0.001$) , as opposed to the gender and the group by gender interaction effects, which proved nonsignificant. Multiple t-tests for the pairwise comparisons confirmed that the scores of the ED patients and their husbands differed significantly from those of the ND and MD spouses (at $p = 0.001$ and $p = 0.006$, respectively). So it appears that, as a group, ED patients and their husbands alike have more potential conflict areas than ND spouses, but fewer than MD spouses.

To determine the *content* of these conflict areas, the relative importance of the items contained in the Problem List was determined for the couples in each group. This was achieved by tallying how often each item received a rating of 2 or 3 (i.e. moderate or severe conflict) from at least one of the partners. Per group, the topics were then ranked on the basis of the frequency of their endorsement. The items that were most often endorsed as conflict-provoking by the ED couples were the sexual relationship, leisure time, the degree of affection in the relationship and the partner's temperament (see Table 6.2). Except for the second, these items mostly concern rather personal issues, which elicit an emotional involvement of the spouses. In this regard, they resembled the MD couples' conflicts, which were also often concerned with personal issues (e.g. the partner's temperament, personal habits and the sexual relation). This resemblance was substantiated by the highly significant rank-order correlation between the data of the two groups (Spearman's $\rho = 0.612$, $p = 0.009$). In contrast, the ND couples most often had conflicts about the instrumental aspects of marriage, such as finances, jobs, household management or child care, or about issues which did not concern the marital relationship itself (e.g. the relationship with relatives). Consequently, their ranking of conflict topics was quite different from those of the ED ($\rho = -0.036$, NS) and MD ($\rho = 0.324$, $p = 0.201$) couples.

In sum, ED couples not only have a greater range of topics that may induce conflict, but given their higher degree of emotional

Table 6.1   Number of conflict topics

	ED (n=21)		ND (n=21)		MD (n=21)	
	M	SD	M	SD	M	SD
Husbands	2.9	3.4	0.9	1.1	4.3	3.2
Wives	3.4	3.1	0.3	0.6	6.0	3.9

Source: Adapted from Van den Broucke *et al.* (1995d)

Table 6.2 Content of conflict topics

Conflict area	ED n	ED %	ND n	ND %	MD n	MD %
Sexual relations	13	62	0	0	12	57
Leisure time	9	43	2	10	14	67
Affection	8	38	0	0	8	38
Temperament	8	38	1	5	15	71
Relatives	7	33	5	24	11	52
Friendships	7	33	1	5	6	29
Values	7	33	0	0	11	52
Personal habits	6	29	2	10	13	62
Child care	5	24	2	10	9	43
Trust	5	24	0	0	8	38
Personal freedom	5	24	0	0	8	38
Job	4	19	2	10	13	62
Household	4	19	2	10	10	48
Attractiveness	4	19	0	0	4	19
Finances	3	14	4	19	5	24
Jealousy	3	14	1	5	6	29
Extramarital relations	2	10	0	0	6	29

Source: Van den Broucke *et al.* (1995d)

involvement with these topics, their conflicts are also likely to be more aversive than in ND couples. It is conceivable, then, that the ED couples try to prevent these aversive feelings by avoiding marital conflicts altogether.

Dominance structure

Within the context of marital interaction research, dominance is usually defined in terms of an asymmetry in the predictability of the spouses' interventions. This means that if the behaviour of partner A is more predictable from partner B's past behaviour than conversely, B is said to be the dominant spouse. If on the other hand both spouses' behaviours are equally predictable from the other's previous behaviours, the relationship is said to be egalitarian (Gottman, 1979; Wampold, 1984). Note that the concept of dominance, defined here as a one-way influence process, does not coincide with the reciprocity notion discussed in the previous chapter: whereas in reciprocity the second person responds with the same behaviour as the first one, this is not necessarily the case in dominance. Furthermore, while it is possible for both partners to reciprocate each other's behaviours and to establish long chains of reciprocal interaction, it is principally *not* possible for both spouses to be dominant at the same time, except when one partner is dominant in one communication channel and the other partner in the other (Mettetal and Gottman, 1980).

Like reciprocity, however, dominance can be assessed from the couple's interactions. To that effect, several approaches have been proposed, based on the use of time-series analysis (Gottman, 1979), on the difference between transitional probabilities (Allison and Liker, 1982; Wampold, 1984), or on the coefficient of cross-covariability as used in information theory (Kerkstra, 1985). The first two approaches assess dominance with regard to specific (combinations of) behaviours; the third yields a more global measure of dominance. The cross-covariability coefficient, which is central to the latter approach, is basically a measure of the reduction of uncertainty in one partner's behaviour when the other partner's preceding behaviour is known (Losey, 1978). Thus, by comparing the cross-covariabilities between the husband's behaviour and the wife's subsequent behaviour and vice versa, one can determine which partner is more dominant in a given relationship.

The latter approach was used to assess the dominance structures of the eating-disordered (ED), nondistressed (ND) and maritally distressed (MD) couples participating in our own study programme (Van den Broucke *et al.*, 1995d), starting from their interactions during a high-conflict discussion as coded by means of the *Kategoriensystem für Partnerschaftliche Interaktion* (KPI; see chapter 5). For the purpose of this analysis, the verbal codes were collapsed into positive (self-disclosure, positive solution, acceptance, agreement and positive listening), neutral (problem statement, metacommunication and neutral listening), and negative communications (criticism, negative solution, justification, disagreement and negative listening). Using these data, cross-covariability coefficients were computed for the husband-to-wife and wife-to-husband transitions for each couple and for both the verbal and nonverbal communication channel. The coefficients of interest are given in Table 6.3.

To infer the couples' dominance structure from this table, one must consider the difference between the cross-covariabilities for both types of transition; the larger this difference, the less egalitarian are the partners' interactions. Accordingly, the greatest differences (albeit not significant) were observed for the ND and, to a lesser extent, the MD couples. In both groups, it was apparent that the men dominated the verbal interactions and the women the nonverbal. Conversely, very similar degrees of predictability were found in the interactions of the ED patients and their husbands, which implies that their dominance structure is in fact highly egalitarian. This clearly contradicts the

Table 6.3   Cross-covariabilities for the husband-to-wife and wife-to-husband
transitions

	Verbal communication				Nonverbal communication			
	H-W	*W-H*	*t*	*p*	*H-W*	*W-H*	*t*	*p*
ED	0.09	0.09	-0.27	0.79	0.08	0.07	0.39	0.77
ND	0.13	0.10	1.34	0.20	0.13	0.16	-1.36	0.19
MD	0.08	0.07	0.90	0.38	0.08	0.10	-1.93	0.07

H-W = husband-to-wife; W-H = wife-to-husband
Source: Van den Broucke *et al.* (1995d)

strategic therapists' view that the occurrence of an eating disorder
reflects a covert struggle for power in the relationship.

It is possible, however, that the observed symmetry of these couples'
interactions is of a submissive rather than a competitive type. Such
interactions are allegedly characterized by mutual coalescence and
surrender, rather than escalation and fighting (Bateson and Jackson,
1968). Unfortunately, our analyses of the dominance structure did not
discriminate between subtypes of symmetry. Alternatively, the
symmetry of ED couples' communication may also reflect the success
of the patients' attempts to restore an unequal power balance in their
relationship by developing the eating disorder. To test for this possibility, it would be necessary to investigate the changes in the couples'
dominance structures over the course of the patients' illness. In want
of such longitudinal studies, however, conclusions about the structural
components underlying the conflicts between these patients and their
partners appear immature. Instead, it may be more fruitful to focus on
their conflict processes.

Conflict interaction patterns

As has already been mentioned, it is mostly assumed that married
eating-disorder patients and their husbands tend to avoid marital
conflicts. To investigate this assumption, Van Buren and Williamson
(1988) used a self-report questionnaire assessing the conflict resolution
styles of 12 bulimic couples and two comparison groups. They found
that the bulimic patients resembled maritally distressed women in that
they endorsed fewer problem-solving skills and reported more withdrawal from conflict than normal control females. Their husbands, on
the other hand, did not differ from the nondistressed males with
regard to their self-reported conflict resolution styles.

While these findings are consistent with the clinical observations,
the scope of the study was limited in some respects. First of all, it was

not based on a theoretical model of marital interaction or conflict, which limits the possibility of interpreting the findings. Second, the patient sample consisted only of bulimic women and their husbands, which restricts the generalizability of the reported findings to one particular eating disorder. Finally, the use of a self-report inventory allows for only a subjective and retrospective assessment of the couples' conflict resolution styles. As such, the data may reveal how the subjects *think* they handle their conflicts, but they tell us very little about their actual behaviours during conflict discussions. For that purpose, the use of observational measures is probably more appropriate (Notarius and Markman, 1989).

Such an observational procedure focusing on the couples' interaction patterns during conflict was employed in our own research programme (Van den Broucke *et al.*, 1995d), starting from the observational data described in the previous section. To detect the couples' conflict patterns from these data, a sequential analysis technique (K-gramm analysis) was used, revealing that for the verbal communication, the conflict interactions of the ED couples resembled those of ND couples with regard to the succession of positive behaviours (positive escalation) and the alternation of negative and neutral interventions (conflict neutralization); they were similar to those of MD couples with regard to the succession of negative interventions (negative escalation). In the nonverbal channel, on the other hand, the ED couples' positive escalations were shorter than those of the ND couples, and their negative escalations shorter than those of MD couples. However, although the ED couples did not emit as many negative nonverbal cues as the MD couples, when they did do so they were more likely to engage in a lengthy neutralization sequence, where one partner attempted to neutralize the other's negative behaviour. The latter seems consistent with the idea that ED patients and their spouses tend to avoid marital conflicts.

This finding was further substantiated by the results of a more holistic, graphical analysis of the data, using a technique that was introduced by Gottman, Markman and Notarius (1977), and refined by Schaap (1982) and Hooley and Hahlweg (1986). The idea of this technique is to plot the course of the spouses' interactions in a two-dimensional space, with the abscissa referring to the sequence of the interventions and the ordinate to the affective quality of the communications. With each successive response, an upward, downward or horizontal move is recorded, depending on whether the intervention is positive, negative or neutral (as decided on the basis of predetermined scoring rules). As a result, two superimposed profiles are obtained, representing the cumulative record of each spouse's interactions.

Using this procedure, interaction profiles were plotted for the 63 couples participating in our study (i.e. 21 ED couples and 42 control couples). Two untrained judges, agreeing in 92 per cent of the cases, then classified these profiles into five categories, each representing a different conflict pattern: (a) *positive interaction* (a parallel increase of the response curves of both partners above the zero value on the ordinate); (b) *negative interaction* (a parallel decrease of the spouses' response curves below the zero value); (c) *neutral interaction* (the curves of the two spouses remain parallel with the abscissa throughout the discussion); (d) *asymmetric negative* (one partner's interventions are increasingly negative, and the other's neutral or positive, counteracting the first's tendency to negatively escalate); and (e) *asymmetric positive* (one partner is positive and the other neutral). Examples of the five interaction types are shown in Figure 6.1.

Table 6.4 shows the results of the classification, in the form of the numbers of ED, ND and MD couples found in each category. It is apparent that the three groups differed considerably with regard to their conflict style ($\chi^2(8) = 28.941$, $p < 0.001$). Whereas the ND couples most often display positive interaction (more than 50 per cent of the couples in this group) and the MD couples negative interaction (nearly 60 per cent), the most frequently observed pattern in the ED group is asymmetric negative interaction. Of the 21 couples in the ED sample, 8 (or 38 per cent) are placed in this category, which is almost double the percentage obtained for the total group. In other words, an ED couple is almost twice as likely to show conflict avoidance than a couple drawn at random from the total sample. We may add that in half of the cases it was the patient who tried to avoid the negative escalation, while in the other half it was the husband. So there seems to be no systematic role effect as to who engages in the conflict and who tries to avoid it.

CONCLUSIONS

In this chapter, we have substantiated the assumption that inefficient conflict styles play a major role in the development or maintenance of an eating disorder by addressing three core aspects of marital conflicts as they occur in these patients' marriages: their conflict topics, their conflict structure and their interaction processes during conflict. With respect to the first, it was seen that anorectic or bulimic patients and their spouses report not only more conflict-producing topics than

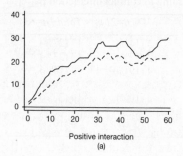

Positive interaction
(a)

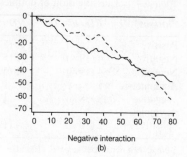

Negative interaction
(b)

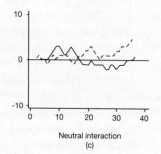

Neutral interaction
(c)

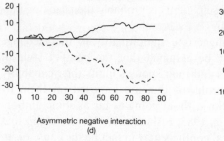

Asymmetric negative interaction
(d)

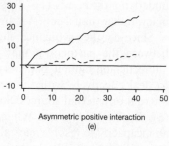

Asymmetric positive interaction
(e)

HUSBAND ———
WIFE – – – – –

Figure 6.1   Conflict interaction types

Table 6.4   Classification of couples according to conflict interaction patterns

Patterns	ED (n=21)	ND (n=21)	MD (n=21)	Total (n=63)
Positive	3 (14%)	11 (52%)	3 (14%)	17 (27%)
Negative	4 (19%)	1 (5%)	12 (57%)	17 (27%)
Neutral	4 (19%)	1 (5%)	4 (19%)	9 (14%)
Asymmetric negative	8 (38%)	4 (19%)	2 (10%)	14 (22%)
Asymmetric positive	2 (10%)	4 (19%)	0 (0%)	6 (10%)

Source: Van den Broucke *et al.* (1995d)

nondistressed couples, but also different ones, which are more concerned with affectively charged issues. This high emotional involvement may make conflicts about these topics more aversive, and therefore the avoidance of conflicts more likely. The latter corresponds with the findings from self-report and observation studies regarding these couples' conflict interaction processes, demonstrating that avoidance is indeed the preferred conflict tactic in most eating-disordered couples. Finally, on a structural level, the conflicts between eating-disordered patients and their husbands were seen to be very egalitarian. This contradicts the strategic therapists' view that the conflicts in these couples are really concerned with the question of who is in command of the relationship, unless it is maintained that the apparent symmetry reflects the success of the patient's attempts to restore the power balance by developing her symptoms. A more plausible explanation, then, is that the main structural characteristic underlying the conflicts of these patients is probably their lack of intimacy, rather than a covert struggle for power.

Since conflict avoidance suggests a static quality to the exchange between the partners, it may be assumed that the conflict style of anorectic and bulimic patients and their spouses limits their capability to deal effectively with the problems that are imposed on them by internal or external sources. So, without going as far as some authors (e.g. Boskind-White and White, 1983; Fishman, 1979), who claim that an incapacity to resolve marital conflicts may in fact be the cause of an eating disorder, we do think that these couples' lack of conflict resolution skills further compounds their already considerable relational and personal difficulties.

7   Sexuality, fertility and parenting

To say that sexuality is an important aspect of a marital relationship is probably a truism. Indeed, sexuality is so intrinsically related to the satisfaction of marital partners with their relationship and to their subjective sense of well-being that it is included in many formal definitions of marital intimacy (e.g. Parelman, 1983; Waring *et al.*, 1981). While more specific empirical studies suggest that sexuality and intimacy are in fact different concepts (Monsour, 1992; Patton and Waring, 1985), it is commonly assumed that a couple's sexual relationship is strongly influenced by their overall marital quality and vice versa.

This 'intimate' connection between marital and sexual quality can also be expected in the relationships of eating-disordered patients, although here the interaction is probably more complex: on the one hand, AN and BN frequently lead to sexual dysfunctions; on the other hand, the eating disorders themselves are sometimes triggered by sexual problems, which are often rooted in a history of sexual abuse. So, whereas the relationship between sexual functioning and the occurrence of AN or BN is an important issue by itself, it is of particular interest for patients who live together with a sexual partner. Given the specific focus of this book on married patients, we will review the existing literature on sexuality in eating-disordered patients in this chapter, distinguishing between clinical assumptions and research-based findings. Because of the importance of the patients' psychosexual history for their current sexual relationship and psychological problems, we will also pay specific attention to the issue of sexual abuse.

A problem that is closely related to sexuality concerns the reproductive functions of patients with AN or BN and their ability to take up their roles as parents. In view of their apparent psychological conflicts with sexuality and body image, and their troubled relationships with their partners and families of origin, it is obvious that pregnancy and parenthood can be very stressful experiences for these women, and as such these deserve specific attention. Therefore, they will also be addressed in this chapter.

SEXUAL FUNCTIONING

Sexual conflicts

In the eating disorder literature, the patients' sexuality is often considered from a psychodynamic perspective, which stresses the conflictual nature of the patients' sexuality and the symbolic function of food and body weight in this regard. It has been suggested, for example, that for women there is a special relationship between food and sex (Kaplan, 1980; Meadow and Weiss, 1992; Pasini, 1995), which would explain why females are more prone to 'disorders of desire' (Liss-Levinson, 1988). With respect to AN, it is traditionally assumed that the patients are sexually inhibited because of their supposed fear of growing up. According to Crisp (1980), 'The link between . . . a change in shape, body weight and sexuality is as much a biological one and one remarked by others, as simply implying a link between orality and sexuality' (p. 64). The anorectic symptoms thus seem to serve the purpose of avoiding sexual feelings that are experienced as threatening. In turn, the developmental arrest in anorectic patients results in an adult unresponsiveness that is expressed by the avoidance of intimacy and sex. In Andersen's (1985) terms, 'Every aspect of sexual life is affected, including libido, performance, and capacity for reproduction. In general, anorectic patients are sexually inhibited and have difficulty experiencing pleasure' (p. 145).

A similarly stereotyped image is found in the literature on bulimic women. More specifically, it is assumed that BN patients are sexually more active, but instead of reaching psychosexual maturity they tend to lead an almost promiscuous life in a search for the satisfaction of their insatiable 'hunger' for recognition and love. Crisp (1980) for example reports that 'Even at low body weights [bulimic patients] may occasionally find themselves sexually preoccupied. Although rarely getting any satisfaction or contentment from sexual relationships they may plunge into them recklessly from time to time' (p. 32). The same is observed by Andersen (1985), who notes that 'bulimic patients, especially those with generalized disorders of impulse control, may show inappropriate sexual activity' (p. 145). As such, this view underscores the standard picture of the 'overcontrolled' anorectic versus the 'loss of control' in bulimic patients.

Sexual activity

While the above views appear clinically attractive, they are probably overgeneralized and should certainly not be taken for granted. Moreover, to the extent that they are true, the question remains as to causality in the relationship between sexual problems and eating disorders. The interpretations of research data in this respect differ a lot according to the reviewers – compare, for instance, Scott (1987) and Coovert, Kinder and Thompson (1989) – although there is a consensus about the fact that during the active phase of AN most women show a considerable decrease of sexual interest due to hypogonadism caused by emaciation (Tuiten *et al.*, 1993).

Another important point is that most of the above data and speculations are concerned with younger patients without a sexual partner. Only a few studies have focused on older adolescent or adult patients who are involved in a heterosexual relationship. The results of these studies yield a mixed picture. For example, an Australian study in which the sexual histories of bulimic patients were compared with those of matched control subjects (Abraham *et al.*, 1985) showed few differences between the samples: bulimics were in some ways more sexually experienced, more likely to achieve orgasm through masturbation and less likely to be orgasmic during intercourse, yet in general the bulimics seemed to be as 'typical' as their peers. The same conclusion was arrived at in a German study with a comparable design (Fichter and Haberger, 1990), although here a slightly lower ability to achieve orgasm was found in bulimics compared to controls. Finally, in a Swiss comparative study the similarities in sexual activity between bulimics and normal controls were confirmed, but a clearly lower sexual satisfaction and more sexual dysfunctions were reported for the patient group (Jagstaidt and Pasini, 1994).

The few studies involving adult women with restricting AN (Haimes and Katz, 1988; Heavey *et al.*, 1989; Raboch and Faltus, 1991; Tuiten *et al.*, 1993) all seem to point into the same direction: these patients are generally slower in their psychosexual development, and report more sexual problems and dissatisfaction.

The problem with the previous findings is, however, that they were all contaminated by a number of interfering variables, such as family background, sexual education, body experience, hormonal status, relationship with partner and history of sexual abuse. This makes it very difficult to summarize the results in terms of diagnostic subgroups. Thus, one should be cautious in drawing conclusions about sexual behaviour in relation to an eating disorder. Nevertheless, it is clear that sexuality is an issue that is of central importance for the development and therapeutic management of eating disorders. This is especially true for the married subjects described in this book. While being married or having a sexual partner does not imply that one has achieved the stage of psychosexual maturity, the presence of a sexual relationship may well exacerbate the patient's sexual insecurity, and thus contribute to her problems.

SEXUAL ABUSE

In the last decade sexual abuse has gained considerable attention in the psychiatric literature. Especially in disorders that are typically 'female', like AN or BN, a history of sexual traumatization is sometimes assumed as a causal factor (Schwartz and Cohn, 1996). In such cases, the eating disorder can be regarded as the scar of a 'violated' body. The problem with this view, however, is that the presence of sexual traumatization in patients with an eating disorder has not yet been unequivocally established. In fact, highly divergent rates of sexual abuse in eating disorders have been reported in the literature (Vanderlinden and Vandereycken, 1997). To explain this divergence, a number of factors may be considered.

A first issue is the *heterogeneity of eating disorders*. Samples of eating-disordered patients may vary a lot with respect to clinical features such as the type and severity of eating disorder, the age of onset and the duration of the illness, and co-morbidity (additional diagnoses). Research data clearly suggest that sexual abuse in eating-disordered women may be related to higher levels of co-morbidity, in particular with mood disorders, anxiety disorders, personality disorders (especially of the borderline type) and dissociative disorders.

A second problem concerns the *definition of trauma and/or sexual abuse*. Some studies report only those sexually abusive experiences that took place before the onset of the eating disorder and where the perpetrator was at least five years older than the victim. Some studies consider only childhood sexual abuse, while others also include more recent traumatic experiences in adolescence or adulthood, where peers are involved. So, in order to allow for more definite conclusions, a consensus about the definition of sexual abuse is badly needed.

Third, findings about sexual abuse in patients with eating disorders also differ according to the *method of assessment*. Personal characteristics of the investigator (e.g. male or female, involved in therapy or not), the timing of the assessment (e.g. before, during or after therapy) and the method that is used to collect information (e.g. self-report questionnaire versus standardized interview) may have an impact on the results. At the moment, no empirical basis is available to recommend the use of any specific assessment method. Moreover, there always remains the problem of memory distortion and induction, especially in this group of highly vulnerable, suggestible and emotionally unbalanced patients.

An important yet complex factor that is seldom addressed in studies about this topic is the *severity and duration of the abuse*. Research data show a relationship between the severity of sexual abuse (for instance: starting before the age of 5, combined with violence or physical abuse, involving multiple perpetrators who are close relatives) and the severity of adult psychopathology. However, evaluation of the severity of abuse remains a difficult issue, for in most cases it can be based only on the victim's subjective experience. Furthermore, one must also pay attention to the perceived response to (attempted) disclosure. Indeed, the absence of reaction or a hostile response to a disclosure about sexual abuse may be as traumatic as the event itself!

Taking into account the above methodological problems, the major findings with regard to sexual abuse in eating disorders can be summarized as follows (for more details, see Vanderlinden and Vandereycken, 1997):

1 A history of sexual abuse in childhood or adolescence is reported in 20 to 50 per cent of women with an eating disorder, but such rates have been found in other psychiatric patients as well.
2 Compared to the general female population, the rate of sexual abuse appears to be higher in eating-disordered patients.
3 The rate of sexual abuse is higher in patients with bulimic symptomatology than in restricting anorectics.
4 Sexual abuse is more often associated with co-morbidity, especially of borderline personality disorder and dissociative symptoms.

By way of conclusion we may note that a specific and direct connection between sexual abuse (or other traumatic experiences) and the subsequent development of an eating disorder has not yet been demonstrated. However, the available research data, as well as our own clinical experiences in therapeutic work with these patients, suggest that serious sexual and/or physical abuse in childhood and early adolescence puts the individual at special risk for developing psychological crises, some of which may lead to psychiatric disorders such as AN and BN.

REPRODUCTIVE FUNCTIONS

Menstrual function

As pointed out in chapter 1, eating disorder patients have important hormonal disturbances that are mostly revealed upon medical screening. One of the most conspicuous symptoms of AN is indeed the disturbance of menstrual function, which is associated with a hypothalamic dysfunction. To account for this disturbance several explanations have been advanced, including the patient's weight loss, decreased body fat, hyperactivity, weight-losing behaviours and neurotransmitter abnormalities. The exact mechanism of amenorrhoea in AN remains unclear (Beumont, 1992; Golden and Shenker, 1994), although there is a consensus about the secondary nature of the menstrual dysfunctioning. From a diagnostic point of view, the value of amenorrhoea as a criterion is questionable (Vandereycken and Meermann, 1987). In fact, findings from two recent studies (Cachelin and Mahrer, 1996; Garfinkel *et al.*, 1996) suggest that amenorrhoea is not a discriminating factor between women with AN and women who have the same features except amenorrhoea, and that the presence of menses is not an indication of lower levels of eating disorder, body-image disturbance or psychopathology. Nevertheless, all major definitions of AN, including DSM-IV (see chapter 1), imply amenorrhoea as a necessary criterion.

Curiously enough, the absence of their menses is not usually considered a problem by the patients themselves; in fact they often feel relieved that they are 'free from this annoying condition'. During recovery menses normally reoccur once the weight is restored to normal (i.e. a BMI consistently above 19). When the menses do not resume after weight restoration, this must be seen as an indication of a nutritional imbalance, due to persisting dieting or anorectic behaviours such as food restriction, purging or excessive physical activity (Abraham and Llewellyn-Jones, 1995; Copeland, Sacks, and Herzog, 1995; Schweiger, Laessle and Pirke, 1988). On the other hand, the recurrence of menstruation does not necessarily mean that the ovulatory functioning has been restored (Beumont, 1992). Ultrasound scans may be useful in indicating a normal multifollicular ovarian morphology as an indication for a full hormonal recovery (Treasure *et al.*, 1988). Full recovery means a satisfactory readjustment in the emotional and social area, and an adequate eating pattern, without hyperactivity or weight-reducing strategies.

One should also be aware of the fact that in sexually active patients oral contraceptives may be prescribed. In addition, an increasing number of patients are on hormonal substitution to prevent osteo-porosis, which is a common and important complication of (chronic) AN. In both cases the use of hormones could be very misleading in the recognition of the diagnosis as well as the recovery of AN.

Although less conspicuously than in AN, patients with BN also suffer from hormonal disturbances. Depending on the study, the prevalence of secondary amenorrhoea in BN patients varies between 20 and 75 per cent (Abraham and Llewellyn-Jones, 1995; Copeland, Sacks and Herzog, 1995). Because the majority of bulimic women have a weight within the normal range, their hormonal disturbances are related to the weight-losing behaviours (intermittent dieting) rather than to low body fat. The few outcome studies that have paid attention to menstrual functioning in BN (Fairburn *et al.*, 1987; Copeland, Sacks and Herzog, 1995) showed that recovery of menstruation was related to less 'restrained eating' and absence of an affective disorder.

Fertility

Relatively little is known about the effects of the hormonal distur-bances of eating-disordered patients on their sexual behaviour, reproductive function and pregnancies. It is well known, however, that many women perceive a pregnancy as a challenge to their body image, to the control of their body weight and to their self-esteem (Franko and Walton, 1993; Abraham and Llewellyn-Jones, 1995; Stewart and Robinson, 1993). Whereas a weight gain of 12.5 kg from conception to childbirth is normal for a healthy woman (Fahy and Morrison, 1993; Davies and Wardle, 1994; Moore and Greenwood, 1995), it is typical for our dieting culture that most women believe they should restrict their weight gain during pregnancy. Fairburn and Welsh (1990) found that about 40 per cent of normal primigravida (first-pregnancy mothers) worried that they might gain too much weight; 28 per cent had negative attitudes to changes in body shape, and 72 per cent reported a fear that they would be unable to return to their former weight after delivery. In multiparas, on the other hand, the attitude towards the postpartum body appears to be more positive (Strang and Sullivan, 1985).

In women with an eating disorder, the above concerns are probably complicated by the many psychological conflicts concerning sexuality, body image, autonomy versus dependency, and relationships with the family of origin that highlight during pregnancy (Stewart *et al.*, 1987; Hall, 1996). A pregnancy or postpartum period is therefore likely to be especially stressful for these patients, and infertility may represent a way to avoid these threatening experiences. It may also reflect the ongoing problems in the marital relationship, whereby the infertility means 'I do not want a child from this man'.

These assumptions are confirmed by research findings. Comparing bulimic patients with women from the general population, Abraham and Llewellyn-Jones (1995) found that twice as many of the bulimic group complained of infertility during the course of their illness. Anorectics are nearly always infertile during the active phase of AN, due to the lack of sexual activity and/or the hormonal disturbances (anovulation due to a changed morphological ovarium structure). Nevertheless, the exception confirms the rule: a few case reports have documented the possibility of pregnancy without menstruation in these patients (Marshall and Palmer, 1988).

One should also be aware that through the rapid evolution of medical techniques in the field of infertility in recent years ovulation may be induced by the use of pulsatile LHRH treatment, even in a stage of emaciation. Of course, such an intervention is not without risks. Even in normal couples a treatment for infertility is a stressful event, which not only affects the daily life experiences of the partners but also impacts on the marital relationship by increasing the likelihood of conflicts and sexual dissatisfaction. Moreover, the stress of a fertility treatment affects the woman's sexual identity, body image and sense of self-efficacy (Andrews, Abbey, and Halman, 1992; Leiblum, 1993). For both spouses, anxiety, depression and lowered self-esteem are common responses to a fertility treatment. Since the adjustment to this experience is related to positive self-esteem and internal locus of control (Koropatnick, Daniluk and Pattinson, 1993; Nachtigall, Becker and Wozny, 1992; Newman and Zouves, 1991), a woman with an eating disorder is especially vulnerable to not coping successfully to the experience. Instead, she may react with an exacerbation of the anorectic or bulimic symptoms. Therefore, like Beumont (1992), we question the acceptability of fertility treatment in non-recovered patients with an eating disorder.

It is likely, however, that many women who ask for technical help do not inform their obstetricians about their past or present eating disorder because they feel guilty and shameful (Fahy and O'Donoghue, 1991; Franko and Walton, 1993; Lemberg *et al.*, 1992; Hall, 1996; Schweiger *et al.*, 1988; Stewart *et al.*, 1990). The following findings are an important warning in this respect: a Canadian (Stewart *et al.*, 1990) and a Swiss study (Thommen, Valach and Kiencke, 1995) revealed a prevalence of eating disorders in 7.6 per cent and 5.8 per cent, respectively, of the women seeking help in a Family Planning Clinic!

After recovery, the fecundity of ex-AN women who want to have children is not different from that of women in the general population. However, a significant proportion of recovered anorectics voluntarily chooses a childless life (Abraham and Llewellyn-Jones, 1995).

PREGNANCY AND PARENTHOOD

Pregnancy

Despite the infertility problems outlined above, AN or BN patients may become pregnant. Given their considerable psychological difficulties, however, it is obvious that pregnancy and parenthood can be very stressful for these women. The effect of the pregnancy on the eating disorder varies according to the patient's condition. Women who conceive during the active phase of AN show an increase of psychological symptoms, including anxiety and depression. Their anxiety at losing control over their weight may result in efforts to prevent weight gain. Although most of these women also fear that their unborn child may be damaged because of their own poor nutrition or other weight-reducing practices, an improvement of the core symptoms is rare. Because of their low self-esteem and their sense of lack of control, many patients have feelings of inadequacy about parenting (Lewis and le Grange, 1994; Georgiou, 1995; Hall, 1996) which result in a persistence or exacerbation of the anorectic or bulimic symptoms during pregnancy (Stewart *et al.*, 1987). Conversely, in one study (Lemberg, Phillips and Fischer, 1992) a beneficial impact of the pregnancy on the AN symptoms was found, with 70 per cent of the women reporting an overall improvement. According to the authors, these positive results were the consequence of the self-selection sampling in their study. But after childbirth there was a great remission, with only a minority of the patients (23 per cent) being able to maintain the improvement of their symptoms. At all events, in the case of serious vomiting during pregnancy, known as *hyperemesis gravidarum*, an association with an eating disorder should be considered, especially when there is a failure to gain weight (Lingam and McCluskey, 1996; Stewart and Robinson, 1993; Vandereycken, 1982).

Since women who are underweight at conception (i.e. a BMI below 19) have an increased risk of delivering infants weighing below the tenth centile (Fahy and Morrison, 1993), it is not surprising that AN patients deliver infants with a lower birth weight, low Apgar scores, a higher incidence of congenital malformations and a higher than expected incidence of prematurity and perinatal mortality (Beumont, 1992; Stewart, 1992; Stewart *et al.*, 1987). If these women become pregnant at a low body weight as the result of an induced ovulation, they have a higher than normal frequency of spontaneous abortions and low-weight newborns, and are more prone to deliver infants with birth defects (Abraham and Llewellyn-Jones, 1995; Burke and Vangellow, 1990; Stewart, 1992; Stewart *et al.*, 1987). However, in two studies where the patients had gained adequate weight during pregnancy, infant birth weights were within normal range (Lemberg *et al.*, 1992; Namir, Melman and Yager, 1986).

While the above findings primarily concern anorectic patients, the literature on pregnancy in BN patients is more equivocal. Nevertheless, the published data about this topic do suggest a relationship between bulimic symptoms and complications of pregnancy and childbirth. Like anorectics, BN patients report a fear of losing control over eating and weight, realize the risks of damaging the unborn child as a result of their unhealthy eating practices, and feel insecure about their ability to cope with a newborn baby (Lewis and le Grange, 1994). Yet this does not prevent them from engaging in bulimic behaviours. The inability to stop their bulimia may actually increase feelings of fear, guilt and shame (Franko and Walton, 1993; Lewis and le Grange, 1994). In such cases, the severity of the bulimic symptoms often remains unchanged during pregnancy. Alternatively, a resurgence of symptoms is often attributed to the anxiety over weight gained during pregnancy and the attendant desperation to return to pre-pregnancy weight (Hollifield and Hobdy, 1990; Lacey and Smith, 1987; Lemberg and Phillips, 1989; Lewis and le Grange, 1994; Woodside and Shekter-Wolfson, 1990). In three studies (Abraham and Llewellyn-Jones, 1995; Lacey and Smith, 1987; Lemberg and Phillips, 1989) a decrease of bulimic symptoms during pregnancy was reported, suggesting that pregnancy might be beneficial!

As in anorectic women, the incidence of foetal abnormalities, multiple pregnancies and obstetrical complications in bulimic women is higher than expected (Copeland, Sacks and Herzog, 1995; Franko and Walton, 1993; Lacey and Smith, 1987; Lewis and le Grange, 1994). In two studies (Abraham and Llewellyn-Jones, 1995; Lemberg and Phillips, 1989) there were no implications to the development of the foetus or to the birthweight of the infants, but a recent well-controlled study demonstrated that infants of mothers with eating disorders were smaller than infants of mothers with postnatal depression (Stein *et al.*, 1996). Table 7.1 summarizes the main complications of pregnancy in anorectic and bulimic women.

Table 7.1   Reported complications of pregnancy in eating-disordered women

	Maternal complications	Birth complications
AN	Inadequate weight gain Vaginal bleeding Decreased uterine size Miscarriage Hyperemesis	Low birth weight Premature birth Perinatal death Delayed development
BN	Increased symptoms Excessive exercise Low and high weight gain Miscarriage Hypertension	Stillbirth Low birth weight Low Apgar scores Breech delivery Cleft palate

Source: Adapted from Franko and Walton (1993) and Stewart and Robinson (1993)

Taking these points into consideration, a delay in pregnancy is strongly recommended until the eating disorder is in sufficient remission. If the eating disorder is in remission or there is a full recovery, an uncomplicated pregnancy and a healthy baby can be expected (Miyake, 1986; Stewart *et al.*, 1987). In recovered AN patients who have no problems with their eating behaviour and show an adequate weight, infant birthweights are within normal range (Rand, Willis and Kuldau, 1987; Abraham and Llewellyn-Jones, 1995). Nevertheless, a follow-up study (Brinch, Isager and Tolstrup, 1988) of 50 women assessed on average 12.5 years after the diagnosis of AN had been made – 36 of whom were considered to have recovered – revealed that the rate of prematurity in infants was twice the expected rate and prenatal mortality was six times the expected number! But these mothers functioned psychologically well during pregnancy and the postpartum period. Involuntary childlessness was of the same size in this sample as in the general Danish population (Brinch, Isager and Tolstrup, 1988).

To conclude, it appears that despite the general tendencies summarized above many findings in this field remain inconsistent. This points to the necessity of increased research efforts in which prospective and longitudinal measures are used to evaluate the impact of pregnancy on eating disorders and vice versa. An unusual but inspiring view on this complex issue has been described by Melanie Katzman (1993), who reports on the reactions of her eating disorder patients to her own pregnancy as a therapist. An aspect which also merits further attention is the mediating role of the marital relationship quality in the effect of the pregnancy on the eating disorder. In some studies, bulimic women who recovered completely while being pregnant tended to have a stable and meaningful relationship, whereas those who continued their bulimic behaviour during pregnancy and afterwards tended to have serious interpersonal problems and a sense of failure (Lewis and le Grange, 1994; Woodside *et al.*, 1993). Further, women who had the most severe eating pathology during pregnancy also seemed to be the ones who subsequently divorced or separated from their husbands (Lewis and le Grange, 1994).

Parenting

A chronic illness such as an eating disorder has profound effects on the psychosocial functioning of a woman, including her ability to raise children. In this regard, we may note that about one-third of the married anorectics have children (Brinch, Isager and Tolstrup, 1988; Woodside *et al.*, 1993). There are two reasons why parenting could become inadequate in these women. First, the core symptoms are quite disruptive to daily life and conflict with sensitive parenting. Second, parents with an eating disorder have difficulties in interpersonal relationships, which may also strongly influence the parent–child relationship.

Mothers with AN may find that their intense preoccupation with weight and shape conflicts with the desire to nurture and feed their child. Whereas a single case report mentioned a positive influence of breast-feeding on the eating-disordered mother's self-esteem (Georgiou, 1995), the majority of these mothers wish to lose weight rapidly after delivery. This morbid preoccupation with food, weight and body shape impairs their responsiveness towards the children's needs (Stewart *et al.*, 1987; Stein and Woolley, 1996; Hall, 1996). The concern that their children could become obese may lead to nutritional deprivation or caloric restriction (Stewart, 1992). In the pioneering Danish follow-up study by Brinch, Isager and Tolstrup (1988), it was demonstrated that 17 per cent of the children failed to thrive during the first year! The observational study by Stein *et al.* (1994) showed mothers with an eating disorder to be more intrusive with their infants, not only during mealtimes but also during playtime. They also expressed more negative emotions towards their infants during mealtimes, and the latter tended to be lighter than controls. But even later on in life an anorectic mother can seriously affect the development of her child, especially when it is a girl. This may eventually lead to 'anorexia by proxy' (Scourfield, 1995) or 'anorexie à deux' (Griffiths *et al.*, 1995).

With regard to the impact of being a parent on the global social functioning of the AN patient, the research findings are controversial.

In the Danish follow-up study (Brinch *et al.*, 1988) it was found that AN patients who are mothers have better scores of all-round functioning than childless ones. In contrast, Woodside *et al.* (1993) reported that patients with children had significant impairments compared with childless patients. These investigators were struck by the frequency with which their patients reported exacerbations of their symptoms, or even initiation of their illness, as a consequence of the changes in weight and body shape associated with pregnancy (Woodside and Shekter-Wolfson, 1990; Fahy and O'Donoghue, 1991). The severity of this parental dysfunction was also reflected by the marital dysfunction (Woodside *et al.*, 1993; Georgiou, 1995).

Although there are very few reports concerning the effect of bulimia on the mother's ability to take care of her child, the issues that were mentioned above with regard to AN may be repeated here. In fact, the study by Woodside *et al.* (1993) also included a number of bulimic mothers. Few of their patients reported happiness with their new role, and they experienced the eating disorder as the main impediment to effective childrearing. Neither were bulimic mothers able to provide adequate nutrition for their young children (Stein and Fairburn, 1989). In one study no birth complications or significant feeding problems were found, although many mothers with bulimia regarded their daughters as being overweight or underweight at some time (Mitchell, Boutacoff and Wilson, 1986).

CONCLUSIONS

In this chapter, we have reviewed the available literature on the issues of sexuality, fertility, pregnancy and parenting in patients with an eating disorder. With regard to sexuality, it was pointed out that the patients' sexual (dys)functioning was of central importance for the development and therapeutic management of the eating disorder, yet the complexity of this issue was also emphasized. Although sexuality should always be addressed in a treatment programme, the manner of dealing with sexual difficulties in eating-disordered patients may vary widely. In adolescent patients a special sex education programme (Van Vreckem and Vandereycken, 1994) or group therapy (Lonergan, 1992) can be very valuable, whereas in other cases some form of sex therapy may be indicated (Guile, Horne and Dunston, 1978; Renshaw, 1990). However, the latter requires special experience in the therapist because of the many biopsychosocial aspects that are involved (Simpson and Ramberg, 1992; Zerbe, 1992). Further, it has been documented that although sexual abuse must not be considered as the major or specific cause of an eating disorder, its significance in the life history of patients should not be underestimated. For the practical aspects of its assessment and treatment we refer to a recent publication of our own group (Vanderlinden and Vandereycken, 1997).

It is a common clinical finding that women with an eating disorder have an increased risk of being infertile during the active stage of their illness. On the other hand, women within the community who have an undiagnosed eating disorder may seek treatment for infertility. Since most of these women are secretive about their eating disorder, obstetricians should be alert for menstrual abnormalities and peculiar weight fluctuations. It was argued that fertility treatment is unacceptable in non-recovered patients because it ignores the psychobiological state of these women and does not take into consideration the complexity of their attitudes towards having children.

Drawing from recent research findings, it was pointed out that pregnancy during an eating disorder may jeopardize both maternal and foetal health. For the mother, the medical complications are mainly associated with the disturbed eating pattern and inadequate weight gain. Although some researchers reported a positive influence of the pregnancy on the eating disorder, most studies showed at best a neutral effect and most often an exacerbation of the anorectic or bulimic symptoms in pregnant patients. For the child, the most common complication is the low birthweight of the newborn. Mental health professionals, family physicians (general practitioners) and obstetricians, as well as eating-disordered women themselves, should be informed about these complications. They also should know that, after delivery, these women are at increased risk for postpartum depression (Abraham and Llewellyn-Jones, 1995).

Finally, we also addressed the parenting abilities of eating disorder patients, pointing out that the interactional problems which characterize all cases of AN or BN become even more complex if the eating-disordered patient is a parent. It was demonstrated that mothers who suffer from an eating disorder often have excessive concerns about their child's weight, and that their children often suffer from inadequate nutrition.

8 Assessment and treatment of eating disorders

In the foregoing chapters, we have described the marital relationships of patients with AN or BN, drawing from existing models of marital interaction and relying as much as possible on findings from empirical research. In addition, we have explored the relationship between the marital characteristics of these patients and the occurrence of the eating disorder. From a practitioner's point of view, however, a description of these phenomena is probably not sufficient; what matters most for clinical practice is how they can be successfully integrated into the assessment and treatment of eating-disordered patients and couples in order to improve the effectiveness of the intervention. This question will be addressed in the remaining chapters of this book. As a preamble, this chapter will present some general guidelines for the clinical assessment and treatment of anorectic and bulimic patients deriving from our own clinical experience. The approach we advocate may be characterized as a family-oriented, cognitive-behavioural one, and is based on the multidimensional process model of eating disorders which takes into account the many somatic, psychological and social factors in the aetiology of these disorders as well as the complex interplay between these factors. It also endorses the principle of the 'scientist–practitioner' approach (Barlow et al., 1984) according to which practitioners should base their interventions on empirical findings and should apply research methods whenever possible, to provide for an empirical feedback system during the therapy process and an evaluation of the outcome. More detailed information about this approach can be found in Vandereycken and Meermann (1987) and in Vanderlinden, Norré and Vandereycken (1992). Elements that are specific for married patients will be discussed in the next two chapters.

ASSESSMENT OF EATING DISORDERS

In chapter 1 we have presented the diagnostic criteria for AN and BN, pointing out that the diagnosis should be based on the patient's behaviour rather than on her physical condition, and emphasizing the importance of a proper differentiation with co-existing disorders. The verification of these issues requires the systematic assessment of the patient's condition. To that effect, both a clinical interview and standardized assessment measures may provide useful information. Both methods will now be discussed in detail.

Clinical interview with the patient

For many anorectic or bulimic patients, the interview conducted on the intake represents the first time that they are expected to talk overtly about their eating behaviour. At first, patients may be inclined to mislead the interviewer by minimizing the symptoms, as they are used to doing with others in their social environment. When the interviewer has reasons to believe that such is the case, it is best to discuss this openly with the patient in a nonblaming way. To that effect, one may reframe her tendency to deny symptoms as a sign of ambivalence or fear of change. Making reference to the inward struggle between the incompatible feelings that 'this cannot go on forever' and that 'something inside prevents me from changing' will strike a familiar chord in most patients, and often makes it easier for them to 'confess' or 'admit' to their behaviour.

To obtain an accurate image of the eating disorder, the interviewer should proceed step by step, checking the different criteria as outlined in chapter 1. This implies that, along with the exploration of the patient's behaviour and her feelings and thoughts about eating, weight and body size, the possibility of other (co-morbid) problems must also be assessed (see Table 1.4). One should realize that asking specific and accurate questions about these items not only provides answers that will help to make the diagnosis, but also gives the patient the confidence-inducing sensation that she is dealing with an 'expert'.

To assess the extent to which the eating disorder has an impact on the patient's psychosocial functioning, it is helpful to get an impression of how she spends an 'average' day. An important element in this context is her past and present relationship with her family of origin and the actual (lack of) intimate relationships. Finally, one should also get an impression of the patient's self-image in relation to her 'ideal' self. Relevant questions in this regard concern how she perceives herself, if she shows excessive self-criticism and whether she tends towards black-or-white thinking. An outline for the clinical interview with the patient is presented in Table 8.1.

Interview with the parents or spouse

Because an eating disorder is usually compounded by numerous interactional problems, information should not only be collected about the patient's eating behaviour and psychological (dys)functioning, but also about her position within the family and/or marital system. Therefore, as part of the intake procedure it is advisable also to have an exploratory interview with the parents and, if the patient is married, with her husband. With regard to the latter, the interview will be discussed in detail in the following chapter. In this chapter, we want to focus on the patient's relationship with her family of origin, especially her parents. Even if the patient is no longer living with them, it is important to pay attention to this relationship, for it is a well-known fact that patients with AN or BN, regardless of their age or marital status, often demonstrate a striking dependence or discordant relationship with their parents (Minuchin *et al.*, 1978; Vandereycken *et al.*, 1989).

An interview with the parent not only provides the necessary information about the patient's family relationship characteristics, but also makes clear to the parents that their co-operation in the treatment is very important. In younger patients, the parents' commitment must even be considered an essential condition if outpatient treatment is to have a reasonable chance of success. It must be explained to them that good progress of the therapy requires the family to restore its normal living pattern as soon as possible, and that their daughter must assume responsibility for her own health. During the interview, it can also be emphasized to the parents that the treatment of an eating disorder is a complicated matter, and that false optimism in quick changes is unwarranted (Herzog, Deter and Vandereycken, 1992). An outline of the parental interview is presented by Perednia and Vandereycken (1989).

Standardized measures

Although a clinical interview is a *sine qua non* for diagnosing AN or BN, the additional use of standardized measures to determine the individual and interactional aspects of the illness is advisable for both practical and research purposes. While such measures cannot replace

Table 8.1   Outline for clinical interview with the patient

Weight

What does the patient think about her present weight?
Has she recently lost weight? How much and in what period of time?
Did she want to lose weight? How much and why?
What is her ideal weight? Does she often 'feel fat'?
Do other people (e.g. at home) think she should lose or gain weight?
Is she afraid of becoming overweight? What does she consider to be
overweight?
Does she ever use laxatives (diuretics) to lose weight?
Has she ever been treated for a weight disorder?

Eating

What does the patient eat? How much? How often? When and where?
Does she ever feel hungry?
Does she prefer eating alone? Does she avoid eating in front of other people?
Does she ever fast? How often? For how long?
Is she ever afraid of not being able to stop eating?
Does she ever eat large amounts of food in a short period of time?
Does she think about food and calories much of the time?
To what extent does eating interfere with her life?
Does she ever induce vomiting after she has eaten?
Does she ever take pills to curb her appetite?
Does she think her eating pattern is normal?
Has she ever been treated for an eating disorder before?

Activity

Does the patient exercise? What types of exercise?
Does she feel tired more quickly than before?
Does she have an active life style (e.g. active or sedentary job; job involved
with food; sports)?

Self-image

How does the patient cope with growing up?
Does she compare herself with others? Does she feel inferior?
Does she think everything she does is not good enough?
Does she often feel empty and worthless?
Is she often unsure about her own feelings (e.g. not sure when she is sad,
anxious or angry)?
Does she often have mood swings?

Interactions

Can the patient make decisions on her own?
Can she express her own personal opinion?
Can she talk about her feelings or does she hide them from others?
Are there any problems at home (e.g. family problems that remain undiscussed
or unresolved)?
Does she have many social contacts outside the family?
Does she have a sexual relationship?

Source: Adapted from Vandereycken and Meermann (1987)

the interview as a diagnostic tool, they can facilitate the systematic description and assessment of the symptoms. When they are applied at various stages during the therapeutic process, standardized instruments allow for the systematic monitoring of the patient's progress over time.

In the last few years, several self-report questionnaires and rating scales have been proposed for the assessment of eating disorder symptoms. It should be pointed out, however, that patients with an eating disorder, AN in particular, are not always reliable in their self-reports, in that their responses can be deformed by a tendency to minimize or even deny their symptoms (Vandereycken and Vanderlinden, 1983). Self-report data should therefore always be interpreted with the necessary caution, and must be considered against the background of information obtained from other sources.

With this limitation in mind, we will briefly present the instruments we prefer to use in our clinical work with eating-disordered patients. Several of these instruments were developed by our own group; others are borrowed from the international literature.

The *Eating Disorder Evaluation Scale* (EDES; Vandereycken, 1993) is a rating scale that can either be included in a (standardized) interview or be presented to the patient in the form of a questionnaire. It allows for a rating (on scale ranging from 0 to 6) of the patient's functioning in various domains relevant to the diagnostic criteria for AN or BN: weight and eating behaviour, attitude towards body and nutrition, sexuality, relationships with parents and friends, current work or studies, and psychiatric status. Scores on these items can be combined into a global clinical score, offering an overall impression of the seriousness of the illness: the lower the score, the more serious the level of dysfunction. Since such a global impression is often misleading, the preferred analysis of the EDES entails the computation of scores on four subscales: (1) anorectic preoccupation; (2) bulimic behaviour; (3) sexuality; and (4) psychosocial adjustment.

The *Eating Disorder Inventory* (EDI; Garner, Olmsted and Polivy, 1983) is a diagnostic questionnaire that is widely used internationally. It consists of 64 items, measuring a broad spectrum of behaviours and attitudes commonly found in AN and BN patients. Items are scored on a six-point scale (ranging from *always* to *never*), yielding scores on eight subscales: (1) drive for thinness; (2) bulimia; (3) body dissatisfaction; (4) ineffectiveness; (5) perfectionism; (6) interpersonal distrust; (7)interoceptive awareness; and (8) maturity fears. An updated version of the instrument (EDI-2; Garner, 1991) contains three complementary subscales: (9) asceticism; (10) impulse regulation; and (11) social insecurity. A large number of studies have shown the EDI to be a reliable and valid measure (see Garner, 1991). In terms of its discriminative validity, however, it should be noted that some of the scales of the EDI, particularly the ones which are not directly concerned with eating and body weight, are not specific to eating disorders, but reflect a high level of psychological distress that may be found in other psychiatric patients as well (Cooper, Cooper and Fairburn, 1985). Also, a test of the possible influence of social desirability has not yet been provided.

The *Body Attitude Test* (BAT; Probst *et al.*, 1995) is a self-report questionnaire that was developed in our own group to measure specific aspects of the body experience of eating disorder patients. It consists of 20 items that must be scored on a six-point scale, yielding scores on three factor-analytically derived subscales with clinical relevance: (1) negative appreciation of body size; (2) general body dissatisfaction; and (3) lack of familiarity with one's body. The reliability and validity of the BAT were demonstrated in a series of studies, showing a high internal consistency (Cronbach's alpha = 0.93) and test-retest reliability (0.72 to 0.95), as well as a high discriminative and convergent validity.

The *Anorectic Behaviour Observation Scale* (ABOS; Vandereycken, 1992; see Appendix 1) is a diagnostic questionnaire that is not intended for the patient but for the parents or partners (spouses). Although the latter can deny the severity of the situation in the same way as the patient, experience has taught that their information is usually more reliable and objective. They also often notice more quickly that something is wrong with the eating behaviour. The ABOS consists of 30 items referring to aspects of the patient's behaviour, and is scored on a three-point categorical scale (yes, no, don't know). Scores can be obtained on three factor-analytically derived subscales: (1) eating behaviour, preoccupation with nutrition and weight, denial of problems; (2) bulimic behaviour; and (3) hyperactivity. The ABOS can be very useful as an aid in early detection, but also acts as a complementary instrument in therapy assessment.

For the assessment of family functioning, one may choose from a large number of inventories, rating scales and observational techniques (for extensive reviews, see Fredman and Sherman, 1987; Jacob and Tennenbaum, 1988). Family questionnaires which have been used in clinical practice to assess the functioning of families with an anorectic or bulimic patient are the *Family Adaptability and Cohesion Scales* (FACES; Olson, Bell and Portner, 1978) and the *Leuven Family Questionnaire* (LFQ; Kog, Vandereycken and Vertommen, 1985). The first, in its most recent version (FACES III; Olson, Portner and Lavee, 1985) is a 20-item self-report questionnaire which measures the degree of family adaptability and cohesion, as contained in Olson's family circumplex model (Olson *et al.*, 1978) and in Minuchin's psychosomatic family model (Minuchin *et al.*, 1978). Scores of various family members referring to the perceived and ideal family situation can be charted in a family profile for interpretation. The FACES III has a moderate internal consistency (0.77 and 0.62 for the cohesion and adaptability scales, respectively) and discriminates between clinical and nonclinical families. The Leuven Family Questionnaire was developed by our own group especially for families of eating disorder patients, and contains 73 items yielding scores on three factor-analytically derived dimensions: (1) conflict; (2) cohesion; and (3) organization within the family. Internal consistencies for the scales range between 0.74 and 0.92, and test-retest reliabilities between 0.73 and 0.89. Apart from high correlations with other scales, the LFQ has been shown to discriminate between families with an anorectic patient and normal families.

Functional analysis

The information deriving from the clinical interviews with the patient and parents and from the standardized measures can be integrated in a functional analysis which, in a hypothetical manner, describes the relationships between the somatic, behavioural, emotional, cognitive and interpersonal aspects of the eating disorder. Specifically, it must answer the question of what function the symptoms have or what gains are achieved through the symptom, both on the part of the patient and for the family. For example, do the eating disorder symptoms act as a sort of 'lightning conductor' for concealed tensions and conflicts between the family members? Is it an indirect way to express aggression or to achieve independence? Does it refer to a rigid education, or is there a history of emotional, physical or sexual abuse in the family? In this regard, one should also consider the possibility of serious mental health problems in other family members, particularly depression and alcohol abuse, and also eating disorders (Vandereycken *et al.*, 1989). The hypothetical relationships assumed in the functional analysis may be viewed as possible 'points of entry' for the treatment, the main principles of which will now be outlined.

TREATMENT OF EATING DISORDERS

Principles of the treatment

Like the 'typical' eating disorder patient, the textbook case for the treatment of an eating disorder is a rarity. The clinical management of eating disorders should therefore always be individualized. Nevertheless, a number of general principles may be outlined to guide this treatment. In our view, the treatment of an eating disorder patient must be:

1 planned on the basis of a multidimensional problem analysis;
2 oriented towards symptoms (weight, eating) as well as psychological and interactional problems;
3 based on clear rules while remaining sufficiently flexible to fit the individual's changing needs;
4 transparent for the patients and their families;
5 involving the family and/or marital partner as much as possible and as is necessary for the therapeutic process;
6 consistent over an extended period of time;
7 evaluated regularly with regard to its immediate and long-term positive and negative effects.

These general principles will now be translated into more specific guidelines which cover the main steps in the treatment process.

Defining treatment goals

Once the diagnosis is made and the role of the eating disorder in its interactional context identified, a plan for the intervention can be developed. Since the patient will assume an active role in the treatment, it is important to involve her in this planning process. This will allow her to become co-responsible for her treatment and to proceed towards more self-determination.

The first step of the treatment plan is to decide on the specific goals for the treatment. These goals largely depend on the seriousness of the eating disorder and, accordingly, on the risk for possible complications. For instance, in seriously underweight AN patients hospitalization can be avoided if weight restoration is obtained quickly. In this case, the treatment plan will initially have a limited purpose, comparable to crisis intervention. On the other hand, when faced with milder forms of an eating disorder, the treatment goal may entail a long-term perspective and be directed at psychosocial adjustment and the maintenance of a normal eating behaviour. This usually requires the patient to look for social support in her own environment and/or to become her own change agent. Indeed, in some cases no treatment may actually be the prescription of choice! Alternatively, for chronic cases, the main goal of the treatment must probably be tertiary prevention, i.e. supporting the patient in her decision to remain anorectic and helping her to stabilize her symptoms and to limit the handicaps she will have to live with.

Apart from the patient's condition, the goals for the treatment will also depend on the experience of the therapist and on his or her preference for particular forms of therapy, as well as on the setting for the therapy. We consider it a leading principle that treatment should be tried on an outpatient basis, unless emergency situations require the patient's hospitalization. These emergencies may concern a life-threatening medical condition (e.g. severe acute or unremitting extreme weight loss, dangerous alterations in vital signs, intercurrent infections in cachectic patients, suicidal tendencies, psychosis), a seriously disturbed psychosocial situation creating a vicious circle for the patient (e.g. serious family disturbance that is inaccessible for treatment, social withdrawal) or psychotherapeutic indications (e.g. previous treatment failures, need for an intensive psychotherapeutic environment). In case of uncertainty, a day treatment programme or partial hospitalization may offer a valuable alternative.

Once the individual treatment goals are selected, they must be translated into specific steps to be attained within a given period of time. This detailed plan not only serves as a guideline for the treatment, but can also be used for evaluative purposes. Of course, sufficient flexibility should be allowed, and the plan may be changed during the treatment process if necessary.

Involving the parents or partner

Although the idea that eating disorders are 'caused' by the patient's family context has been abandoned by most clinicians, parents or husbands are usually very sensitive to being blamed as responsible for the patient's problems. It is important to pay attention to these feelings for, irrespective of the nature of their relationship with the patient, it is always recommendable for the therapist to work *with* rather than *against* the family. In our practice, we therefore make it a point to involve the parents or spouses in the treatment process from the very onset, i.e. from the exploratory interview. This creates an opportunity to explain to both the patient and her parents or partner about the treatment contract and to point out the consequences of this contract (e.g. the possibility of hospitalization if the condition does not improve), as well as the importance of a sufficiently long follow-up.

In the case of BN, it is not uncommon that the parents (or partners) do not know about the existence of the binge eating, vomiting or purging behaviour, and that the patient wants to keep her treatment secret from them as well. This is generally not acceptable, for it only reinforces her problem-avoidance strategies. Once the taboo is broken and the parents or partner are informed, it is important that they support the treatment. Many parents insist on a rapid remittance of the bingeing behaviour, because of its disturbing influence on family life (e.g. disappearing food, smell of vomit in the toilet, waste of money). It must be explained to them that only a gradual 'detoxification' has a chance of succeeding, which means that binges will not disappear immediately, and even that the patient should have the opportunity to binge without interfering with family life.

Involving the parents in the treatment does not necessarily imply family therapy. The need for such a therapy depends on the functional analysis of the problems and on the role of the family system therein. Whereas the basic rationale is to seek some form of collaboration with the family, in practice this co-operation can be achieved through different types of family sessions. In younger patients (under 18 years old), family sessions are usually more central to the treatment. As such, they may take the form of either 'real' family therapy sessions or individual sessions for the patient combined with parallel sessions for the parents. The presence of siblings during these sessions depends on the particular issues that are on the agenda. In older patients (over 18 years old), the emphasis lies more on the individual change processes, which allow them to learn for themselves to what extent and in what ways their family contributes to the eating disorder. Parents or spouses can be oriented towards a specific group therapy to support them during these changes.

Gaining the patient's collaboration

Anorectic patients are seldom motivated to enter therapy. Whereas bulimics often seek treatment by themselves without informing their family, in anorectics it is usually the parents or partners who insist on the treatment. The patients themselves typically deny their problems and resist treatment, probably because they perceive it as a way of surrendering control over their eating and weight. To overcome this resistance, the therapist may try to convince the patient that she actually 'suffers' from her condition but finds it hard to admit this. In this manner it is possible to avoid a power struggle in the therapy: once the patient realizes that her weight obsession has become a 'straitjacket' which causes great physical and psychosocial discomfort, she is ready to accept that the therapy can offer a favourable outcome.

Unlike anorectic patients, bulimics are usually willing to accept professional help. This may be due to a variety of motives. Some patients are driven by physical complaints, such as dental decay, disturbed digestion or fatigue. Others are disturbed by the fact that their food preoccupation leads to concentration problems which interfere with their work or studies; the bulimic eating pattern can indeed be so overwhelming and time-consuming that they are no longer able to keep up their daily routines. Another motive may be the secrecy of the eating pattern, which makes the patient feel ashamed and afraid for the impact on her social life.

Especially in AN, but also in BN, the need for professional assistance may be amplified by the growing tensions in the family or marital relationship. Family members or spouses are mostly (over)concerned about the disturbed eating behaviour. Although they cannot understand the behaviour, they want to intervene or 'help' by way of controlling their daughter or partner. Thus, they start keeping track of how much she weighs, whether she eats enough, whether she is going to vomit, and so on. Sometimes this need to interfere with the patient's behaviour becomes excessive: in the case of AN, the parents may force their daughter to eat; in BN, food may be hidden or locked away. When the patient resists these interferences, the control over the eating behaviour or weight becomes a real struggle which upsets the delicate balance in the family or relationship.

It is unusual, however, for eating disorder patients or for those in their immediate environment to actually request help in areas other than the eating behaviour. Instead, it is mostly assumed that a normalization of the eating or weight problem will resolve all other problems. BN patients in particular often expect an immediate and almost 'magical' intervention, which reflects their unrealistic expectations and aspiration for performance in general. Such expectations provide a pitfall for the therapist, who may feel tempted to assume the position of an omnipotent rescuer. Since compliance with the patient's request confirms her idea that the problem is 'just a bad eating habit', it is recommendable first to test the patient's reasons for asking for help, and to strengthen her motivation. For that purpose, motivational assignments can be elaborated during the first exploratory sessions. The rationale and contents of these assignments can be summarized as follows.

Overt discussion of the eating problem with relatives (parents, partner)

Having to admit that one's daughter or wife has an eating disorder nearly always creates feelings of guilt in the parents or spouse. They feel responsible for the situation and, as they are not able to change it, ask themselves what they are doing wrong. To avoid these painful feelings, parents or partners sometimes refuse to be confronted with the seriousness of the illness or reject co-operation with the treatment. As has been pointed out, however, their support and confidence in the treatment is badly needed, for only a combined effort may remedy the anorexia or bulimia, especially in younger patients who still live at home. For most patients, it is very difficult to discuss their symptoms openly in front of their parents or partner, especially when this concerns bulimic behaviour (vomiting/purging). Nevertheless, admitting to these symptoms is a way to break the 'taboo' of the problems. In case the patient finds it too difficult to discuss these issues at home, the therapist may suggest making the 'confession' during a family or couple session. It is important, however, that the patient should do it herself.

Confrontation with the seriousness of the illness

Eating disorder patients are often unaware of the gravity and complexity of their illness. AN patients tend to label their thin figure as 'normal' or 'healthy', and BN patients often reduce their problem to a 'bad eating habit' or a mere 'lack of character'. It is therefore important to explain to them the mental and physical consequences of starvation or bulimic behaviour. This explanation can be supported by an educational brochure (Vanderlinden *et al.*, 1992), while the seriousness of their situation is also emphasized by the thorough medical examination which the patients undergo in the diagnostic phase. In addition, they must be made aware of the possibility of therapy failure. Specifically, it can be pointed out to them that outpatient therapy is not always successful, and that an absence of significant change after two months of therapy means that a further continuation of the outpatient treatment is senseless and an admission to a hospital may be indicated. This possibility can be stipulated in the treatment contract.

Priority of the treatment

Patients should realize that the treatment can only succeed if it is given full priority. This is especially important for AN patients, who often find it difficult to give the treatment priority over their studies, sports or work because of their inclination to deny their problem and their aspiration for high performance. For that reason, it is sometimes necessary to 'impose' this priority upon them with the help of the parents or spouse. For BN patients, the priority of the treatment can be emphasized by the high frequency of sessions (e.g. twice a week at the beginning of the treatment) and by the obligation to keep a diary.

No drastic changes in eating behaviour

It is important to point out to the patients that the primary aim of the therapy is not to achieve a rapid and drastic change of the symptoms (i.e. rapid weight increase in AN and the disappearance of the bulimic eating behaviour in BN) but to work gradually towards a remission of all relevant problems. This is often reassuring for AN patients but can be disappointing for bulimic patients, whose general tendency to perform well and to think in extremes makes them expect a rapid improvement. Moreover, they may secretly hope that the therapy will help them to lose weight rapidly. The first binge after the start of the therapy is then experienced as a painful failure, and undermines both their negative self-image and the credibility of the therapy ('nothing can help me'). In that case, the therapist may explain that the chances of long-term success are greater when a gradual change is allowed.

Life without the eating disorder

Many patients not only have trouble abandoning their eating problem, which offers them security or a diversion from other problems, but even find it difficult to imagine their life without the eating disorder. To test their expectations, the therapist may ask the patients to write down the positive and negative consequences of the disappearance of the eating disorder. AN patients may thus realize that change can also bring about advantages; for BN patients, in contrast, it is important to learn that getting rid of the bingeing and vomiting may also imply the loss of certain advantages. By highlighting these issues, important information may be obtained about possible obstacles for the change process.

Contracting

An important way to structure the therapy process is to make use of a formal contract. While offering a high degree of transparency for both the patient and her family or spouse, such contracts also provide a framework for the therapy in which the patient herself can assume responsibility, thus increasing her feeling of self-efficacy. The specific clauses of the contract must of course be agreed upon in consultation with the patient and her parents or spouse. Nevertheless, a number of general issues can be outlined here.

The treatment contract for AN patients

With regard to the treatment contract for AN patients, the following elements are important:

1 As a goal for weight increase, the contract has to define the patient's 'normal' weight as a function of her age and height. In patients under 15 years of age the paediatric growth curve may be used as an indicator; in older patients one may refer to the (internationally accepted) data of the Metropolitan Life Insurance Company. The average population weight specified in this table minus 2 kg is considered as the minimum target weight. No bargaining about this target weight is tolerated, although patients often tempt the thera-pist to do so. They may argue that 'they have never been that fat' or that 'everybody in the family is lightly built', but psychologically this is where the struggle for control over the therapy starts. Our one and only argument is of a medical-scientific nature: a normal production of female hormones and growth hormones requires a minimum weight. The only exception in our experience is a very rare one – when a patient is menstruating at a lower weight while it appears from tests that the hormonal functions are normalized.

2 The contract has to stipulate how often and by whom the weight is to be controlled. Preferably, the therapist will do this him or herself. However, if the patient is so seriously emaciated that her physical condition needs to be monitored, an appeal can be made to the physician or paediatrician. The seriousness of the weight loss also determines how soon a weight increase must be attained. For most AN patients an average increase of 100 grams per day is a reasonable and attainable norm. Because a patient's weight may fluctuate strongly, the average increase is calculated weekly. If the situation is less acute, it may be left to the patient to decide for herself how much weight she wants to put on. However, the therapist should see to it that the goal is realistic, i.e. not too slow (a minimum being 350 grams per week, i.e. 50 grams per day) and not too fast (a maximum of 3 kg per week). In this regard, it may be necessary to explain to the patient that one wants to avoid a lapse into binges and/or overweight.

3 To restore the patient's self-determination, the contract should mention that the parents (or spouse) must give up their control of their daughter's (or wife's) eating behaviour, and that the responsibility over what to eat and how much to eat lies with the patient ('nobody can eat in her place'). It must be realized, however, that AN patients have often lost their hunger sensations. In order to restore their biorhythm, fixed mealtimes must be agreed upon, and it must be made clear that no meal can be skipped and no snacks can be taken between meals. Patients who are seriously underweight may initially have difficulties in digesting large quantities of food because of the slow emptying of their stomach; 'forcing' eating may therefore induce involuntary vomiting. To ensure sufficient nourishment we propose the following schedule for the first part of the treatment (until they have put on 5 kg): fixed meals around 8 a.m., 1 p.m. and 6 p.m.; and some liquid 'complementary food' in standard wrapping (e.g. Sustagen, Metrecal, Carnation Instant Breakfast) around 10 a.m., 4 p.m. and 9 p.m. The patient must decide for herself what is eaten during the fixed mealtimes, on the condition that her meals do not include diet products and that they correspond as much as possible with the food that is eaten by the other family members. In most cases it is also proposed that the patients no longer run errands or cook until they are able to eat 'normally' again. In the case of bingeing, vomiting and/or purging, agreements are made such as in the case of BN (see below).

4 Finally, the contract should also mention the consequences in case the agreements are not lived up to. If the patient resists the treatment, these consequences may be determined in consultation with the parents, but preferably the patient herself is also involved. It can be explained to her that a certain amount of pressure is necessary to overcome her fear of weight and her 'slimming obsession' that has gone out of control. Since many AN patients strongly aspire for performance in study, work or leisure (e.g. sports, fitness, ballet) the consequences of non-agreement with the contract are often chosen in this domain. Practically, this may imply that the patient is allowed to continue certain physical or intellectual activities only as long as a minimum weight increase is attained. Another type of consequence concerns the 'limits' of the therapy. It must be determined that when the progress is too slow (e.g. 1 kg increase in two months) or when the situation does not improve or even worsens (e.g. weight under a pre-determined risk limit), the continuation of outpatient treatment becomes senseless and inpatient therapy is indicated. To prevent arguments or appeals to the therapist to make

concessions, these consequences are fixed in writing at the start of the treatment and in the presence of the parents (or spouse).

The treatment contract for BN patients

The treatment contract for BN patients usually contains specific clauses regarding the patient's eating behaviour, based on the information obtained during the assessment phase. Other issues that may be considered for inclusion in the contract are:

1 The use of a diary, to be delivered to the therapist before each treatment session;
2 The use of a 'withdrawal schedule' to reduce and eventually stop the vomiting and purging behaviour, whereby regular blood tests (for potassium level) can be used as a monitoring tool;
3 The use of a schedule (e.g. three meals at fixed times and two snacks) to restore a balanced eating pattern;
4 The introduction of weight controls and the fixing of weight limits, minimum and maximum, in the case of large weight variations (in the case of underweight, a schedule similar to the one in AN can be agreed on; in the case of overweight, the eating behaviour should first be normalized before starting a diet of not less than 1,500 Kcal);
5 The stipulation of the consequences of failing to meet the agreements of the contract, including the termination of therapy and the decision to hospitalize (comparable with point 4 of the AN contract).

The involvement of the parents or spouse

During the discussion of the contract, the involvement of the parents or spouse is of crucial importance in order to gain their confidence and co-operation in the treatment. In the case of younger AN patients, the contract may stipulate that the parents are assigned the role of co-therapists. Instead of making remarks about their daughter's eating behaviour or attempting to influence it, they are told to exert their parental authority in executing the consequences registered in the contract. Giving up the fighting over eating behaviour enables these parents to bring in other conversation topics and to alter the family's eating pattern, which often has been disturbed by the patient's interferences with the food supplies, the choice of the menu, and the way of cooking. Ultimately, family meals should again become a pleasant social event.

Naturally it is impossible for parents *not* to pay attention to their daughter's behaviour. The therapist may therefore ask them to monitor the energy expenditure of their daughter and to try restricting this behaviour in accordance with the agreements. In turn, the patient is expected to report all non-agreed interventions from family members in connection with her eating or weight. Indeed, some parents are not able to give up their inefficient strategies to make the patient eat, and cannot or will not admit that they have 'failed' in some way. They may even try to sabotage the treatment or undermine the contract with the (non-pronounced) intention or hope that the 'expert' will fail as well, which would safeguard them against their guilt or a fear that the expert might reveal some family problem. When parents do not live up to the agreements, the therapist should confront them with this as soon as possible and, if necessary, mention the possibility of terminating the treatment. This may enhance their dedication or make them realize the gravity of the issue.

In the case of bulimics, it is sometimes useful to make an agreement in the contract on the use of a 'bulimic cupboard', where food for binges is kept. In consultation with the parents (or spouse) it may be agreed which food supplies are provided in this cupboard and how the stock is replenished (possibly with financial contribution from the patient). This paradoxical agreement breaks the taboo, structures the bulimia and facilitates the patient's self-control, in that she may binge only food from the 'bulimia cupboard'.

Evaluation

From a scientist–practitioner's point of view, it is important to evaluate the extent to which the goals of the treatment are obtained. Apart from the standardized measures referred to in our discussion of the assessment phase, a simple and practical method of structuring and evaluating the therapy process is the *Goal Attainment Evaluation* (Vanderlinden *et al.*, 1992). In this method, problem areas or therapy aims are determined on three levels: eating/weight problems, self-perception and interactions. For each level, the patient must indicate three specific steps which must be attained in the short term. This treatment plan is then regularly evaluated and adjusted accordingly. An example of such a treatment plan is given in Table 8.2.

CONCLUSIONS

In this chapter, we have given a comprehensive account of the main principles and guidelines for the assessment and treatment of patients

Table 8.2 Goal attainment evaluation

Area A   *Eating/weight problems*

Aim 1   *Regaining confidence in my hunger and appetite*
Step (a)   To dare to eat when I am hungry
Step (b)   To dare to eat what I like, even when it is calorie-rich
Step (c)   To dare to eat what I like for myself without letting myself be influenced by what others eat

Aim 2   *Becoming less preoccupied with food*
Step (a)   I avoid eating alone, for in company I am less occupied with food
Step (b)   I buy whatever I like to eat without reading the calories on the wrapping
Step (c)   I put away all my cook and diet books

Area B   *Self-perception*

Aim 1   *Feeling equal to others*
Step (a)   I stick to my choice or decision even if others have a different opinion
Step (b)   I try to be active in company to avoid 'reading their minds'
Step (c)   I dare to speak my mind to my sister

Aim 2   *Keeping my mood under control*
Step (a)   When I feel irritable, find out who or what is upsetting me
Step (b)   When I feel sad or depressed, accept it and look for the reason for it

Area C   *Interactions*

Aim 1   *Becoming more independent from my parents*
Step (a)   Spend the following weekend without my parents
Step (b)   Go out for an evening even if I think that my parents would prefer me to stay with them
Step (c)   See somebody for myself instead of going out with my sister

Aim 2   *Building more social contacts*
Step (a)   Sign up to a course or join a club
Step (b)   Agree on a fixed evening out with a girlfriend

---

with AN or BN. These guidelines were not presented as simple 'do's' and 'don'ts', but rather as suggestions and recommendations that need to be further supplemented by the therapist's own creativity, taking into consideration one's own experience and work setting as well as the idiosyncratic needs of the patient and her family or spouse. In spite of these individual accents, however, the main emphasis in the treatment approach proposed here lies on its systematic, research-guided and goal-oriented nature, and on the need for transparency and the active involvement of the patient and her family or spouse. In the next two chapters, we will discuss how these principles can be applied to the specific needs of married anorectics or bulimics and their husbands.

9 Assessment of the marital relationship

In chapters 3 to 7 it was shown that the occurrence of AN or BN in a married patient is often complicated by marital problems, such as a low level of marital intimacy, a deficient communication style, conflict avoidance and sexual difficulties. These shortcomings not only cause a great deal of psychological distress in the patients and their husbands, but may also be an important obstacle for the constructive evolution of the eating disorder. Hence, a careful assessment of the marital relationship quality and of its impact on the eating disorder (and vice versa) should be part of the standard intake procedure for married eating disorder patients.

For the assessment of these issues, a variety of methods may be used, ranging from the clinical interview with the couple to marital questionnaires and observation procedures. In the following paragraphs we will review these various methods from a clinician's point of view, pointing out their possibilities and limitations for application in clinical work with eating disorder patients. First, however, we will highlight the similarities and differences between the various types of methods for marital assessment.

MARITAL ASSESSMENT PROCEDURES

Reviews of marital assessment procedures (e.g. Fredman and Sherman, 1987; Jacobson, Elwood and Dallas, 1981; Jacob and Tennenbaum, 1988) generally distinguish between two types of method that may be used to obtain information about the properties of a marital relationship: (1) reports of the marital relationship based upon the spouses' perceptions of past behaviour and events; and (2) reports of the marital relationship based upon someone else's observation of ongoing behaviour and events. Within these two general types, several variations are possible.

Eliciting the spouses' perceptions of their relationship is no doubt the most frequently used type of marital assessment. Typically, this approach involves the application of self-report methods or instruments such as interviews, questionnaires and standardized tests, which all have in common that they yield information about an individual's feelings or attitudes towards the relationship. While these procedures thus give access to the subjects' innermost experiences, the information they provide is inevitably subjective. An alternative approach is to ask one or both members of the dyad to count or monitor their own or their spouse's specific behaviours as they occur in their day-to-day interactions. This assessment technique, which is mostly referred to as behavioural self-report, self-observation or self-monitoring (whereby the term 'self' refers to the relationship rather than to the individual), has the advantage of yielding more objective data than subjective self-report procedures. Like these procedures, however, it is still open to self-report bias, as in both cases the person who supplies the information is him or herself a member of the marital dyad.

Observational methods, on the other hand, rely on information supplied by an outsider who reports about the ongoing interaction between the partners. The observer's information may again consist of subjective impressions or of more objective registrations. Marital therapists, for instance, often rely on their own 'clinical' interpretation of observed interactions to draw conclusions about their clients' relationships. As such, they make use of a (subjective) observer report method. Some marital investigators, on the other hand, have developed rating scales or scoring procedures to quantify their observation data. As opposed to the subjective and qualified data obtained by means of observer report methods, the systematic scoring of the spouses' behaviour generally yields a more objective record of the marital interactions, but is also very time-consuming.

As noted by Cromwell *et al.* (1976), the above methods differ from one another with regard to at least one of two aspects: the *type of data* which are obtained (subjective or objective), and the *reporter's frame of reference* (insider or outsider). A combination of these two dimensions yields a 2 x 2 classification table of marital assessment procedures (see Table 9.1).

Because these four types of marital assessment take different perspectives and generate different sorts of data, one should not expect agreement across methods. Indeed, the application of different assessment procedures to the same marriages may yield divergent or even conflicting information. This does not imply, however, that this information must be discarded as unusable. On the contrary: the diversity of the

Table 9.1   Classification of marital assessment procedures

Observer's frame of reference	Type of data	
	subjective	*objective*
Insider	subjective self-report methods	self-observation methods
Outsider	observer's subjective report methods	systematic behaviour observation methods

Source: Cromwell *et al.* (1976)

information obtained from different perspectives has its proper value. Rather than getting caught in a controversy over which of the above approaches offers the best operationalization of the 'true' characteristics of a marriage, one should consider them as supplementary information sources from which a therapist may draw to obtain a more comprehensive understanding of the marital relationship. In the next section, we will expand on this issue by discussing the possibilities for assessing the marital characteristics of anorectic or bulimic patients, paying attention to the strength and weaknesses of each type of method.

THE COUPLE INTERVIEW FOR EATING-DISORDERED PATIENTS

Function of the couple interview

When an eating-disordered patient is married or lives together with her boyfriend or fiancé, it should be a normal part of the intake procedure to invite the patient with her partner to a conjoint interview. Such a couple interview serves several purposes.

First, it gives the husband the opportunity to tell *his* story about the eating disorder. Being confronted with the symptoms of the eating disorder usually causes a great deal of personal distress and may trigger all kinds of emotional reactions in the husband. For example, he may act in an overprotective and almost 'parent-like' way to help his wife, or he may be shocked by the absurdity of the eating disorder. Often, his confidence is shaken by the secrecy of the symptoms. The interview creates an opportunity for the husband to express these feelings.

Second, meeting the husband for the interview allows for an assessment of *his* psychological functioning. Particularly relevant in this regard are his way of coping with the eating disorder and his general psychological make-up. Although the empirical evidence reviewed in chapter 3 suggested that, in general, husbands of eating-disordered patients are not more psychologically distressed than normal men, it is not impossible that in individual cases the husband may show a psychiatric pathology, either as a primary problem or as secondary to the eating disorder. Since psychiatric distress in the husband influences his capability to react constructively to his wife's problems, it should be detected as soon as possible.

Third, the couple interview may give the therapist an idea of the quality of the marital relationship, either by asking the spouses directly about it (e.g. asking about their satisfaction with the relationship, conflicts, sexuality and their relationship with the parents) or by looking at the way they communicate, handle disagreements or show affection to one another. Sometimes information about the relationship must also be inferred from the patient's or the husband's behaviour. For example, the husband's reluctance to see the therapist or his opposition to the treatment may suggest the presence of rescue phantasies ('no one else can help my partner better than I can'). On the other hand, the avoidance or sabotage of the conjoint interview by the patient may indicate that she wants to keep her eating disorder as something personal, and that she is afraid of her husband's interference. She may also fear the consequences for the relationship when the eating disorder, or its severity, is brought into the open, which suggests a low level of openness between the spouses.

In connection with the above, the couple interview may also serve to explore the possible functions of the eating disorder within the marriage. Evidently, this should be done in a hypothetical way, without overreliance on unproven clinical assumptions, and with an emphasis on circular rather than unidirectional causalities, given the dynamic nature of marital processes. Also, one should beware of inducing guilt in either of the partners.

The couple interview also provides an opportunity to inform the husband about the physical and psychological consequences of the eating disorder. Husbands seldom realize the severity and complexity of the anorexia or bulimia. For some it is just a 'foolish idea' or a matter of 'not enough will-power'. Others expect the therapist to produce some sort of wonder drug or magic trick. But the majority of husbands usually feel helpless, sometimes concealing this behind aggression or criticism, and are looking for advice about what they can or should do to help their partner. This need for information gives the clinician an entry to explain both the necessity and the possibilities and limitations of the treatment.

Finally, the couple interview may help the clinician to evaluate and strengthen the husband's motivation to collaborate in the treatment. In

Table 9.2   Outline for the couple interview

The role of food and physical appearance
The eating disorder's impact on the relationship
The history of the relationship
The sexual relationship
The relationship with the families of origin
Fertility, pregnancy and parenting

this regard, a minimum requirement is that the husband be present when the treatment contract is made. Possibilities for a more active involvement in the therapy process depend on the functional analysis of the eating disorder, and will be discussed in chapter 10.

Format of the couple interview

The interview with a couple in which one of the partners has AN or BN resembles the standard marital interview in that it focuses on the individual, family-of-origin and couple history and on the current strengths and weaknesses in the relationship, yet with an additional focus on the couple's eating pattern and its influence on the relationship. Practical outlines for the couple interview with eating-disordered patients have been presented by Woodside *et al.* (1993), who describe a number of areas to be covered during the interview, and by Van den Broucke and Vandereycken (1989b), who propose questions for a standardized interview (see Appendix 2). An overview of the main areas to be included in the couple interview is given in Table 9.2. We will now consider each of these topics, and illustrate their importance by referring to cases from our own clinical practice.

The role of food and physical appearance

Food, weight and shape are of crucial interest not only to eating disorder patients but also to their husbands. Their importance for the couple should be explored during the interview: How do the partners deal with food and mealtimes? How much time do they both spend on physical exercise or sports? What is the husband's attitude towards body weight and shape? In an overwhelming majority of couples, these issues appear to be the main themes of their conversations and the focal point of most interactions. Many husbands go to extreme lengths to try and understand their wife's 'obsession' and to 'talk it out of her head'. Their patience towards their wife's disorder is sometimes inexhaustible, as is illustrated by the following examples.

Elisabeth, a 32-year-old married woman, had starved herself for many years. She always complained about feeling ugly and fat. Her husband spent literally hundreds of hours convincing her that she was not fat and trying to make her eat more. At the time of the first interview, he considered himself the loser in the battle against her illness.

Catherine, a 26-year-old bulimic, told her boyfriend about the bingeing and vomiting when they decided to live together (a decision she had delayed for a while). From then on he rearranged his working schedule so that they could eat together most of the time. He took care of the shopping and cooking, and even ate all the leftovers from dinner to prevent her from bingeing.

During the interview, specific attention should also be given to the role of physical appearance in the relationship. Many anorectics and bulimics want to please others, including their husbands. They are convinced that looking good is the best guarantee for an enduring relationship, to the point where appearing physically attractive becomes an obsession. In this way, the eating disorder helps them cope with the fear of being deserted. This is illustrated by the following cases:

Laura, a 25-year-old bulimia nervosa patient, lived together with her boyfriend, who insisted on her being attractive and sexy as a way of showing his love. Giving in to these demands, she dressed only as he liked, cut her hair according to his preference and wore little make-up, following his directives. The very idea that he might prefer another woman was a powerful trigger to her bulimia.

Monica, 29 years of age, felt her bulimia was the cause of everything that went wrong in her otherwise 'excellent' marriage. During the interview it was revealed that she was in fact scared of her husband, who frequently put her on the scales to control her eating behaviour. If her weight went up, he punished her by not taking her out. If she dared to show any resistance, he was physically aggressive to her.

The eating disorder's impact on the relationship

In many cases, it takes a long time before the husband notices the presence of an eating disorder, especially in the case of BN. Unbelievable as it may seem, bulimics often manage to keep their bingeing and purging behaviour a total secret from their husbands for years. When the eating problems are finally revealed, the husband may at first feel relieved, as a 'food problem' seems rather insignificant compared with the problems he may have suspected, for example an extramarital affair. However, as the symptoms remain present, bewilderment, suspicion and anger gradually take over. These distressed feelings are often accompanied by a lack of understanding of the patient's problems. For example, the husband may define the eating problem as a lack of will-power and label his wife as 'weak', thus giving a blow to her already low self-esteem. As such, eating disorders often cause a great deal of relational distress, as shown in the following case:

> Marion, a 34-year-old bulimic, told her husband two years ago that she had binged and vomited since the birth of their youngest child (now 6 years old). He was shocked and could not understand her behaviour, because 'she had all she needed'. He urged her to stop her behaviour immediately by showing the same will-power he evidenced in his (highly competitive) cycling. Because of his reaction, she pretended that she had overcome her eating disorder, but secretly continued her bingeing and vomiting as before.

As this example illustrates, the lack of mutual understanding between the partners with regard to the eating disorder can be very severe. It is therefore important to elicit both partners' views of their relationship and its changes due to the eating disorder. Asking for this information may also shed light on the openness of their communication and on the way they deal with conflicts: do they discuss differences of opinion openly, or do they avoid them?

The history of the relationship

To understand the current marital relationship and its connection with the eating disorder, it is often informative to look at the history of the relationship. An issue that is particularly relevant in this regard is that of partner choice. When and how did the patient and her partner meet? What caused the initial attraction? How did they decide to get married? The answers to these and similar questions may have implications for the treatment. For example, to the extent that physical appearance, body weight or shape were key factors in the initial partner choice, the husband may (c)overtly want his wife to maintain her thin figure and may therefore obstruct the therapy process. Of related interest is the question of the timing of the eating disorder: was it already present before the relationship, or did it occur after the marriage? Despite the fact that in our own research we found no significant differences between the characteristics of the husbands and marriages of patients with a pre- or postmarital disorder onset, the question of why, in the case of a premarital onset, the husband chose to marry an ill woman and to what extent his motives (e.g. rescue phantasies) could interfere with the therapy, remains thought-provoking.

In her relationship with her boyfriend, Catherine (described earlier) accepted the role of the identified patient, but she was ambivalent about his excessive concern: she liked his attention, but it also reinforced her idea of being 'weak'. For him, in contrast, helping others boosted his self-esteem.

Alternatively, in the case of a postmarital disorder onset, the interview can explore which particular events elicited the eating disorder, and to what extent they were related to the marriage (e.g. a marital conflict, an extramarital affair, pregnancy, concerns about intimacy, etc.).

The anorexia nervosa of Elisabeth (described earlier) started four years after her marriage, when she realized that she was not able to reveal her emotions and thoughts to her husband. She had never shared her experiences with anyone, neither friends nor parents, except for her grandfather, who took care of her when she was a little child. Being intimate with someone had always been frightening for her.

The sexual relationship

Given the importance of sexuality for marital relationship quality in general, it is important to assess the quality and history of these couples' sexual relationship. Relevant questions in this regard are: When did the couple become sexually active? Who took the initiative? How do the partners currently feel about their sexual relationship? Do they relate specific sexual problems to the eating disorder? When exploring these issues, it is important to ask for both partners' opinions, and to avoid suggesting any causal relationship between the eating disorder and the sexual relationship. As explained in chapter 7, AN patients are often insecure about their sexuality and may show a decreased sexual interest related to their disturbed hormonal balance, negative body image and – presumably – their fear of (sexual) intimacy. BN patients may have a more active and sometimes promiscuous sex life. This is exemplified by the following two cases:

Elisabeth, who had met her husband on holiday, refused sexual intercourse before her marriage. Once they were married, she complied with her husband's sexual desires but looked upon it as duty. Soon after the anorexia developed, all sexual activity disappeared rapidly. At the time of the intake interview there had been no sexual contact for more than a year.

Wendy, a 30-year-old bulimia nervosa patient, had had several sexual experiences with other men since her marriage six years before the treatment. Her promiscuity was not so much a matter of interest in sex; it was more that she was pleased with the attention from these men. Having sex with other men also compensated for the loneliness she experienced in her marriage. At the same time, it reassured her that she was not dependent on her husband, yet only for as long as she was attractive! The fear of rejection and abandonment fuelled her need to control her weight by purging.

Talking about sexual experiences can be a new experience for both partners, and may induce mixed feelings like anger or disgust (Woodside *et al.*, 1993). This is particularly true for patients who have had negative or traumatic sexual experiences, which is not uncommon among eating-disordered women (see chapter 7).

Mary's main reason for seeking help was being overweight (16 stone). She binged almost daily, without any purging. In the individual assessment it was noticed that she had frequent memory gaps; several times, she found herself in a place without knowing how she had arrived there or what she was supposed to do there. She also reported having been sexually abused by her father, and admitted that she was very dissatisfied with her marriage. Her husband also felt uncomfortable with intimate contact; Mary was mostly very distant, which reminded him of his 'cool' mother. When he tried to be nice and gentle to her, it reminded her of the seducing 'sweetness' of her father.

In case of an (assumed) history of sexual abuse – known or unknown to the husband – one should proceed with caution, and attention should be paid to overt or subtle rehearsal of traumatic experiences in the current sexual relationship which may prohibit other therapeutic work. For practical guidelines regarding this specific issue, see Vanderlinden and Vandereycken (1997).

The relationship with the families of origin

In order to assess the intimacy between the patient and her spouse, it is also important to consider the relationship between the couple and their families of origin. Indeed, the fact that a couple live physically separated from the spouses' families of origin does not necessarily mean that they have achieved sufficient autonomy. The eating disorder may in fact mask a problematic individuation in one or both partners, whereby dysfunctional relational patterns in the family of origin recur in the couple's interaction. This is illustrated by the following case:

> Sarah, a 24-year-old bulimic, had frequent quarrels with her husband about the time he spent with his parents. She accused him of not really being married to her. When her husband came home from work, he first visited his parents' farm to see 'whether they needed any help'. Sarah usually spent her evenings waiting for him while phoning her mother or bingeing and vomiting. When there were important decisions to make, her husband would always insist on asking advice from his parents first. The only thing he did not want his parents to know about was Sarah's eating disorder!

To evaluate the current relationship with the family of origin during the couple interview, see Vandereycken *et al.* (1989).

Fertility, pregnancy and parenting

As explained in chapter 7, it is common for women with an eating disorder to have problems with fertility and to have ambivalent feelings about the possibility of becoming a mother. Sometimes, pregnancy or childbirth is actually the event which triggers the eating disorder, as in Marion's case:

> Marion (described earlier) started binge eating after the birth of her second child. She wanted to resume her pre-pregnancy weight and discovered that vomiting could help her to achieve this goal. Because of her husband's busy professional life she alone had to take care of her two children. The bingeing also brought some relief in the lonely evening hours.

During the couple interview, the role of pregnancy and parenthood can be assessed by asking both the patient's and her partner's feelings about these issues. One should be aware of the fact that a mother with an eating disorder may also influence her children's eating habits or their development in general. This is illustrated by the following case.

> Diana, a 32-year-old anorectic mother of two daughters aged 11 and 8, considered childrearing as the most distressing task of her life. She wanted to be a 'good mother' by being perfect in her housekeeping.

This created heavy conflicts with her older daughter, who was upset with her mother's rigid living standards. Diana's husband also thought his wife was controlling the girls' lives too much. For Diana, this criticism reinforced her idea that she was a failure as a mother.

Limitations of the couple interview

While the clinical interview with the partners may provide valuable information about the topics outlined above, it also has its limitations. First, interview data by their very nature are always subjective, for they only concern the couple's own accounts of their marital characteristics. Second, an interview is not a very systematic way to assess marital characteristics, since it relies on the interviewer's idiosyncratic registrations. As such, it is less suitable to monitor any changes in marital quality over time. To obtain more systematic and quantifiable data, the interview data may therefore be complemented with other data deriving from standardized measures. These measures will now be discussed.

MARITAL QUESTIONNAIRES

Possibilities and limitations of marital questionnaires

Self-report questionnaires are probably the most convenient and time-efficient procedure for systematically assessing marital characteristics. Indeed, the administration of a questionnaire does not usually require much time or effort from either the subjects or the assessor, yet unlike the clinical interview it produces standardized and quantifiable data about the couple's relationship properties. Furthermore, like the interview – yet unlike observational procedures, which by definition are concerned only with observable phenomena – self-report questionnaires may yield information concerning covert aspects, such as the spouses' private thoughts and feelings about their marriage. Finally, most marital questionnaires have a high face validity, or at least appear to offer an adequate operationalization of the constructs they are intended to measure. It is not surprising, then, that self-report questionnaires are widely used by marital therapists and researchers.

Unfortunately, the questionnaire method is also afflicted with a number of shortcomings which the clinician should be aware of. The most obvious one is that questionnaire data are highly vulnerable to response styles such as social desirability, defensiveness, acquiescence, carelessness and (particularly with regard to marital questionnaires) pseudomutuality. Unless the impact of such response styles on the scales of a given instrument is known and controlled for, it is very difficult to interpret a subject's scores on these scales in an unambiguous way.

A more fundamental concern is that questionnaires do not capture the dynamic aspect of relationships. While a marital relationship by definition involves dynamic interactions between two partners, questionnaire items make abstraction of this dynamic feature by asking the subjects to report about the *overall* status of their relationship, as based upon a retrospective summary of all that has happened up to the moment of enquiry. The information thus obtained is inevitably selective and incomplete. It is impossible to know, for example, whether the spouses' reports about their relationship are primarily a function of very recent experiences, such as the fight they may have had on the way to the therapist's office, or of more distant but influential issues, such as an extramarital affair that occurred several years before. Moreover, questionnaire data do not contain any information about the sequencing of interaction processes or about the variability of the spouses' behaviours.

A third limitation, which is unique to questionnaires measuring aspects of the marital or family functioning, is the discrepancy between the unit of measurement and the unit of study: whereas marital concepts are typically concerned with dyadic issues, questionnaires can only produce scores for the individual members of the dyad. Husbands' and wives' perceptions of their relationship may differ greatly. Although this problem may be circumvented by combining the spouses' individual scores into 'second-order' couple scores (e.g. mean or sum scores, minimum or maximum scores, or interspouse correlations or discrepancy scores), such operations always result in a loss of information. For example, there is no way of telling whether an 'average' couple score is the result of combining a very low and a very high score, or of two moderate ones. In a way, this example illustrates the correctness of the system theorists' axiom that 'a system is more than the sum of its components'!

Marital questionnaires for eating disorder patients

Despite these limitations, marital questionnaires, if correctly applied and interpreted, are very convenient assessment tools which may produce relevant data about relationship issues with relatively little time investment and without demanding too much effort from either the subjects or the assessor. Referring to the marital constructs outlined in chapters 2 to 7 (i.e. spousal psychiatric distress, marital satisfaction, intimacy, communication, conflict and sexuality) a number of specific questionnaires may be proposed for use in clinical work with eating-disordered patients.

A first aspect concerns the degree of psychological distress in the husband, which together with the patient's psychiatric condition may be considered as the individual level of the marital system. To assess this issue, it is preferable to determine the husband's position on a series of relevant symptom dimensions rather than making a categorical diagnosis. An instrument which allows such an assessment is the *Symptom Checklist* (SCL-90; Derogatis, 1977). This multidimensional self-report inventory of current psychiatric problems consists of 90 items to be scored on a five-point Likert scale, which in the American version yields scores on nine primary symptom dimensions: (1) somatization; (2) obsession-compulsion; (3) interpersonal sensitivity; (4) depression; (5) anxiety; (6) hostility; (7) phobia; (8) paranoid ideation; and (9) psychoticism. Several studies have documented the reliability of the SCL-90 (i.e. high factor invariance for eight out of nine scales) as well as its ability to discriminate between psychologically distressed and nondistressed subjects.

For the assessment of marital (dis)satisfaction one has access to a large number of questionnaires. The most popular ones are the 15-item *Marital Adjustment Test* (Locke and Wallace, 1959) which measures the couple's global adjustment; the 32-item *Dyadic Adjustment Scale* (Spanier, 1976), which measures dyadic consensus, satisfaction, cohesion and affectional expression; the 280-item *Marital Satisfaction Inventory* (Snyder, 1981) which yields information on eleven possible sources of marital distress; and the 40-item *Relationship Belief Inventory* (Eidelson and Epstein, 1982), which assesses cognitive factors that are dysfunctional for the marital relationship. For detailed information about these instruments, see the reviews by Fredman and Sherman (1987) and Jacob and Tennenbaum (1988). A marital satisfaction questionnaire used in our own clinical practice is the (modified) *Maudsley Marital Questionnaire* (MMQ; Crowe, 1978), which contains 20 items to be scored on an eight-point scale, measuring the spouses' experienced maladjustment in their current marital, sexual and social relationships. Research has demonstrated the MMQ scales to have a high internal consistency and sufficient test-retest reliability and validity, and to be only moderately influenced by social desirability (Arrindell *et al.*, 1983).

Various self-report instruments also exist for the assessment of marital intimacy. The *Personal Assessment of Intimacy in Relationships*

(PAIR; Schaefer and Olson, 1981) is a 36-item questionnaire which measures the expected and perceived degrees of intimacy in five areas (emotional, social, sexual, intellectual and recreational), allowing for an analysis of the scores both in terms of the differences within each partner's perceived and expected intimacy and in terms of the differences between the two partners. The *Waring Intimacy Questionnaire* (WIQ; Waring and Reddon, 1983) is a 90-item true–false questionnaire measuring the eight dimensions implied in Waring's marital intimacy model described in chapter 3 (affection, expressiveness, compatibility, cohesion, sexuality, conflict resolution, autonomy and identity). A new intimacy questionnaire, developed by our own group, is the *Marital Intimacy Questionnaire* (MIQ; Van den Broucke *et al*, 1995e; see Appendix 3). It contains 56 items to be scored on a five-point Likert-type scale, producing scores on five factor-analytically derived dimensions: (1) intimacy problems (lack of intimacy); (2) consensus, generally exemplifying cognitive and behavioural aspects of intimacy; (3) openness, which also measures authenticity (i.e. the individual components of intimacy); (4) affection; and (5) commitment (i.e. the social group component of intimacy). The scales of the MIQ have been demonstrated to have a high internal consistency (Cronbach alphas above 0.80 for all scales except commitment), as well as a good convergent and discriminant validity.

While the above instruments mostly refer to covert (cognitive and/or emotional) constructs, the couple's communication process essentially refers to overt phenomena. As such, this construct may be assessed directly by means of observational procedures, as will be discussed. Nevertheless, there are also a number of convenient self-report instruments which tap relevant dimensions of communication as perceived by the spouses. The best known are the *Primary Communication Inventory* (Navran, 1967), which assesses the quality of the couple's verbal and nonverbal communication using 25 items, and the 48-item *Marital Communication Inventory* (Bienvenu, 1970), which produces a total appreciation of the couple's communication adequacy accounting for aspects like self-disclosure, hostility, regard, empathy and discussion. More information about the psychometric properties of these instruments is provided in Fredman and Sherman (1987) and Jacob and Tennenbaum (1988).

Questionnaires have also been developed to assess aspects of marital conflict. The couple's conflict topics can be assessed by means of the *Problem List* (Hahlweg *et al.*, 1980), which is a 17-item inventory of possible problem areas in a marriage (relatives, finances, job, household, child care, leisure time, personal habits, friendships, temperament, jealousy, values, affection, attractiveness, trust, personal freedom, sexual relations and extramarital relations). The items must be rated on a five-point scale (0 = no problems; 1 = problems, but we can usually solve them; 2 = problems which are difficult to solve and which we often quarrel about; 3 = problems we don't even discuss any more, since we cannot find any solutions for them). An overall 'conflict score', which measures the number of significant conflict-producing areas, is obtained by summing the items for which the category 2 or 3 is endorsed. The Problem List has a sufficient degree of reliability (test-retest reliability after a six-month interval = 0.66), and has a proven capacity to discriminate between maritally distressed and nondistressed couples. With regard to the conflict styles, a frequently used measure is the *Conflict Tactics Scale* (CTS; Straus, 1979), which measures three strategies to resolve conflicts in a marriage or family: (1) reasoning; (2) verbal aggression; and (3) violence. Because of its short length (19 items) the CTS can be conveniently applied in clinical practice, but the reliability scale lacks internal consistency (alphas between 0.50 and 0.69). Alternative measures are the *Conflict Inventory* (Margolin *et al.*, cited in Van Buren and Williamson, 1988), which also measures three conflict-resolution styles (problem-solving, withdrawal and aggression); and the *Interactional Problem Solving Inventory* (Lange *et al.*, 1991), which is a 17-item, five-point scale assessing the couple's problem-solving capacity. For the latter instrument, good reliability (internal consistency of 0.90) and validity data (convergent and discriminative) have been reported.

Finally, with regard to the couple's sexuality there is the *Sexual Interaction Inventory* (LoPiccolo and Steger, 1974), which contains 17 items covering a broad range of sexual behaviours, and provides information on the satisfaction with the frequency of sexual behaviours, self-acceptance, the overall pleasure derived from sexual activity, the perceptual accuracy and the acceptance of one's partner. Test-retest reliability (*r*s between 0.67 and 0.90) and internal consistency (Cronbach alphas of 0.85 to 0.93) are high, as well as the instrument's ability to discriminate between sexually distressed and satisfied couples.

OBSERVATIONAL METHODS

Possibilities and limitations of observational methods

Observational methods essentially differ from self-report techniques such as interviews or questionnaires in that the actual interaction behaviour of the couple, rather than the spouses' evaluation of their relationship, is the subject of investigation. The observation may be done either by the spouses themselves (self-observation or quasi-observational procedures) or by one or more outsiders (for example, the therapist). In the former case, the observation usually takes place in a naturalistic setting (e.g. at home). In the latter case, the interaction is mostly generated in the assessor's office. In the typical procedure the couple is instructed to discuss a certain topic (usually a problem they consider as relevant for their relationship), and their interaction is observed directly (e.g. through a one-way mirror) or indirectly (by means of audio or videotape) by trained outsiders. To enhance standardization, these outsiders may employ a rating or coding system by means of which the interactions can be scored on a series of pre-defined dimensions or codes, which serve as the 'raw' material for further analysis.

There are compelling conceptual as well as methodological arguments for using observational methods for the study of marital interaction. From a conceptual point of view, nearly all theories of marital functioning focus upon couple interaction patterns as important determinants of marital distress and spouse psychopathology. While most other assessment methods fail to accommodate to this interactional focus, observation does (Markman and Notarius, 1987). Furthermore, by looking directly at the couple's interaction processes, observational methods do justice to not only the dynamic aspects of marital interaction but also the dyadic nature of the marital unit. Hence, unlike self-report methods, observational methods allow for an assessment of the spouses' interaction sequencing. From a methodological perspective, observational methods generally yield more reliable and objective data than more traditional methods of assessment (Gottman, 1979). Since observation implies that the interactional processes of interest are assessed without the intermediary of the subjects' perception, the data are not contaminated by self-report bias. Although this does not eliminate the problem of subjectivity altogether (since the responders' subjectivity is replaced by that of the observers), it is possible to control the objectivity of the data by computing the interobserver reliability.

The main disadvantage of interactional observation, however, concerns its practical applicability. If it is done in a standardized way, marital observation is indeed a very elaborate and costly procedure, which not only requires expensive equipment and the intensive training of the observers in order to attain sufficient reliability, but also takes up a large amount of time when actually applied. This is especially true for micro-analysis, where the spouses' discrete behavioural interventions are coded act for act. Learning how to use a micro-analytic coding system may take two to three months of weekly instruction and practice, and then it takes approximately 25 to 30 minutes to code 1 minute of interaction! On the other hand, the use of larger coding units to rate the interactions (macro-analysis) generally yields lower levels of interscorer reliability.

Taken together, this makes the use of systematic observational approaches prohibitive for clinical practice. This does not mean, however, that observational systems are of no use to clinicians at all. On the contrary, therapists may benefit from the valuable experience that has been accumulated from observational studies to make their observations as 'participant observers' more systematic. Specifically, by focusing their attention on the codes or dimensions identified in existing coding systems or rating scales, they have a serviceable reference system at their disposal for rating the couple's interactions on dimensions with a demonstrated validity.

Marital observation systems for eating disorder patients

In the marital literature, a number of specific coding systems have been proposed to assess marital interaction. Since these instruments have been devised mainly for research purposes, their use for clinical application is very limited. Hence, we will mention them only briefly here. The most widely used coding system is the *Marital Interaction Coding System* (MICS-III; Weiss and Summers, 1983), which includes 30 codes describing verbal and nonverbal behaviours observed in marital problem-solving discussions. The *Couples Interaction Scoring System* (CISS; Gottman, 1979) contains the same codes as the MICS, but allows for an assessment of the sequential patterning of the interactions. In our own work, we have used the *Kategoriensystem für Partnerschaftliche Interaktion* (KPI; Hahlweg *et al.*, 1984b), which contains 12 verbal and 3 nonverbal codes measuring specific communication skills (see chapter 5). All three coding systems require an intensive training to attain reliability.

As contrasted with these coding systems, couple interaction rating scales may offer more possibilities for clinical application. Examples of such rating scales are the *Marital Communication Rating Scale* (MCRaS; Borkin, Thomas and Walter, 1980), which provides a concise assessment of communication problems by rating the couple's interaction in 37 categories using seven- and four-point scales; and the *Communication Rapid Assessment Scale* (CRAS; Joanning, Brewster and Koval, 1984), which specifies a number of criteria to rate the overall constructiveness of the couple's verbal and nonverbal communications on a five-point scale. Given sufficient training (which may require up to 20 hours of instruction and practice) both rating scales attain reasonable degrees of reliability.

Finally, within a clinical context, effective use can be made of self-observational procedures, where the spouses are asked to observe and record the behaviour of their partner. The most frequently used instrument for this purpose is the *Spouse Observation Checklist* (SOC; Weiss and Perry, 1979), which assesses the pleasing and displeasing behaviour of the spouse in terms of the following 12 categories: affection, companionship, consideration, sex, communication, coupling activities, child care and parenting, household management, financial decision-making, employment and education, personal habits and appearance, and independence. Both spouses independently complete the scales at a given moment of the day. Despite the rather low inter-spouse agreement levels (46–62 per cent), the SOC has proved to be a useful assessment tool which discriminates between maritally distressed and nondistressed couples and accounts for significant variations of marital satisfaction.

CONCLUSIONS

The assessment of marital characteristics and processes is probably one of the major challenges faced by clinicians who work with married eating disorder patients. While it is generally agreed that a careful assessment of the marital relationship should be part of the standard intake procedure for these patients, it is less clear *how* this assessment should be done and which measures should be used to tap the relevant constructs of interest. Because of the particular difficulties associated with marital assessment, therapists often refrain from systematically assessing marital constructs altogether, and rely on clinical hermeneutic methods to acquire information about these patients' marriages. From a researcher–practitioner point of view, however, it is evident that a precise and logical understanding of these couples' marital functioning requires the use of more quantifiable and objective measures, in addition to the 'clinical' methods, for planning the therapy and evaluating its effects over time.

In this chapter we have provided an overview of the various types of measures that may be used for this purpose, focusing on the couple interview, marital questionnaires and observation procedures in particular. For each type, the main assets and limitations were considered from a clinician's perspective, and examples of specific measures or interview topics were given. This should enable the therapist to combine assessment tools into a multimethod approach, capturing the complexity of the relationships.

It may be pointed out here that such an assessment of the patient's marriage in itself represents a significant intervention. By bringing the relevant issues of their intimate relationship out into the open, the couple can place the eating disorder in the context of other problems in their personal or marital life. This improved understanding of the eating disorder is an important step towards planning an appropriate treatment. It also may be the starting point for the husband's involvement in the treatment, the different modalities of which will be described in the next chapter.

10 Involving the husband in the therapy

For many years, the treatment of patients with an eating disorder has been dominated by the idea that anorectic or bulimic symptoms are an expression of dysfunctions in the patient's family, and that changing the family interactions will result in a disappearance of the symptoms. The same idea is also found with regard to married anorectics or bulimics: inspired by the popularity of marital therapy, it has almost become an axiom that the marital relationship of these patients is in some way disturbed, and must therefore be treated. In our view, this axiom must be seriously challenged: marital therapy is not a panacea nor a mandatory component of the treatment. Whereas it is true that the relationships between eating-disordered patients and their spouses are often distressed in the ways described elsewhere in this book, the actual need for marital therapy depends on the results of the assessment of the patient and the couple. This does not imply, however, that the partner should not be involved in the treatment. On the contrary: one of the basic principles of our multimodal treatment approach is that, irrespective of the problem situation, the therapist must work *with* instead of against the partner.

In practice, this co-operation can take many forms, ranging from periodic meetings with the partner to counselling groups or actual marital therapy. In this chapter, we will discuss these various possibilities and offer guidelines for the decision about the mode of involvement. In addition, we will expand on the marital issues that may be considered during the therapy, providing illustrations from our own clinical practice. First, however, we will briefly indicate the need to involve the partner in the treatment.

IMPORTANCE OF THE HUSBAND'S INVOLVEMENT

Involving the spouse of a married anorectic or bulimic patient in the therapy is important for the following reasons.

Giving support

Being married to an anorectic or bulimic wife usually causes a great deal of distress in the husband. Feelings of frustration, guilt, anxiety or isolation are often present in these men, but are seldom expressed. To learn how to deal with these emotions, most husbands would benefit from a form of counselling which the therapist may offer.

Gaining compliance

Although the idea that the husband is the 'architect' of his wife's eating disorder must be regarded as one-sided, husbands are usually very sensitive to being blamed for the patient's problems. It is important to pay attention to these feelings, which can seriously obstruct the treatment. By emphasizing that 'it is not easy to live with an eating-disordered woman' (just as it is not easy for the patient's parents or siblings), the therapist can show his or her interest in the husband's well-being and in the quality of the marital relationship, which will make him feel accepted and enhance his confidence in the therapist and the therapy.

Helping the husband understand the eating disorder

Some men want to know everything about the eating disorder in order to help their wives as much as possible; others hide their feelings of frustration behind the attitude that they have already done everything they could to make her happy. In the latter case, it is important to motivate the husband to co-operate in the treatment by providing specific information about the characteristics, causes, physical and psychological consequences, possible treatments and prognosis of the eating disorder.

Preventing post-therapy distress

While it is clear that the presence of an eating disorder severely challenges the marital relationship, the same also holds true for the treatment and subsequent improvement of an eating disorder

(Roberto, 1991). According to Andersen (1985), problems which may result from an improvement of the eating disorder include: (a) an increased assertiveness on the part of the ill spouse, which threatens the stability of the relationship; (b) a sudden discharge of long-repressed anger by the patient, effecting a counter-reaction by the husband, who feels unappreciated; (c) expressions of anger by the husband, who had previously stored up his feelings out of fear of harming his ill spouse; and (d) demands for separation or divorce by either partner. By involving the husband in the treatment from the onset, these reactions can be curbed and used for enhancing growth in both partners.

One should be cautious, however, in engaging the husband too quickly in some form of psychotherapy, because this may upset his self-esteem and/or the fragile marriage. Dally and Gomez (1980) have suggested that, from the outset, while the therapist explores the problem and develops rapport with the eating-disordered woman, the husband can be interviewed by a co-therapist. Later, joint interviews can be set up with the patient, the husband and the two therapists, during which the couple are encouraged to recognize each other's needs and to improve their communication.

WAYS OF INVOLVING THE HUSBAND

Indications

The way in which the husband is involved in the treatment largely depends on the outcome of the marital assessment, and particularly on the perceived need to focus on the marital relationship. In this regard, four possible outcomes can be considered.

1 If the assessment reveals that neither of the spouses reports a significant dissatisfaction with the relationship and that the interactions do not show any major deficiencies, the focus of the therapy should be placed on the patient's symptoms rather than on the marital relationship. However, as a privileged companion of the patient, the husband may contribute to the treatment by assuming the role of a *co-therapist*, following the therapist's instructions to help the patient gain control over her symptoms. At the same time, this co-operation will allow the therapist to monitor the changes in the marital relationship as the treatment progresses.

2 A second possibility is that neither the patient nor her partner considers their relationship distressing, but that the 'objective' ther-

apist finds their interactions (e.g. communication and/or conflict resolution skills) inadequate. In this case, the therapist should beware of imposing his or her own attribution of the problem onto the couple by labelling the cause of the patient's symptoms a 'relational' one. Instead, it is recommended that the patient and the spouse can learn for themselves how and to what extent their way of relating contributes to the disorder. For the patient, this awareness can be stimulated during the therapy, particularly when this includes participation in some form of group therapy. For the husband, a concomitant *support programme* may provide a useful adjunct to the patient's therapy. Apart from fulfilling his need for information, such a programme may help him to ventilate his feelings of frustration, guilt, anxiety or isolation. This support may take the form of group sessions (Kapoor, 1989; Leichner, Harper and Johnson, 1985). It should be mainly educational and supportive in focus and may only shift to a more interactional and therapeutic level when the marital bond is sufficiently strong and when the group members are willing to explore more personal issues.

3 If only one of the partners thinks the marital relationship quality is an important aspect of the problem, the therapist's role is to address the marital issues of interest and to provide a support for the 'distressed' partner, while acknowledging the other partner's position. For both purposes, the patient's therapy sessions and/or a support programme for the husband may again provide a useful medium.

4 A final possibility is that, either at the time of the initial assessment or as a result of the previous steps in the treatment, both partners are able to disengage from the exclusive focus on the patient's symptoms and to explore the relational issues of the disorder. In this case, there is a strong argument for starting *marital therapy*, either as the treatment of choice or in addition to individual therapy of the anorectic/bulimic spouse. Foster (1986) mentioned four indications for couple therapy in eating disorders: (a) when the onset is at the beginning of the relationship or at a serious relational crisis; (b) when individual therapy has failed; (c) when marital conflicts are identified as a problem by both partners; and (d) when the husband seems stable enough to tolerate changes in the marital relationship. But real marital therapy is only possible when the couple are prepared to see the focus of the treatment as an improvement of the marital relationship rather than as treatment of the eating disorder, with a passive stance allowed to the 'well' husband (Andersen, 1985).

Marital issues can also be addressed in individual or group psychotherapy, although these can only deal with the patient's point of view. One of us (J.N.) has long experience of combining weekly group psychotherapy for eating-disordered patients with parallel sessions of marital therapy once every two or three weeks. The aim of this combined approach is to help the patient and the spouse redefine the eating disorder as an interpersonal problem. The patient usually explores a theme in the group session and then discusses it in the marital therapy session, or vice versa. Since the same therapist is conducting both the group and the marital therapy sessions, there is no danger of splitting mechanisms and/or playing off one therapist against the other. On the other hand, the therapist must make sure that the husband feels accepted as an equal party and does not fear a coalition between his wife and the therapist.

The husband's involvement as a gradual process

While the above outlines may give the impression that the indication for the involvement of the spouse is a static issue, one should be aware of the fact that a therapy process is dynamic in nature, and that a flexible approach is appropriate. Thus, involving the husband in the treatment is usually a gradual process, the first step of which is to give information and support. All spouses need at least some form of (psycho)education about the nature and course of the eating disorder, and most of them need counselling to deal with their emotional reactions to their wife's eating disorder. Giving information and support enhances the spouses' readiness to engage in the treatment, which will not only increase the wife's motivation to stop the eating disorder, but also make her feel encouraged and supported during difficult phases in therapy.

A next step in the process can be a form of general counselling, in which the couple are stimulated to talk openly about the eating disorder. When they are encouraged to explore the meanings and functions of the disorder in their personal, marital and social life, any shortcomings in their relationship (e.g. a lack of intimacy, deficient communication or conflict regulation, dissatisfaction with the sex life) will inevitably surface. On the basis of this exploration, specific goals for the individual and/or couple therapy can be specified within the framework of the more global therapy plan.

In general, we prefer to start with some kind of *spouse-aided therapy* for the eating disorder, based upon our experiences with a similar approach in married agoraphobics (Vandereycken, 1983). This means that the eating disorder is advanced as the focus of treatment, and that the husband is involved as much as possible as a 'co-therapist' from the very beginning of the therapy. Since the existence and extent of marital problems is seldom known in advance, such an approach may have several outcomes:

1 In some cases, the treatment of the eating disorder may improve the marital relationship, making a separate marital therapy unnecessary;
2 In other cases, the improvement of the eating disorder will not affect the marital problems that are present, nor make them more prominent. The partial success of the symptom-oriented treatment may then motivate the couple to engage in marital therapy which they might have rejected if it had been offered in the beginning;
3 Finally, in some cases the treatment of the eating disorder may fail because of severe marital discord or a marital crisis. By this time, however, a supportive and non-threatening therapeutic relationship may have been established, so that patient and/or husband are more willing to work on their marital interaction.

ISSUES IN THE MARITAL TREATMENT OF EATING DISORDERS

Marital dissatisfaction

The presence of an eating disorder usually causes a great deal of tension in the patient's relationship with her spouse. In many cases, these recurrent tensions are the main reason why the patient seeks professional help: she may fear that the eating disorder is becoming too much of a burden for her spouse, and that it threatens the marriage itself. Indeed, most men have tried in their own way to be their wife's 'therapist' once they learned about the existence of the eating disorder, but have soon become frustrated because they failed to change their wife's behaviour.

A year before the beginning of her treatment, 27-year-old Pamela confessed to her husband that she had been bingeing and vomiting for ten years. This confession gave a serious blow to their three-year-old 'harmonious' relationship. Her husband decided to leave the house for a while. Completely desperate, she went – for the first time – to a specialist in eating disorders.

Besides experiencing the marital tensions that occur as a direct consequence of the eating disorder, the couple can also report marital conflicts which already existed before the onset of the eating disorder or which are experienced as a separate problem. But usually both spouses consider their marital problems secondary to the eating disorder.

Partner choice

When the anorexia or bulimia developed prior to the start of the relationship, one may question the motives of the partner choice. It is likely that the patient's and the partner's choice of each other have been influenced by their unfulfilled needs, rooted in unresolved individual problems. The husband may have been attracted to the patient's 'weakness' because of his own rescue phantasies, whereas the patient may have looked for a 'protective and understanding' husband. The complementarity of these motives may lead to a homeostatic function of the eating disorder, in which case the improvement of the symptoms will affect the fundamental features of the relationship. During therapy the patient may realize that she never would have chosen her husband if she had not been ill. In that case, the husband's willingness and capability to change is of crucial importance for the future of the relationship.

> Elise, a 34-year-old married woman with bulimia nervosa, went into therapy without informing her husband. She did not want him to be involved in the treatment in any way, because 'it is my problem which I have to cure on my own'. Moreover, she was convinced that her husband would never understand her problems. She was convinced that her marital situation would never change, but she claimed she had learned how to live with it.

Communication and conflict resolution

Couples with an eating-disordered partner often demonstrate a lack of communication skills and an avoidance of open conflicts. In this regard, the disturbed eating pattern may be part of a maladaptive system to cope with relational distress. The first step in marital therapy is then to learn to understand each other's thoughts and feelings about the eating disorder.

> During a group therapy session Catherine (introduced in chapter 9) realized that she did not want to go to a family meeting she had promised her boyfriend John she would attend. At first she was reluctant to bring up this subject with John, for she knew the meeting was very important to him. But after she was encouraged

by the other group members she confronted him with her opinion. They discussed the topic for a whole evening and finally came to the agreement that John would cancel the visit. During the next couple session, their discussion was evaluated. They said that in the beginning they had both felt strange and insecure, but once they were able to reveal their different opinions, they experienced a growing feeling of mutual respect. They were surprised to see that their difference of opinion was not threatening the stability of the relationship. The therapist congratulated them with this positive experience, although he also warned them that it would be more difficult to reach an agreement on intimate matters.

In this example the group therapy helped a patient to realize her conflict-avoiding behaviour, which probably was also one of the functions of her eating disorder. The group can also offer a setting for the patient to prepare her discussion with the husband if she is afraid of an open confrontation. In this case, role playing can be a way to help her overcome her hesitation.

Boundaries

An important issue in couples with an eating-disordered partner is the relationship with both partners' families of origin. Many patients and/or their spouses are still searching for a comfortable emotional distance from their families. Since a successful separation and individuation is a necessary condition to attaining intimacy in one's relationship (Van den Broucke *et al.*, 1995a), the close emotional relationship with the parents obstructs the intimacy of the partners, particularly with regard to exclusiveness and openness. Because of the lack of clear boundaries with the parents, the relationship is not experienced as an exclusive one. Moreover, the partners will not share their thoughts or feelings towards one another because they fear that the spouse will disclose private matters to his or her parents.

> Since his parents had divorced, John had assumed a sustaining and helping role towards his mother. When he met Catherine this interaction pattern persisted; it was even reinforced once he knew about her bulimia. He only became aware of it when Catherine grew angry about the fact that he spent so much time with his mother. He then realized that he had to make a profound change himself by redefining his relationship with his mother. It also became clear that he acted towards his 'ill' wife in the same supporting and nursing way as he did towards his 'lonely' mother.

This example illustrates the importance and necessity of a major change for the husband in this phase of the therapy. It was his responsibility to resolve the loyalty conflict with his mother and to establish firmer boundaries. Once the rehearsal of the interaction patterns was recognized, the couple's codependency could be redefined. To enhance intimacy within their relationship, it was important for them to learn how to function as two autonomous individuals with different expectations and needs, instead of continuously trying to please each other by fulfilling their partner's desires. This led to a new crisis of instability and insecurity within their relationship.

> During the next session John was totally confused. He expressed his feelings of insecurity and asked for help, for he did not understand what Catherine wanted from him. Now that she had recognized his nursing and pleasing behaviour, she encouraged him to formulate his own needs and feelings instead of persisting in finding out hers. This was something new for him and he could not specify his own needs, except for feeling good by helping others. However, this had changed by the next session, during which he mentioned that he had troubles at work. Now he was able to recognize his emotional needs and asked for Catherine's support. But she was upset by his now being dependent on her and felt unable to cope with it.

At this moment in the therapy Catherine and John's co-dependency (i.e. their being caught in the mutually sustaining roles of 'helper' and 'patient') was being questioned. He was allowed to be 'weak' and she had to learn to deal with his emotional needs. It was the beginning of defining individual boundaries within an intimate relationship, which is possible only if the false safety of fixed role-patterns is abandoned.

Power and autonomy

For eating-disordered women the issues of power and control are of major importance in their interactions with the outside world. Often, the marital interaction is a repetition of the patterns that were present in the family of origin. The struggle for power and control is based on the desire for autonomy, and the way an anorectic or bulimic woman tries to expand her autonomy within the marriage reflects the way the separation-individuation process within the family of origin has taken place. Will the parents (husband) tolerate individual differentiation and assertiveness in the child (wife) or do they cherish 'peaceful harmony' at the price of an eating disorder? When the couple live in a satisfactory codependency with a caretaking husband and a dependent 'sick' wife, the issues of power and control are latently present in their way of dealing with the eating disorder.

> Catherine's binges reinforced John's caretaking behaviour. She felt comfortable and safe by controlling his predictable behaviour, as she would like to shape him into the figure of the perfect husband. The therapist had to confront John with this pitfall of persistently pleasing and indulging Catherine. He was encouraged to oppose her desires. Stepping out of their nurse/patient or parent/child roles was a necessary condition for achieving more autonomy for both of them.

In couples with an anorectic wife, the struggle for power and control is not limited to food intake and weight. She wants to control the relationship, and in most cases the husband seems to accept it. In this regard, their interaction strongly resembles that of marriages of obsessive-compulsive or phobic patients.

> Referring to her perfectionist standards, Elisabeth (introduced in chapter 9) always criticized her husband's way of cleaning the house. In the beginning he defended himself, but soon he felt how useless it was to oppose her, for this would only make her angry. And anger was something he could not tolerate, so he became the obedient and silent husband.

Intimacy and sexuality

Enhancing the intimacy within the couple is the main underlying purpose of couple therapy for eating disorders. Working together on all major issues will implicitly influence the level of intimacy within the marital relationship. But the therapeutic work can be inhibited by fear of intimacy in one or both partners, as reflected in the fear, for example, of becoming dependent upon the partner or losing one's identity (i.e. being identified as 'the spouse of' the other).

> For Elisabeth it was quite normal to keep something hidden from her husband. She was very reluctant to share personal matters with him: when he knew too much about her, she felt too vulnerable. He seemed not to bother and was not inclined to self-disclose himself.

> Catherine had overcome her anxiety for sexual feelings, but was still afraid of sharing her experiences with John. Being confronted with his desires, she became confused and could not enjoy sex any more. For her, it would have been easier to have sex with a stranger!

Sexual problems may often be revealed in an indirect way. For example, the more negative the patient's attitude towards her own body, the greater the likelihood of sexual dysfunctioning ('How can you enjoy sex when you feel disgusted with your own body?'). The eating disorder may also be a good excuse for both partners not to engage in sex. Especially with anorectic women, we have often seen husbands who 'with great patience and love' did not complain about the fact that there was no sexual contact any more – sometimes there had not been any for many years!

Already, in the very first interview, Wendy, a 31-year-old bulimic, had spoken about her disgust for sexual contact with her husband. From the very beginning of the relationship she avoided physical intimacy. Although she felt attracted to other men, these experiences were also unsatisfactory. Her husband had accepted her 'frigidity' as a part of her illness.

Although sexuality should already have been explored during the assessment stage, dealing with this issue must usually be postponed to a later phase of the marital therapy (except for some rules to be agreed upon by the couple in order to avoid negative sexual interactions). First, the patient must have improved her weight and nutritional status, because weight loss and malnutrition reduce her sexual desire (see chapter 7). Then she has to deal with body-image related issues and with her personal sexual history, during individual or group therapy. This involves a learning process of giving up the cognitive overcontrolling attitude towards emotions and associated bodily experiences. However, becoming sexually 'alive' again may provoke the fear of losing control. At this point one should always be concerned about a history of negative experiences, especially of sexual abuse (see Vanderlinden and Vandereycken, 1997).

Fertility

As discussed in chapter 7, all kinds of fertility problems may be connected to (a history of) an eating disorder. In several cases the issue of whether or not to have children is not a physiological but a psychological one. Becoming a parent oneself implies a further step in the psychological separation from the family of origin, which is often a problematic issue in eating-disordered women. Because of their fragile self-esteem patients may also doubt their abilities to be a good parent, and may be afraid of the responsibilities of childrearing. Sometimes patients are afraid of making the same mistakes as their mothers, i.e.

controlling the life of their children. If connected with fertility problems, the eating disorder itself helps the couple to avoid a direct confrontation with the desire for a child. The same may be true for the argument that 'I cannot become pregnant as long as I have an eating disorder'. Although in itself this is a healthy rationale in view of the dangers discussed in chapter 7, it is also an avoidance reaction which may reinforce the continuation of the eating disorder and thus resistance to therapeutic change. These underlying conflicts should be explored together with the husband in order to face the possibility of procreation as a conscious and shared decision by both spouses. In some couples a child serves as the 'natural solution' for all problems, even for the eating disorder!

In the assessment interview the only thing Elisabeth said about children was that it was 'a matter for the future'. At that moment she did not want to say anything more about it. During her weight restoration, five months later, she spontaneously began to write in her diary about this topic. The increasing weight confronted her with her female body, especially her growing belly and the possibility of menstruating again, which she detested. She never talked to her husband about the possibility of having children for fear of hurting him. She believed he liked children but had to admit that she did not know his real feelings. They never discussed this topic. When she had explored her feelings during several group sessions, she was prepared to take up this subject with her husband. In the next couple session, the therapist stimulated both spouses to express their ideas and feelings about children. The husband was astonished about the convincing way Elisabeth explained her decision to stay childless. He admitted that he had never made up his mind because 'I never wanted to push her in any direction'. The therapist asked him to write down his ideas and discuss the matter explicitly in the next session.

Alice had always avoided psychological therapies for her anorexia nervosa or had stopped them prematurely. Soon after her marriage she went to a gynaecologist with a 'desperate' wish to become pregnant and, if possible, to give birth to a daughter. In the fertility clinic she accepted seeing the psychologist 'to prepare me for pregnancy'; if the eating disorder had been put forward as the main reason for referral, she probably would have refused. Avoiding tackling the anorexia in a direct way, the psychologist was able to establish a therapeutic rapport with Alice. During the sessions it soon became clear that in Alice's eyes a pregnancy would solve three major problems in her life: she would accept eating 'for the little baby', her mother would no longer treat her like a child, and her husband would pay more attention to her.

Of course contraceptive practices should also be discussed. Ideally, hormonal contraceptives are only advisable after a natural restoration of the hormonal function. Even when the couple makes a clear decision to stay childless, we dissuade them from choosing an irreversible solution (sterilisation) before the age of 35. If this relationship ends, for whatever reason, the desire for a child can reappear in a new relationship.

Tina, a 34-year-old woman with a long history of anorexia nervosa, had reached her target weight about five months previously but was still amenorrhoeic. When she found she had reached the age for making a final decision about becoming a mother, this became the central issue in her therapy. She came to the conclusion that it was better not to have children. It was only at this point that her husband clearly stated that he had had the same idea for many years. He had never discussed this with her 'because it would conflict with a woman's natural desire for children'. It was a relief for both of them to find out that they had had the same opinion without knowing it. They agreed to tell her mother about this decision, because she was waiting to become a grandmother. Six weeks later, Tina's menses resumed after a period of eight years.

When the couple decide to have children and there are fertility problems, a referral for specialized treatment should be postponed until the eating disorder has disappeared, because a fertility treatment may interfere with the eating disorder and vice versa (see chapter 7).

Pregnancy and childbirth

After a long history of mixed anorexia and bulimia nervosa, at the age of 29, Sandra came for help when she was eight weeks pregnant. Her husband, Ron, was involved in the treatment from the beginning. At the start, body image issues were the focus of the therapy. Sandra could not accept the changes her body would go through during the pregnancy. Would all these efforts be worthwhile, she asked herself. In fact she was afraid that something would go wrong. She revealed that she had had a miscarriage in a previous relationship when she was 21 years old. Working through these feelings with Ron was an essential step towards looking more positively to the future. She grew more confident about her body and the pregnancy. At the same time, she was able to re-establish healthy eating habits and to stop bingeing and vomiting. In the next phase of the marital therapy, Sandra and Ron learned to talk more openly about their feelings and no longer protected each other. Now Ron could express his frustration about Sandra's mother's frequent interference with their marital life. They agreed to reduce the frequency of contacts (phone calls and visits) with her mother and to make all necessary preparations for the child-to-come without asking her mother's advice first. At this stage the bulimic behaviour disappeared; Sandra realized her binges were a way of coping with her anger and disappointment towards her mother.

Becoming pregnant can be the motivation for an eating-disordered woman to look for professional help. This does not mean that the pregnancy will have a 'healing' influence by itself. On the contrary, the pregnant anorectic or bulimic woman confronts the therapist with specific difficulties, as discussed in chapter 7. Both she and her husband should be informed about the risks of disturbed eating and weight-controlling behaviour for the foetus. This may of course increase an irrational fear of malformation of the foetus and provoke guilt feelings. In addition, the weight changes may induce considerable anxiety and strong negative feelings towards the body. Therefore, it is important to help the woman to have a realistic view of the changes in her body during pregnancy. We also stress that the couple should inform the obstetrician about the eating disorder. In addition, this can be the occasion for the wife to disclose more about the symptoms of her eating disorder to her husband. Finally, becoming a mother can also help the patient to separate from her family of origin. But memories of disappointment and frustration with respect to one's own childhood can also lead to the almost obsessional idea of becoming a 'better' parent. Questions about new roles and responsibilities must therefore be shared openly within the relationship (parents should stay partners).

Lisa, a 26-year-old married woman with bulimia nervosa, was pregnant at the end of the group therapy. She became depressed and her old negative feelings about herself came back. She was disappointed about this relapse. Now the issue of her dependence on her mother re-emerged. In spite of repeated invitations by the therapist and the group members, Lisa had up to now resisted discussing her relationship with her mother. They were 'like good friends', sharing everything. The pregnancy, however, had put this 'ideal' bond in a completely new perspective: there was a new person who needed

Lisa, unlike her husband who had always been in the background, absorbed by his work. For the first time Lisa realized she was afraid of the emotional distance that would grow between herself and her mother, and of the feeling 'of being left alone'. Fortunately the group therapy made her aware of the necessity to separate her own needs from those of her growing child; otherwise she might use the child to fill the 'loneliness' in her life. Probably her bulimia had had a similar function before.

Parenting

The relationship between children and parents cannot escape being affected by the reality of the eating disorder. In patients with AN or BN the negative self-image and their strong feelings of insufficiency undermine their perception of being a good parent. In addition, the quality of the marital relationship also affects this perceived ability. These feelings of inadequacy and ineffectiveness exacerbate the eating disorder. Efforts by the husband (or family) to support the wife in the education of the children may at first be experienced as helpful, but can also reinforce her perceived insufficiency as a parent. The main therapeutic goal is therefore to enhance the patient's sense of personal effectiveness in parenting, and to reduce the distress within the couple by reaching common ideas about the education of their children.

Diana (introduced in chapter 9) started every morning in a bad mood. Her older daughter refused to help prepare breakfast, no matter what punishment was given. Diana felt that her authority towards her daughter was not respected. Discussing this issue with her husband in the marital therapy, she realized that she wanted too much control over the behaviour of her daughter. This was probably related to her feeling completely responsible for raising the children. Moreover, the husband only criticized her for being too rigid. He thus undermined her authority but avoided taking educational responsibility himself. Without blaming anyone, the therapist explained this negative interaction and stressed that both spouses should first agree about their parental roles. Soon it became clear that underneath this problem there was a serious lack of intimacy and communication.

It is important that a mother takes her own eating disorder seriously, without cherishing the illusion that she can completely conceal it from her children. When eating-disordered women become aware of the possible effect of their problems on the well-being of their children, this may be the crucial incentive for seeking treatment. However, this motivation, which is quite common, may also be misleading: therapy is not meant to get rid of guilt feelings or to produce an 'ideal' mother. Whether or not the eating-disordered mother reports child-rearing to be an important stressor, the husband should always be involved in the evaluation of current family life. Without making his wife a scapegoat for all the problems with the children, he should at least be aware of the potential influences of an eating disorder upon the children's eating pattern, growth and well-being in general. At the same time his part in taking responsibility for the children's education has to be discussed.

> Since puberty, Elly had been alternating between anorectic and bulimic episodes but always refused treatment. Her husband Fred had given up saying anything about it. Since the birth of their daughter Sabine, who was now 4 years old, Elly had meticulously watched her child's food intake. All meals were calculated, no snacks were allowed in between, and sweets were banned completely. Sabine grew up as a rather thin girl, but each time the paediatrician asked questions about the child's food intake, Elly convincingly stated that Sabine was eating well. After a routine examination at the school health centre (obligatory for all children going to kindergarten), the family doctor was contacted over Sabine's growth retardation. Quite by chance, a few days later Fred went to the family doctor with a continuing headache. When the doctor expressed his concerns about Sabine's growth problem, Fred started to cry and immediately told him about Elly's 'food obsession'. That same evening the couple had a big fight about it, but the next day Elly phoned the doctor: 'Could you send me to a specialist in eating disorders?'

PITFALLS IN THE MARITAL TREATMENT OF EATING DISORDERS

In their book on married overweight people, Stuart and Jacobson (1987) have described factors that can motivate a man to keep his wife fat, such as: unwillingness to change his own bad habits (e.g. drinking), use of weight to divert attention from marital and sexual problems, and fear of his wife's infidelity. Similar 'benefits' can be assumed in husbands of anorectic and bulimic women. When therapy of the eating disorder brings about changes, this inevitably affects the relationship. The husband can ignore any improvement and persist in the idea that he is living with a 'sick' wife. He can also oppose his wife's 'talking with a stranger', or criticize her individual psychotherapy as 'a waste of money' or, more subtly, never ask about it. In such cases the therapist has to weigh carefully the pros and cons of every possible strategy: ignoring the husband may be seen as a reinforcement of his position; questioning his attitude may confront the wife with a loyalty conflict; involving the husband could mean inviting a Trojan Horse into therapy. . . . Some of these pitfalls are now discussed in more detail.

Ambivalence of the patient

The involvement of the husband in the treatment may be desirable from the therapist's viewpoint, but is not therefore always indicated or beneficial. Many eating-disordered women show ambivalent feelings towards therapy and change. Part of this ambivalence can be their wish to keep the husband out of the therapy. We give these patients the benefit of the doubt by agreeing on a time-limited contract with well-determined goals. After they have gained trust in the therapist and motivation for change has grown, they are more likely to realize the necessity of their husbands' involvement in the treatment. Otherwise dropping out is the outcome to expect.

> Sandra, a 33-year-old bulimic, was very sceptical about psychotherapy. Although she bitterly complained about the quality of her marriage, she strongly resisted bringing her husband with her to the sessions. In her view, he 'would only humiliate me and treat me like a child'. The therapist adopted her point of view to avoid a battle and proposed some treatment goals with regard to her eating behaviour. After a few sessions Sandra suddenly stopped the therapy. Everything was fine now with her marriage, because unexpectedly they had bought a house. And 'for financial reasons' she could not afford to continue therapy.

Opposition by the husband

What are the therapeutic implications when the husband persists in refusing any co-operation in treatment? First of all, the therapist must take into consideration how the wife will cope with this reality. One can consider stopping therapy in those cases where the role of the husband in the maintenance of the eating disorder is so evident that it explains previous failures of individual therapy. Stopping treatment, with the message that it can only be meaningful when the husband is ready to engage in therapy, may then have a confrontational impact on the husband and perhaps even create a fruitful crisis. In contrast, when the therapist decides to continue individual therapy in spite of the husband's opposition, the possible consequences of the latter's attitude on the course of the treatment have to be discussed. If the patient feels better, through further therapy, the husband may become curious about the therapy or may abandon his scepticism. Alternatively, the patient may also learn how to cope with his reactions, or how to distance herself from his influence, or how to question her further life (including the relationship) if things remain unchanged.

> After two sessions, the husband of Mary-Lou left the marital therapy with the message that such an approach was useless, and that it was up to her to get rid of her anorexia. She decided to go on by herself in group therapy. There she learned to become more self-confident and assertive. One day she dared to openly express her feelings and thoughts to her husband. Instead of the big fight she had expected, he ran away! When he came back, he no longer seemed to be the strong man with the big mouth. He realized that he had to take her seriously, otherwise she could leave him. From then on they frequently had difficult discussions, especially about her wish to be more independent. Gradually, he accepted her 'new identity' and they both found a new balance in their relationship.

> Just before seeing a therapist for the first time, Christine confessed to her husband that she had had a well-concealed bulimia nervosa for about ten years, since before she had met her husband. He reacted with anger and felt cheated. Christine had feared such a reaction and was now even more anxious that her eating disorder would trouble their marriage. It reminded her of her parents' divorce when she was 17 years old – the start of her eating disorder. Having a wife with a 'silly' eating problem was not only incomprehensible for the husband, he also saw it as a personal insult, 'because I have done everything to make her happy'. He didn't want to hear anything about her therapy, but she seemed determined to overcome her bulimia alone. She abruptly stopped bingeing and vomiting but soon became depressed. Now, again, he reacted angrily ('there is no reason at all to be unhappy') and he blamed her for continuing a 'ridiculous' therapy. In the next sessions she appeared to question the idealized picture of her marriage. Soon after this, the husband cancelled the therapy with the message that 'everything is all right now'.

Opposition by both partners

One of the 'classical' difficulties in marital therapy will occur when one or both partners resists real change and protects the other. If, for instance, their relationship is characterized by a mutual dependency between the 'strong' and the 'helpless' one, they create a rigid boundary between their marriage and the treatment. While they at first seem collaborative, they avoid discussing intimate matters to protect themselves; the eating disorder is the only problem! Some couples 'survive' as long as they have a common enemy: the eating disorder. If the therapist pursues the goal of bringing the relationship into the therapeutic focus, in many cases the woman silently accepts this move while the husband will oppose it. Such a situation can lead to a serious loyalty conflict.

Sarah and Tom (introduced in chapter 9) agreed to engage in couple therapy because they both acknowledged difficulties in their communication. After a few sessions, Tom made it clear what he expected from life and Sarah's position in it. Afterwards, she was completely upset by his candour but she only expressed her concerns in the parallel group therapy. She began to realize that Tom was staging the relationship according to his needs and that between them there would never be the intimacy she had hoped for. In the group therapy she came to the frightening conclusion that she would never be cured of her eating disorder as long as she continued this marriage. But she was afraid to take such a decision because she was not able to face life on her own. After the group session she spoke to Tom about her dissatisfaction with their marriage. He could not understand what she was talking about, because he felt he did his best to please her. Very angrily he shouted that he never wanted to see that therapist again and – 'if this is the result of treatment' – even forbade her to continue her group therapy. Nevertheless she came to the next session and briefly explained what had happened. But two weeks later, she dropped out.

After ten years of bulimia nervosa, Mary realized that she was sacrificing herself for her two children. In silence she had undergone the frequent humiliations and physical violence from her husband. He always criticized her treatment and refused to be involved in any way. Although she often thought about leaving him, she stayed 'to offer the children a normal family life'. In the group therapy she became aware that precisely for this same reason she should get a divorce. When she finally left him, he felt completely lost and started drinking heavily. He went to Mary's therapist, begging him to repair their marriage. But for her 'it is much too late'.

Sexual or physical abuse

When it becomes clear during the assessment that there is sexual abuse or physical violence in the marriage (although normally this information will be disclosed in a further stage of therapy) the first aim should be to stop it. Whether, when and how the husband can be confronted with his abusive behaviour is a matter of careful evaluation. The patient may refuse to take any action against the husband because of fear or feelings of loyalty. This might be an indication for hospitalization as a protective measure.

At the eighth session, Monica (described earlier) ashamedly confessed the physical violence she suffered at the hands of her boyfriend, something she had always hidden from the outside world, even after two admissions to an emergency unit. She considered herself guilty for this violence and her idea of being responsible was reinforced by her boyfriend's accusation that she always 'pushes me to my limits'. In an individual session he minimized the seriousness of his violence and refused any further co-operation as long as the therapist could not guarantee the immediate stopping of her bulimic behaviour.

CONCLUSIONS

In this chapter we have emphasized the importance of involving the husbands of married eating-disordered patients in the treatment, and have described the different ways in which this involvement can take place. We have pointed out that this involvement is not a 'technical' matter of deciding for or against a marital therapy, but is rather finding a way to meet the couple's needs to the extent they ask for and at the level they are willing to accept. The assessment of the couple should then guide the therapist in the decision about the desirability of focusing on the marital relationship during the treatment. In this regard, we have discussed marital dissatisfaction, partner choice, communication and conflict regulation, boundaries, power and autonomy, intimacy and sexuality, fertility, pregnancy and childbirth and parenting as the main issues to focus on during therapy. Finally, we have explained how the therapist may deal with possible pitfalls in the treatment of these couples, notably the patient's ambivalence, the husband's or the couple's opposition, and sexual or physical abuse in the relationship.

Appendix 1

Anorectic Behaviour Observation Scale for parents or spouse

W. Vandereycken (1992)

Name of patient: .... Date:........

Completed by

- both parents together
- mother
- father
- spouse
- someone else (who? ....)

Instructions

Rate the following items on the basis of observations of the patient made during the last month at home. Rate an item 'YES' or 'NO' only if you are sure about it (for instance, if you yourself saw it happening). Rate '?' if you are not sure (for instance, if you did not have the opportunity to observe it yourself, if you only heard about it or if you can only suppose it happened).

	YES	NO	?
1 Avoids eating with others or delays as much as possible before coming to the dinner table.	( )	( )	( )
2 Shows obvious signs of tension at mealtimes.	( )	( )	( )
3 Shows anger or hostility at mealtimes.	( )	( )	( )
4 Begins by cutting up food into small pieces.		( )	( )
( )			
5 Complains that there is too much food or that it is too rich (fattening).	( )	( )	( )
6 Exhibits unusual 'food faddism'.	( )	( )	( )

7 Attempts to bargain about food (for example,
'I'll eat this if I don't have to eat that'). ( ) ( ) ( )

8 Picks at food or eats very slowly. ( ) ( ) ( )

9 Prefers diet products (with low calorie content). ( ) ( ) ( )

10 Seldom mentions being hungry. ( ) ( ) ( )

11 Likes to cook or help in the kitchen, but avoids
tasting or eating. ( ) ( ) ( )

12 Vomits after meals. ( ) ( ) ( )

13 Conceals food in napkins, handbags or clothing
during mealtimes. ( ) ( ) ( )

14 Disposes of food (out of window, into dustbin,
or down sink or toilet). ( ) ( ) ( )

15 Conceals or hoards food in own room or
elsewhere. ( ) ( ) ( )

16 Eats when alone or secretly (for example
at night). ( ) ( ) ( )

17 Dislikes visiting others or going to parties
because of the 'obligation' to eat. ( ) ( ) ( )

18 Sometimes has difficulties in stopping eating or
eats unusually large amounts of food or sweets. ( ) ( ) ( )

19 Complains a lot about constipation. ( ) ( ) ( )

20 Frequently takes laxatives (purgatives) or asks
for them. ( ) ( ) ( )

21 Claims to be too fat regardless of weight loss. ( ) ( ) ( )

22 Often speaks about slimming, dieting or ideal
body forms. ( ) ( ) ( )

23 Often leaves the table during mealtimes (for
example, to get something from the kitchen). ( ) ( ) ( )

24 Stands, walks or runs about whenever possible. ( ) ( ) ( )

25 Is as active as possible (for example, clearing
tables or cleaning the room). ( ) ( ) ( )

26 Does a lot of physical exercise or sports. ( ) ( ) ( )

27 Studies or works diligently. ( ) ( ) ( )

28 Is seldom tired and takes little or no rest. ( ) ( ) ( )

29 Claims to be normal, healthy or even better
than ever. ( ) ( ) ( )

30 Is reluctant to see a doctor or refuses medical
examinations ( ) ( ) ( )

Appendix 2
Standardized couple interview for eating-disordered patients

S. Van den Broucke and W. Vandereycken (1989)

Identification data

- Name
- Age
- Education
- Profession
- Age of cohabitation
- Age of marriage
- Age of first AN/BN symptoms
- Number and age of children

Questions with reference to the spouse

1 Did the spouse ever experience any of the following symptoms prior to the marriage? And after the marriage?

(a) obesity (> 20 per cent overweight), (b) severe weight loss, (c) loss of appetite, (d) digestive problems, (e) alcohol or drug abuse, (f) depression, (g) neurotic symptoms, (h) psychotic symptoms, (i) psychosomatic problems.

2 Was the spouse familiar with the syndrom of AN before the marriage?

(a) never heard about it, (b) heard or read about it, (c) learned about it through his wife's condition, (d) learned about it through another patient.

3 Were there ever any serious problems in the spouse's family? If so, what?

Questions regarding the partner choice and onset of the relationship

4 At what age did each parter start dating members of the opposite sex?
5 Did they have other relationships prior to the present one?

(a) platonic love, (b) loose relationship without sexual contact, (c) loose relationship with petting, (d) loose relationship with intercourse, (e) steady relationship without sexual contact, (f) steady relationship with petting, (g) steady relationship with intercourse, (h) none of the above.

6 If the answer was 'yes' on item (e), (f) or (g) of the previous question:

(a) was the previous partner younger/same age/older? (b) was the previous partner experienced/inexperienced? (c) who broke up the relationship? (d) what was the reaction of the parents to the relationship and its breakup?

7 Who took the initiative for the following steps in the present relationship:

(a) first contact, (b) engagement, (c) sexual approach, (d) sexual intercourse, (e) marriage?

8 What in particular attracted the partners to each other?
9 Was there any evidence of eating/weight problems in the patient at the start of the relationship?
10 What was the parents' attitude towards the relationship?

Questions regarding the marital relationship quality

11 How do both partners evaluate the time they spend together as a couple?
12 What topics do they agree about most?
14 Do they tell each other what they like or dislike?
15 Do they consider their partner attractive? In which sense (physical or other)?
16 Do they consider themselves attractive to their partner? In which sense?
17 Have there been any extramarital contacts?
18 What do they consider the main qualities of a good spouse (a) in general, (b) socially, (c) sexually?

Questions regarding the impact of the AN/BN on the relationship

19 When did the partners become aware of the eating or weight problem?
20 Did the patient try to hide the eating habits or symptoms?
21 When was the term 'anorexia nervosa' or 'bulimia' first used to describe the problem or as a diagnosis?
22 When, why and on whose initiative was professional help sought?
23 Which form of treatment was considered appropriate at the time of the first consultancy?
24 How did the spouse *overtly* react to the eating/weight problem?
25 How did the spouse *emotionally* react to the eating or weight problem? (Rate: 1 = not at all, 2 = not very, 3 = fairly, 4 = very, 5 = extremely)

(a) patient, (b) supportive, (c) understanding, (d) worried, (e) helpless, (f) sad, (g) guilty, (h) authoritative, (i) angry, (j) distrusting/controlling, (k) threatening with divorce.

26 In what respect did the eating disorder influence the relationship between the partners (e.g. communication, disclosure of feelings, mutual trust)?
27 In what respect did the eating disorder influence the physical and sexual relationship between the partners?
28 In what respect did the eating disorder influence the relationship with the children (if any) and/or the wish for a child?
29 In what respect did the eating disorder influence the relationship with the family of origin?
30 In what respect did the eating disorder influence the practical arrangements in the relationship (e.g. household matters)?
31 In what respect did the eating disorder influence the way the couple spend their leisure time?
32 In what respect did the eating disorder influence the couple's eating habits?
33 In what respect did the eating disorder influence the quality of the marital relationship?

Questions regarding the attribution of the eating disorder

34 Which factors do the partners think elicited the disorder? List one or more of the following:

(a) problems at work/school, (b) moving, (c) conflict between parents, (d) conflict between patient and parents, (e) conflict with brother/sister, (f) first sexual contact, (g) engagement, (h) cohabitation or marriage, (i) pregnancy/miscarriage/childbirth, (j) marital conflicts, (k) children's education, (l) dissatisfaction with appearance, (m) medical reason, (n) other (specify).

35 What is the partners' view on the cause of the eating disorder? (Rate: 1 = not true at all, 2 = probably not true, 3 = perhaps, 4 = probably true, 5 = definitely true)

(a) the eating disorder is a physical disease for which one is not responsible; (b) the eating disorder is of psychological nature and is rooted in childhood experiences; (c) the eating disorder represents a lack of will-power; (d) the eating disorder is something the patient has done to herself by trying to lose weight; (e) the eating disorder is a form of obsession or addiction; (f) the eating disorder represents an inability to accept the female body; (g) the eating disorder represents a fear of the responsibilities of adulthood; (h) the eating disorder is a reaction to marital distress; (i) the eating disorder is a way to avoid sexual intercourse; (j) the eating disorder is a way to draw attention; (k) other (specify).

36 In which way would the partners react differently if they had the chance to do everything over again?
37 In which way would they want their spouse to react differently if they had the chance to do everything over again?
38 How do they think the spouse can help to solve the problems and to avoid future relapses?
39 What will happen to the marriage if there is no real improvement of the eating disorder?
40 Do the partners believe that a complete recovery is possible?

Appendix 3
Marital Intimacy Questionnaire

S. Van den Broucke, H. Vertommen and W. Vandereycken (1995)

You will find below a number of statements describing the relationship between (marital) partners. Please indicate for each statement to what degree it applies to the relationship between yourself and your partner by choosing among the following possibilities:

- not true at all
- untrue
- undecided
- true
- very true.

Some of the statements refer to you, others to your partner and some to both you and your partner. For the latter, you may choose an intermediate answer if the statement does not apply equally to both of you.

---

1 My partner and I enjoy being together.
❑ not true at all
❑ untrue
❑ undecided
❑ true
❑ very true

2 My partner and I agree about most issues.
❑ not true at all
❑ untrue
❑ undecided
❑ true
❑ very true

3 I can be myself in the relationship with my partner.
 ❑ not true at all
 ❑ untrue
 ❑ undecided
 ❑ true
 ❑ very true

4 My partner and I remain faithful to each other.
 ❑ not true at all
 ❑ untrue
 ❑ undecided
 ❑ true
 ❑ very true

5 My partner and I give each other tenderness.
 ❑ not true at all
 ❑ untrue
 ❑ undecided
 ❑ true
 ❑ very true

6 My partner and I do not need many words to understand each other.
 ❑ not true at all
 ❑ untrue
 ❑ undecided
 ❑ true
 ❑ very true

7 My partner and I like to do things together.
 ❑ not true at all
 ❑ untrue
 ❑ undecided
 ❑ true
 ❑ very true

8 If my partner or I have a problem, we ask each other for advice.
 ❑ not true at all
 ❑ untrue
 ❑ undecided
 ❑ true
 ❑ very true

9 The relationship between my partner and me is sometimes less close than the ones with our parents.
   ❏ not true at all
   ❏ untrue
   ❏ undecided
   ❏ true
   ❏ very true

10 My partner has all the qualities I expect a good spouse to possess.
   ❏ not true at all
   ❏ untrue
   ❏ undecided
   ❏ true
   ❏ very true

11 My partner and I could easily live without each other.
   ❏ not true at all
   ❏ untrue
   ❏ undecided
   ❏ true
   ❏ very true

12 My partner and I often have a different opinion.
   ❏ not true at all
   ❏ untrue
   ❏ undecided
   ❏ true
   ❏ very true

13 I can entrust the most intimate things to my partner.
   ❏ not true at all
   ❏ untrue
   ❏ undecided
   ❏ true
   ❏ very true

14 I think others have more to offer to their partner than I can offer mine.
   ❏ not true at all
   ❏ untrue
   ❏ undecided
   ❏ true
   ❏ very true

15 My partner and I leave each other free to engage in other relationships.
   ❏ not true at all
   ❏ untrue
   ❏ undecided
   ❏ true
   ❏ very true

16 My partner and I share each other's feelings.
   ❏ not true at all
   ❏ untrue
   ❏ undecided
   ❏ true
   ❏ very true

17 My partner and I are not on the same wavelength.
   ❏ not true at all
   ❏ untrue
   ❏ undecided
   ❏ true
   ❏ very true

18 My partner and I don't always know what we can expect from
   each other.
   ❏ not true at all
   ❏ untrue
   ❏ undecided
   ❏ true
   ❏ very true

19 My partner and I completely understand each other.
   ❏ not true at all
   ❏ untrue
   ❏ undecided
   ❏ true
   ❏ very true

20 My partner and I accept each other the way we are.
   ❏ not true at all
   ❏ untrue
   ❏ undecided
   ❏ true
   ❏ very true

21 My partner and I can easily make joint decisions.
- ❑ not true at all
- ❑ untrue
- ❑ undecided
- ❑ true
- ❑ very true

22 I prefer to keep very personal things hidden for my partner.
- ❑ not true at all
- ❑ untrue
- ❑ undecided
- ❑ true
- ❑ very true

23 I think I have little to offer to my partner.
- ❑ not true at all
- ❑ untrue
- ❑ undecided
- ❑ true
- ❑ very true

24 The relationship between my partner and me is more important than our relationships with other persons.
- ❑ not true at all
- ❑ untrue
- ❑ undecided
- ❑ true
- ❑ very true

25 I don't think there are couples who are happier than my partner and me.
- ❑ not true at all
- ❑ untrue
- ❑ undecided
- ❑ true
- ❑ very true

26 My partner and I try to please each other.
- ❑ not true at all
- ❑ untrue
- ❑ undecided
- ❑ true
- ❑ very true

27 My partner and I can sense what the other thinks or feels, even if he/she does not say so.
   ❑ not true at all
   ❑ untrue
   ❑ undecided
   ❑ true
   ❑ very true

28 I try to tell my partner only those things I think he/she will like to hear.
   ❑ not true at all
   ❑ untrue
   ❑ undecided
   ❑ true
   ❑ very true

29 If I have a different opinion than my partner, I speak up.
   ❑ not true at all
   ❑ untrue
   ❑ undecided
   ❑ true
   ❑ very true

30 There are things my partner and I prefer to discuss with our parents rather than with each other.
   ❑ not true at all
   ❑ untrue
   ❑ undecided
   ❑ true
   ❑ very true

31 My partner and I share the same view about our relationship.
   ❑ not true at all
   ❑ untrue
   ❑ undecided
   ❑ true
   ❑ very true

32 My partner and I complement each other.
   ❑ not true at all
   ❑ untrue
   ❑ undecided
   ❑ true
   ❑ very true

33 My partner and I talk to each other about sex.
   ❏ not true at all
   ❏ untrue
   ❏ undecided
   ❏ true
   ❏ very true

34 My partner and I need other personal relationships than ours.
   ❏ not true at all
   ❏ untrue
   ❏ undecided
   ❏ true
   ❏ very true

35 My partner and I understand each other.
   ❏ not true at all
   ❏ untrue
   ❏ undecided
   ❏ true
   ❏ very true

36 If there are problems, my partner and I can usually solve them together.
   ❏ not true at all
   ❏ untrue
   ❏ undecided
   ❏ true
   ❏ very true

37 When I say personal things to my partner I often feel sorry afterwards.
   ❏ not true at all
   ❏ untrue
   ❏ undecided
   ❏ true
   ❏ very true

38 I think I am attractive for my partner.
   ❏ not true at all
   ❏ untrue
   ❏ undecided
   ❏ true
   ❏ very true

39 There is a great distance between my partner and me.
❏ not true at all
❏ untrue
❏ undecided
☒ true
❏ very true

40 Sometimes I just pretend I am listening to my partner.
☒ not true at all
❏ untrue
❏ undecided
❏ true
❏ very true

41 I think my partner accepts me as I am.
❏ not true at all
☒ untrue
❏ undecided
❏ true
❏ very true

42 Where important things are concerned, my partner and I have little in common.
❏ not true at all
❏ untrue
❏ undecided
❏ true
☒ very true

43 I show my true feelings to my partner.
❏ not true at all
❏ untrue
❏ undecided
☒ true
❏ very true

44 My partner and I sometimes tell personal things about each other to friends.
❏ not true at all
❏ untrue
❏ undecided
☒ true
❏ very true

45 My partner and I consider it important to show our love to each other.
   ❑ not true at all
   ❑ untrue
   ☒ undecided
   ❑ true
   ❑ very true

46 My partner and I often try to impose our own ideas onto each other.
   ❑ not true at all
   ❑ untrue
   ❑ undecided
   ☒ true
   ❑ very true

47 My partner and I go our own ways.
   ❑ not true at all
   ❑ untrue
   ❑ undecided
   ☒ true
   ❑ very true

48 My partner and I discuss personal things.
   ❑ not true at all
   ❑ untrue
   ☒ undecided
   ❑ true
   ❑ very true

49 I often lose myself in the relationship with my partner.
   ❑ not true at all
   ❑ untrue
   ❑ undecided
   ☒ true
   ❑ very true

50 My partner and I understand each other intuitively.
   ❑ not true at all
   ❑ untrue
   ❑ undecided
   ☒ true
   ❑ very true

51 My partner and I usually need much time to get tuned in to each other when performing certain tasks.
    ❑ not true at all
    ❑ untrue
    ☑ undecided
    ❑ true
    ❑ very true

52 In our relationship everything can be discussed openly.
    ❑ not true at all
    ☑ untrue
    ❑ undecided
    ❑ true
    ❑ very true

53 The relationship with my partner inhibits my self-development.
    ❑ not true at all
    ❑ untrue
    ❑ undecided
    ☑ true
    ❑ very true

54 Faith is an important aspect of the relationship between my partner and me.
    ❑ not true at all
    ❑ untrue
    ☑ undecided
    ❑ true
    ❑ very true

55 My partner and I long for each other when we are apart.
    ❑ not true at all
    ❑ untrue
    ❑ undecided
    ☑ true
    ❑ very true

56 My partner and I count each other in when we make plans.
    ☑ not true at all
    ☑ untrue
    ❑ undecided
    ☑ true
    ❑ very true

Scale composition of the Marital Intimacy Questionnaire

Intimacy problems: 9, 14, 17, 18, 23, 30, 37, 39, 40, 42, 46, 49, 51, 53

Consensus: 2, 6, 12(-), 19, 20, 21, 27, 31, 32, 35, 36, 41

Openness: 3, 8, 13, 22(-), 28(-), 29, 33, 38, 43, 48, 50, 52

Affection: 1, 5, 7, 16, 26, 45, 55, 56

Commitment: 4, 10, 11(-), 15 (-), 24, 25, 34 (-), 44 (-), 47 (-), 54

Scoring key
not true at all = 1
untrue = 2
undecided = 3
true = 4
very true = 5

Reverse the scoring for items 11, 12, 22, 15, 28, 34, 44 and 47

References

Abraham, S. and Llewellyn-Jones, D. (1995). Sexual and reproductive function in eating disorders and obesity. In K.D. Brownell and C.G. Fairburn (eds), *Eating Disorders and Obesity* (pp. 281–286). New York/London: Guilford Press.

Abraham, S., Bendit, N., Mason, C., Mitchell, H., O'Connor, N., Ward, J., Young, S. and Llewellyn-Jones, D. (1985). The psychosexual histories of young women with bulimia. *Australian and New Zealand Journal of Psychiatry*, 19, 72–76.

Abraham, S., Mira, M. and Llewellyn-Jones, D. (1990). Should ovulation be induced in women recovering from an eating disorder or who are compulsive exercisers? *Fertility and Sterility*, 53, 566–568.

Acitelli, L.K. and Duck, S.W. (1987). Postscript: intimacy as the proverbial elephant. In D. Perlman and S.W. Duck (eds), *Intimate Relationships: Development, Dynamics, and Deterioration* (pp. 297–308). Beverly Hills: Sage Publications.

Agulnik, P.L. (1970). The spouse of the phobic patient. *British Journal of Psychiatry*, 117, 59–67.

Allison, P.D. and Liker, J.K. (1982). Analyzing sequential categorical data on dyadic interaction: comment on Gottman. *Psychological Bulletin*, 91, 393–403.

Altman, I. and Taylor, D.A. (1973). *Social Penetration: The Development of Interpersonal Relationships*. New York: Holt, Rinehart and Winston.

American Psychiatric Association (1980). *Diagnostic and Statistical Manual of Mental Disorders, Third Edition*. Washington, DC: American Psychiatric Press.

——(1994). *Diagnostic and Statistical Manual of Mental Disorders, Fourth Edition*. Washington, DC: American Psychiatric Association.

Andersen, A.E. (1985). *Practical Comprehensive Treatment of Anorexia Nervosa and Bulimia*. Baltimore: Johns Hopkins University Press.

——(ed.) (1990). *Males with Eating Disorders*. New York: Brunner/Mazel.

Andrews, F.M., Abbey, A. and Halman, L.J. (1992). Is fertility-problem stress different? The dynamics of stress in fertile and infertile couples. *Fertility and Sterility*, 57, 1247–1253.

Argyle, M. and Dean, J. (1965). Eye contact, distance, and affiliation. *Sociometry*, 28, 289–304.

Arrindell, W.A. and Emmelkamp, P.M.G. (1985). Psychological profile of the spouse of the female agoraphobic patient: personality and symptoms. *British Journal of Psychiatry*, 146, 405–414.

——(1986). Marital adjustment, intimacy and needs in female agoraphobics and their partners: a controlled study. *British Journal of Psychiatry*, 149, 592–602.

Arrindell, W.A. and Ettema, J.M. (1986). *SCL-90. Handleiding bij een Multidimensionele Psychopathologie-indicator* [Manual for a multidimensional psychopathology-indicator]. Lisse, The Netherlands: Swets and Zeitlinger.

Arrindell, W.A., Boelens, W. and Lambert, H. (1983). On the psychometric properties of the Maudsley Marital Questionnaire (MMQ): evaluation of self-ratings in distressed and 'normal' volunteer couples based on the Dutch version. *Personality and Individual Differences*, 4, 293–306.

Bakeman, R. and Gottman, J.M. (1986). *Observing Interaction: An Introduction to Sequential Analysis*. Cambridge: Cambridge University Press.

Barlow, D.H., Hayes, S.C. and Nelson, R.O. (1984). *The Scientist Practitioner: Research and Accountability in Clinical and Educational Settings*. New York: Pergamon.

Barrett, M.J. and Schwartz, R. (1987). Couple therapy for bulimia. In J.E. Harkaway (ed.), *Eating Disorders* (pp. 25–39). Rockville, MD: Aspen.

Basco, M.R., Prager, K.J., Pita, J.M., Tamir, L.M. and Stephens, J.J. (1992). Communication and intimacy in the marriages of depressed patients. *Journal of Family Psychology*, 6, 184–194.

Bateson, G. and Jackson, D. (1968). Some varieties in pathogenic organization. In D.D. Jackson (ed.), *Communication, Family and Marriage* (pp. 210–215). Palo Alto, CA: Science and Behavior Press.

Beach, S.R.H. and O'Leary, K.D. (1993). Marital discord and dysphoria: for whom does the marital relationship predict depressive symptomatology? *Journal of Social and Personal Relationships*, 10, 405–420.

Beach, S.R.H., Sandeen, E.E. and O'Leary, K.D. (1990). *Depression in Marriage*. New York: Guilford Press.

Beach, S.R.H., Whisman, M. and O'Leary, K.D. (1994). Marital therapy for depression: theoretical foundation, current status, and future directions. *Behavior Therapy*, 25, 345–371.

Berscheid, E. (1983). Emotion in close relationships. In H.H. Kelley, E. Berscheid, A. Christensen, J.J. Harvey, T.L. Huston, G. Levinger, E. McClintock, L.A. Peplau and D.R. Peterson (eds), *Close Relationships* (pp. 110–168). New York: Freeman.

Beumont, P.J.V. (1992). Menstrual disorder and other hormonal disturbances. In W. Herzog, H.C. Deter and W. Vandereycken (eds), *The Course of Eating Disorders* (pp. 257–272). Berlin: Springer-Verlag.

Beumont, P.J.V., George, G.C.W. and Smart, D.E. (1976). 'Dieters' and 'vomiters and purgers' in anorexia nervosa. *Psychological Medicine*, 6, 617–622.

Bienvenu, M.J. (1970). Measures of marital communication. *Family Coordinator*, 19, 26–31.

Biglan, A., Hops, H., Sherman, L., Friedman, L.S., Arthur, J. and Osteen, V.

(1985). Problem solving interactions of depressed women and their spouses. *Behavior Therapy*, 16, 431–451.

Billings, A.G., Kessler, M., Gomberg, C.A. and Weiner, S. (1979). Marital conflict resolution of alcoholic couples during drinking and nondrinking sessions. *Journal of Studies on Alcohol*, 40, 183–195.

Birchler, G.R., Weiss, R.L. and Vincent, J.P. (1975). Multimethod analysis of social reinforcement between maritally distressed and nondistressed spouse and stranger dyads. *Journal of Personality and Social Psychology*, 31, 349–360.

Birtchnell, J. (1986). The imperfect attainment of intimacy: a key concept in marital therapy. *Journal of Family Therapy*, 8, 153–172.

Birtchnell, J. and Kennard, J. (1983). Marriage and mental illness. *British Journal of Psychiatry*, 142, 193–198.

Bland, K. and Hallam, R.S. (1981). Relationship between response to graded exposure and marital satisfaction in agoraphobics. *Behaviour Research and Therapy*, 19, 335–338.

Borkin, J., Thomas, E.J. and Walter, C.L. (1980). The marital communication rating schedule: an instrument for clinical assessment. *Journal of Behavioral Assessment*, 2, 287–307.

Boskind-White, M. and White, W.C. (1983). *Bulimarexia: The Binge-Purge Cycle*. New York/London: W.W. Norton.

Brinch, M., Isager, T. and Tolstrup, K. (1988). Anorexia nervosa and motherhood: reproductive pattern and mothering behaviour of 50 women. *Acta Psychiatrica Scandinavica*, 77, 98–104.

Brown, G.W. and Harris, T. (1978). *Social Origins of Depression: A Study of Psychiatric Disorder in Women*. London: Tavistock.

Brownell, K.D. and Fairburn, C.G. (eds) (1995). *Eating Disorders and Obesity: A Comprehensive Handbook*. New York: Guilford Press.

Buglass, D., Clarke, J., Henderson, A.S., Kreitman, N. and Presley, A.S. (1977). A study of agoraphobic housewives. *Psychological Medicine*, 7, 73–86.

Burke, M.E. and Vangellow, J. (1990). Anorexia nervosa and bulimia nervosa: chronic conditions affecting pregnancy. *Clinical Issues in Perinatal Woman's Health Nursing*, 1, 240–254.

Byng-Hall, J. (1980). Symptom bearer as marital distress regulator: clinical implications. *Family Process*, 19, 355–365.

Cachelin, F.M. and Mahrer, B.A. (1996). 'Is amenorrhea a critical criterion for anorexia?' Paper presented at the 7th International Conference on Eating Disorders, New York, April 26–28, 1996.

Canary, D.J. and Cupach, W.R. (1988). Relational and episodic characteristics associated with conflict tactics. *Journal of Social and Personal Relationships*, 5, 305–325.

Carpenter, J. (1986). And so they lived happily ever after: intimacy and the idealization of marriage. A comment on Birtchnell. *Journal of Family Therapy*, 8, 173–177.

Cermak, T. (1986). Diagnostic criteria for codependency. *Journal of Psychoactive Drugs*, 18, 15–20.

Chambless, D.L. and Goldstein, A.J. (1980). The treatment of agoraphobia. In A.J. Goldstein and E.B. Foa (eds), *Handbook of Behavioral Interventions* (pp. 322–411). New York: John Wiley.

Chelune, G.J. and Waring, E.M. (1984). Nature and assessment of intimacy. In P. McReynolds and G.J. Chelune (eds), *Advances in Psychological Assessment, Volume 6* (pp. 277–311). San Francisco: Jossey-Bass.

Chelune, G.J., Robison, J.T. and Kommor, M.J. (1984). A cognitive interaction model of intimate relationships. In V.J. Derlega (ed.), *Communication, Intimacy, and Close Relationships* (pp. 11–40). New York: Academic Press.

Christensen, A. (1987). Detection of conflict patterns in couples. In K. Hahlweg and M.J. Goldstein (eds), *Understanding Major Mental Disorders: The Contribution of Family Interaction Research* (pp. 250–265). New York: Family Process Press.

Clark, M.S. and Reis, H.T. (1988). Interpersonal processes in close relationships. *Annual Review of Psychology*, 39, 609–672.

Cloninger, C.R., Reich, T. and Guze, S.B. (1975). The multifactorial model of disease transmission: III. Familial relationships between sociopathy and hysteria (Briquet's syndrome). *British Journal of Psychiatry*, 127, 23–32.

Coleman, R.E. and Miller, A.G. (1975). The relationship between depression and marital maladjustment in a clinical population: a multitrait-multimethod study. *Journal of Consulting and Clinical Psychology*, 43, 647–651.

Cooper, Z., Cooper, P. and Fairburn, C. (1985). The specificity of the Eating Disorder Inventory. *British Journal of Clinical Psychology*, 24, 129–130.

Coovert, D.L., Kinder, B.N. and Thompson, J.K. (1989). The psychosexual aspects of anorexia nervosa and bulimia nervosa: a review of the literature. *Clinical Psychology Review*, 9, 169–180.

Copeland, P.M., Sacks, N.R. and Herzog, D.B. (1995). Longitudinal follow-up of amenorrhea in eating disorders. *Psychosomatic Medicine*, 57, 121–126.

Costello, C.G. (1982). Social factors associated with depression: a retrospective community study. *Psychological Medicine*, 12, 329–340.

Coyne, J.C. (1976). Toward an interactional description of depression. *Psychiatry*, 39, 28–40.

Coyne, J.C., Kessler, R.C., Tal, M., Turnbull, J., Wortman, C.B. and Greden, J.F. (1987). Living with a depressed person. *Journal of Consulting and Clinical Psychology*, 55, 347–352.

Crago, M.A. (1972). Psychopathology in married couples. *Psychological Bulletin*, 77, 114–128.

Crisp, A.H. (1980). *Anorexia Nervosa: Let Me Be*. London/New York: Academic Press/Grune and Stratton.

Crisp, A.H., Kalucy, R.S., Lacey, J.H. and Harding, B. (1977). The long-term prognosis in anorexia nervosa: some factors predictive of its outcome. In R.A. Vigersky (ed.), *Anorexia Nervosa* (pp. 5–65). New York: Raven Press.

Cromwell, R.E. and Peterson, G.E. (1983). Multisystem-multimethod assessment in clinical contexts. *Family Process*, 22, 147–164.

Cromwell, R.E., Olson, H. and Fournier, D.G. (1976). Tools and techniques for diagnosis and evaluation in marital and family therapy. *Family Process*, 15, 1–49.

Crowe, M.J. (1978). Conjoint marital therapy: a controlled outcome study. *Psychological Medicine*, 8, 623–636.

Dally, P. (1984). Anorexia tardive: late onset marital anorexia nervosa. *Journal of Psychosomatic Research*, 18, 423–428.

Dally, P. and Gomez, J. (1979). *Anorexia Nervosa*. London: Heinemann Medical Books.

———(1980). *Obesity and Anorexia Nervosa: A Question of Shape*. London/Boston: Faber and Faber.

Davies, K. and Wardle, J. (1994). Body image and dieting in pregnancy. *Journal of Psychosomatic Research*, 38, 787–799.

Derlega, V.J. and Chaikin, A.L. (1975). *Sharing Intimacy: What We Reveal to Others and Why*. Englewood Cliffs, NJ: Prentice Hall.

Derlega, V.J. and Margulis, S.T. (1982). Why loneliness occurs: the interrelationship of social-psychological and privacy concepts. In L.A. Peplau and D. Perlman (eds), *Loneliness: A Sourcebook of Current Theory, Research and Therapy* (pp. 152–165). New York: John Wiley.

Derogatis, R.L. (1977). *SCL-90: Administration, Scoring and Procedures Manual-I for the Revised Version*. Baltimore: Johns Hopkins University School of Medicine, Clinical Psychometric Research Unit.

Dohrenwend, B.P. and Dohrenwend, B.S. (1969). *Social Status and Psychological Disorder: A Causal Inquiry*. New York: John Wiley.

Duck, S.W. (1990). Relationships as unfinished business: out of the frying pan and into the 1990s. *Journal of Social and Personal Relationships*, 7, 5–28.

Duck, S.W. and Perlman, D. (eds) (1985). *Understanding Personal Relationships: An Interdisciplinary Approach*. Beverly Hills: Sage.

Duck, S.W., Locke, A., McCall, G., Fitzpatrick, M.A. and Coyne, J.C. (1984). Social and personal relationships: a joint editorial. *Journal of Social and Personal Relationships*, 1, 1–10.

Eidelson, R.J. and Epstein, N. (1982). Cognition and relationship maladjustment: development of a measure of dysfunctional relationship belief. *Journal of Consulting and Clinical Psychology*, 50, 715–720.

Emmelkamp, P.M.G. and Gerlsma, C. (1994). Marital functioning and the anxiety disorders. *Behavior Therapy*, 25, 407–429.

Emmelkamp, P.M.G., de Haan, E. and Hoogduin, C.A.L. (1990). Marital adjustment and obsessive-compulsive disorder. *British Journal of Psychiatry*, 156, 55–60.

Emmelkamp, P.M.G., van Dyck, R., Bitter, M., Heins, R., Onstein, E.J. and Eisen, B. (1992). Spouse-aided therapy with agoraphobics. *British Journal of Psychiatry*, 160, 51–56.

Eysenck, H.J. (1974). Personality, premarital sexual permissiveness, and assortative mating. *Journal of Sex Research*, 10, 47–51.

Fahy, T.A. and O'Donoghue, G. (1991). Eating disorders in pregnancy. *Psychological Medicine*, 21, 577–580.

Fahy, T.A. and Morrison, J.J. (1993). The clinical significance of eating disorders in obstetrics. *British Journal of Obstetrics and Gynaecology*, 100, 708–710.

Fairburn, C.G. and Cooper, Z. (1993). The eating disorder examination. In C.G. Fairburn and G.T. Wilson (eds), *Binge Eating: Nature, Assessment, and Treatment* (pp. 333–360). New York/London: Guilford Press.

Fairburn, C.G. and Welsh, S.L. (1990). The impact of pregnancy on eating habits and attitudes to shape and weight. *International Journal of Eating Disorders*, 10, 153–160.

Fairburn, C.G., Kirk, J., O'Connor, M., Anastasiades, P. and Cooper, P.J.

(1987). Prognostic factors in bulimia nervosa. *British Journal of Clinical Psychology*, 26, 223–224.

Fairburn, C.G., Jones, R., Peveler, R.C., Hope, R.A. and O'Connor, M. (1993). Psychotherapy and bulimia nervosa: longer-term effects of interpersonal psychotherapy, behavior therapy, and cognitive behavior therapy. *Archives of General Psychiatry*, 50, 419–428.

Feldman, L.B. (1979). Marital conflict and marital intimacy: an integrative psychodynamic-behavioral-systemic model. *Family Process*, 18, 69–78.

Fichter, M. and Haberger, R. (1990). Bulimia nervosa: Psychosexuelle Entwicklungsstörungen [Bulimia nervosa: Disturbances of psychosexual development]. In H.J. Vogt, W. Eicher and V. Herms (eds), *Praktische Sexualmedizin* (pp. 155–174). Wiesbaden: Medical Tribune.

Fincham, F.D. and Bradbury, T.N. (1988). The impact of attributions in marriage: empirical and conceptual foundations. *British Journal of Clinical Psychology*, 27, 77–90.

Fisher, M. and Stricker, G. (eds) (1982). *Intimacy*. New York/London: Plenum Press.

Fishman, H.C. (1979). Family considerations in liaison psychiatry: a structural approach to anorexia nervosa in adults. *Psychiatric Clinics of North America*, 2, 249–263.

Fitzpatrick, M.A. (1988). *Between Husbands and Wives: Communication in Marriage*. Beverly Hills: Sage Publications.

Foster, S.W. (1986). Marital treatment of eating disorders. In N.S. Jacobson and S. Gurman (eds), *Clinical Handbook of Marital Therapy* (pp. 575–593). New York: Guilford Press.

Franko, D.L. and Hilsinger, E. (1995). Depression and bulimia in a pregnant woman. *Harvard Review of Psychiatry*, 2, 282–287.

Franko, D.L. and Walton, B.E. (1993). Pregnancy and eating disorders: a review and clinical implications. *International Journal of Eating Disorders*, 13, 41–48.

Fredman, N. and Sherman, R. (1987). *Handbook of Measurements for Marriage and Family Therapy*. New York: Brunner/Mazel.

Fry, W.F. (1962). The marital context of an anxiety syndrome. *Family Process*, 7, 245–252.

Gadlin, H. (1977). Private lives and public order: a critical view of the history of intimate relations in the United States. In G. Levinger and H. Raush (eds), *Close Relationships: Perspectives on the Meaning of Intimacy* (pp. 33–72). Amherst: University of Massachusetts Press.

Garfinkel, P.E. and Garner, D.M. (1982). *Anorexia Nervosa: A Multidimensional Perspective*. New York: Brunner/Mazel.

Garfinkel, P.E., Lin, E., Goering, P., Spegg, C., Goldbloom, D., Kennedy, S., Kaplan, A.S. and Woodside, D.B. (1996). Should amenorrhoea be necessary for the diagnosis of anorexia nervosa? Evidence from a Canadian community sample. *British Journal of Psychiatry*, 168, 500–506.

Garner, D.M. (1991). *Eating Disorder Inventory-2, Manual*. Odessa: Psychological Assessment Resources.

Garner, D.M., Olmsted, M.P. and Polivy, J. (1983). Development and validation of a multidimensional Eating Disorder Inventory for anorexia nervosa and bulimia. *International Journal of Eating Disorders*, 2, 15–24.

Georgiou, E. (1995). Hypnotherapy in the treatment of anorexia tardive. *Australian Journal of Clinical and Experimental Hypnosis*, 23, 14–24.

Golden, N.H. and Shenker, I.R. (1994). Amenorrhea in anorexia nervosa. Neuro-endocrine control of hypothalamic dysfunction. *International Journal of Eating Disorders*, 16, 53–60.

Goldstein, A.J. and Chambless, D.L. (1978). A reanalysis of agoraphobia. *Behavior Therapy*, 9, 47–59.

Gotlib, I.H. and Whiffen, V.E. (1989). Depression and marital functioning: an examination of specificity and gender differences. *Journal of Abnormal Psychology*, 98, 23–30.

Gottman, J.M. (1979). *Marital Interaction: Experimental Investigations*. New York: Academic Press.

Gottman, J.M. and Levenson, R.W. (1987). The social psychophysiology of marriage. In P. Noller and M.A. Fitzpatrick (eds), *Perspectives on Marital Interaction*. Philadelphia: Multilingual Matters.

Gottman, J.M., Markman, H.J. and Notarius, C.I. (1977). Topography of marital conflict: a sequential analysis of verbal and nonverbal behavior. *Journal of Marriage and the Family*, 39, 361–377.

Gove, W.R. (1984). Gender differences in mental and physical illness: the effects of fixed roles and nurturant roles. *Social Science and Medicine*, 19, 77–91.

Griffiths, R.A., Beumont, P.J.V., Beumont, D., Touyz, S.W., Williams, H. and Lowinger, K. (1995). Anorexia à deux: an ominous sign for recovery. *European Eating Disorders Review*, 3, 2–14.

Grissett, N.I. and Norvell, N.K. (1992). Perceived social support, social skills, and quality of relationships in bulimic women. *Journal of Consulting and Clinical Psychology*, 60, 293–299.

Grove, W.M. and Andreasen, N.C. (1982). Simultaneous tests of many hypotheses in exploratory research. *Journal of Nervous and Mental Disease*, 170, 3–8.

Guile, L., Horne, M. and Dunston, R. (1978). Anorexia nervosa, sexual behaviour modification as an adjunct to an integrated treatment programme: a case report. *Australian and New Zealand Journal of Psychiatry*, 12, 165–167.

Guerney, B.G. (ed.) (1977). *Relationship Enhancement*. San Francisco: Jossey-Bass.

Haaken, J. (1990). A critical analysis of the co-dependency construct. *Psychiatry*, 53, 396–406.

Hafner, R.J. (1977a). The husbands of agoraphobic women: assortative mating or pathogenic interaction? *British Journal of Psychiatry*, 130, 233–239.

——(1977b). The husbands of agoraphobic women and their influence on treatment outcome. *British Journal of Psychiatry*, 131, 289–294.

——(1979). Agoraphobic women married to abnormally jealous men. *British Journal of Medical Psychology*, 52, 99–104.

——(1986). *Marriage and Mental Illness: A Sex Roles Perspective*. New York: Guilford Press.

Hahlweg, K. and Jacobson, N.S. (eds) (1984). *Marital Interaction: Analysis and Modification*. New York: Guilford Press.

Hahlweg, K., Kraemer, M., Schindler, L. and Revenstorf, D. (1980).

Partnerschaftsprobleme: eine empirische Analyse [Partner problems: an empirical analysis]. *Zeitschrift für Klinische Psychologie*, 9, 159–169.

Hahlweg, K., Schindler, L., Revenstorf, D. and Brengelmann, J.C. (1984a). The Munich marital therapy study. In K. Hahlweg and N.S. Jacobson (eds), *Marital Interaction: Analysis and Modification* (pp. 3–26). New York: Guilford Press.

Hahlweg, K., Reisner, L., Kohli, G., Vollmer, M., Schindler, L. and Revenstorf, D. (1984b). Development and validity of a new system to analyze interpersonal communication: Kategoriensystem für Partnerschaftliche Interaktion. In K. Hahlweg and N.S. Jacobson (eds), *Marital Interaction: Analysis and Modification* (pp. 182–198). New York: Guilford Press.

Haimes, A.L. and Katz, J.L. (1988). Sexual and social maturity versus social conformity in restricting anorectic, bulimic, and borderline women. *International Journal of Eating Disorders*, 7, 331–341.

Haley, J. (1964). *Ordeal Therapy. Unusual Ways to Change Behavior*. San Francisco: Jossey-Bass.

Hall, A. (1982). Deciding to stay anorectic. *Postgraduate Medical Journal*, 58, 641–647.

——(1996). Anorexia nervosa, bulimia and other eating disorders. In M. Göpfert, J. Webster and M.V. Seeman (eds), *Parental Psychiatric Disorder* (pp. 251–256). Cambridge: Cambridge University Press.

Hand, I. and Lamontagne, Y. (1976). The exacerbation of interpersonal problems after rapid phobia-removal. *Psychotherapy: Theory, Research, and Practice*, 13, 405–411.

Hands, M. and Dear, G. (1994). Co-dependency: a critical review. *Drug and Alcohol Review*, 13, 437–445.

Hatfield, E. (1982). Passionate love, companionate love, and intimacy. In M. Fisher and G. Stricker (eds), *Intimacy* (pp. 267–292). New York: Plenum Press.

Hautzinger, M., Linden, M. and Hoffman, N. (1982). Distressed couples with and without a depressed partner: an analysis of their verbal interaction. *Journal of Behavior Therapy and Experimental Psychiatry*, 56, 440–447.

Heavey, A., Parker, Y., Bhat, A.V., Crisp, A.H. and Gowers, S.G. (1989). Anorexia nervosa and marriage. *International Journal of Eating Disorders*, 8, 275–284.

Heim, S.C. and Snyder, D.K. (1991). Predicting depression from marital distress and attributional processes. *Journal of Marital and Family Therapy*, 17, 67–72.

Herzog, W., Deter, H.C. and Vandereycken, W. (eds) (1992). *The Course of Eating Disorders: Long-term Follow-up Studies of Bulimia and Anorexia Nervosa*. Berlin: Springer-Verlag.

Hickie, I., Wilhelm, K., Parker, G., Boyce, P, Hadzi-Pavlovic, D., Brodaty, H. and Mitchell, P. (1990). Perceived dysfunctional intimate relationships: a specific association with the non-melancholic depressive subtype. *Journal of Affective Disorders*, 19, 99–107.

Hinchliffe, M.R., Hooper, D., Roberts, F.J. and Vaughan, R.V. (1975). A study of interaction between depressed patients and their spouses. *British Journal of Psychiatry*, 126, 164–172.

Hinde, R. (1978). Interpersonal relationships: in quest of a science. *Psychological Medicine*, 3, 378–386.

Hobfoll, S. (1988). *The Ecology of Stress*. Washington, DC: Hemisphere.

Hoek, H.W. (1993). Review of the epidemiological studies of eating disorders. *International Review of Psychiatry*, 5, 61–74.

Hollifield, J. and Hobdy, J. (1990). The course of pregnancy complicated by bulimia. *Psychotherapy*, 27, 249–255.

Hooley, J.M. and Hahlweg, K. (1986). The marriages and interaction patterns of depressed patients and their spouses: comparison of high and low EE dyads. In M.J. Goldstein, I. Hand and K. Hahlweg (eds), *Treatment of Schizophrenia: Family Assessment and Intervention* (pp. 85–95). Berlin/Heidelberg: Springer-Verlag.

Hooley, J.M. and Teasdale, J.D. (1989). Predictors of relapse in unipolar depressives: expressed emotion, marital distress, and perceived criticism. *Journal of Abnormal Psychology*, 89, 229–237.

Ineichen, B. (1976). Marriage and neurosis in a modern residential suburb: an application of the Ryle Marital Patterns Test. *British Journal of Psychiatry*, 129, 248–251.

Jacob, T. and Krahn, G.L. (1988). Marital interactions of alcoholic couples: comparison with depressed and nondistressed couples. *Journal of Consulting and Clinical Psychology*, 56, 73–79.

Jacob, T. and Tennenbaum, D.L. (1988). *Family Assessment: Rationale, Methods, and Future Directions*. New York: Plenum Press.

Jacobson, N.S. and Margolin, G. (1979). *Marital Therapy: Strategies Based on Social Learning and Behavior Exchange Principles*. New York: Brunner/Mazel.

Jacobson, N.S. and Moore, D. (1981). Behavior exchange theory of marriage: reconnaissance and reconciliation. In J.P. Vincent (ed.), *Advances in Family Intervention, Assessment, and Theory, Volume II* (pp. 183–213). Greenwich, CT: JAI Press.

Jacobson, N.S., Elwood, R.W. and Dallas, M. (1981). Assessment of marital dysfunction. In D.E. Barlow (ed.), *Behavioral Assessment of Adult Disorders* (pp. 439–479). New York: Guilford Press.

Jacobson, N.S., McDonald, D.W., Follette, W.C. and Berley, R.A. (1985). Attributional processes in distressed and nondistressed married couples. *Journal of Consulting and Clinical Psychology*, 9, 35–50.

Jagstaidt, V. and Pasini, W. (1994). Boulimie et sexualité [Bulimia and sexuality]. *Médecine et Hygiène*, 52, 701–704.

Joanning, H., Brewster, J. and Koval, J. (1984). The Communication Rapid Assessment Scale: developments of a behavioral index of communication quality. *Journal of Marital and Family Therapy*, 8, 463–468.

Jones, W.H. and Perlman, D. (1991). *Advances in Personal Relationships, Volume 2*. London: Jessica Kingsley Publishers.

Jourard, S.M. (1971). *Self-disclosure: An Experimental Analysis of the Transparent Self*. New York: John Wiley.

Kantor, D.A. and Okun, B.F. (eds) (1989). *Intimate Environments: Sex, Intimacy and Gender in Families*. New York: Guilford Press.

Kaplan, J.R. (ed.) (1980). *A Woman's Conflict: The Special Relationship between Women and Food*. Englewood Cliffs, NJ: Prentice Hall.

Kapoor, S.A. (1989). Help for the significant others of bulimia. *Journal of Applied Social Psychology*, 19, 50–66.

Katzman, M.A. (1993). The pregnant therapist and the eating-disordered woman: the challenge of fertility. *Eating Disorders*, 1, 17–30.

Kelley, H.H. (1978). *Personal Relationships: Their Structure and Processes.* Hillsdale, NJ: Lawrence Erlbaum Associates.

Kelley, H.H., Berscheid, E., Christensen, A., Harvey, J.J., Huston, T.L., Levinger, G., McClintock, E., Peplau, L.A. and Peterson, D.R. (eds) (1983). *Close Relationships*. New York: Freeman.

Kerkstra, A. (1985). *Conflicthantering bij Echtparen* [Conflict management in married couples]. Amsterdam: VU Press.

Kleiner, L., Marshall, W.L. and Spevack, M. (1987). Training in problem-solving and exposure treatment for agoraphobics with panic attacks. *Journal of Anxiety Disorders*, 1, 219–238.

Kog, E., Vandereycken, W. and Vertommen, H. (1985). The psychosomatic family model: a critical analysis of family interaction concepts. *Journal of Family Therapy*, 7, 31–44.

Koropatnick, S., Daniluk, J. and Pattinson, H.A. (1993). Infertility: a non-event transition. *Fertility and Sterility*, 59, 163–170.

Kreitman, N. (1964). The patient's spouse. *British Journal of Psychiatry*, 110, 159–173.

L'Abate, L. (1986). *Systemic Family Therapy*. New York: Brunner/Mazel.

Lacey, J.H. (1992). Homogamy: the relationships and sexual partners of normal-weight bulimic women. *British Journal of Psychiatry*, 161, 638–642.

Lacey, J.H. and Smith, G. (1987). Bulimia nervosa: the impact of pregnancy on mother and baby. *British Journal of Psychiatry*, 150, 777–781.

Lange, A., Markus, E., Hageman, W. and Hanewald, G. (1991). Status inconsistency, traditionality and marital distress in the Netherlands. *Psychological Reports*, 68, 1243–1253.

Lazarus, A. (1966). Broad-spectrum behavior therapy and the treatment of agoraphobia. *Behaviour Research and Therapy*, 4, 95–97.

Lederer, W.J. and Jackson, D.D. (1968). *The Mirages of Marriage*. New York: W.W. Norton.

Leiblum, S.R. (1993). The impact of infertility on sexual and marital satisfaction. *Annual Review of Sex Research*, 6, 99–120.

Leichner, P.P., Harper, D.E. and Johnson, D.M. (1985). Adjunctive group support for spouses of women with anorexia nervosa and/or bulimia. *International Journal of Eating Disorders*, 4, 227–235.

Lemberg, R. and Phillips, J. (1989). The impact of pregnancy on anorexia nervosa and bulimia. *International Journal of Eating Disorders*, 8, 285–295.

Lemberg, R., Phillips, J. and Fischer, J.E. (1992). The obstetric experience in primigravida anorexic and bulimic women – some preliminary observations. *British Review of Bulimia and Anorexia Nervosa*, 6, 31–37.

Levinger, G. (1988). Can we picture love? In R.J. Sternberg and M.L. Barnes (eds), *The Psychology of Love* (pp. 139–158). New Haven: Yale University Press.

Lewis, L. and le Grange, D. (1994). The experience and impact of pregnancy in bulimia nervosa: a series of case studies. *European Eating Disorders Review*, 2, 93–105.

Linden, M., Hautzinger, M. and Hoffman, N. (1983). Discriminant analysis of depressive interactions. *Behavior Modification*, 7, 403–422.

Lingam, R. and McCluskey, S. (1996). Eating disorders associated with hyperemesis gravidarum. *Journal of Psychosomatic Research*, 40, 231–234.

Liss-Levinson, N. (1988). Disorders of desire: women, sex, and food. In E. Cole and E.D. Rothblum (eds), *Women and Sex Therapy* (pp. 121–129). New York: Haworth Press.

Locke, H.J. and Wallace, K.M. (1959). Short-term marital adjustment and prediction tests: their reliability and validity. *Marriage and Family Living*, 21, 251–255.

Lonergan, E.C. (1992). Using group therapy to foster the psychosexual development of patients with eating disorders. *Group*, 16, 85–94.

LoPiccolo, J. and Steger, J.C. (1974). The Sexual Interaction Inventory: a new instrument for assessment of sexual dysfunction. *Archives of Sexual Behavior*, 3, 585–595.

Losey, G.S. (1978). Information theory and communication. In P.W. Colgan (ed.), *Quantitative Ethology* (pp. 43–78). New York: John Wiley.

Love, D.R., Brown, J.J., Fraser, R., Lever, A.F., Robertson, J.I.S., Timbury, G.C., Thomson, S. and Tree, M. (1971). An unusual case of self-induced electrolyte depletion. *Gut*, 12, 284–290.

Madanes, C. (1981). *Strategic Family Therapy*. San Francisco: Jossey-Bass.

Margolin, G. and Wampold, B.E. (1981). Sequential analysis of conflict and discord in distressed and nondistressed marital partners. *Journal of Consulting and Clinical Psychology*, 47, 554–567.

Markman, H.J. (1984). The longitudinal study of couples' interactions: implications for understanding and predicting the development of marital distress. In K. Hahlweg and N.S. Jacobson (eds), *Marital Interaction: Analysis and Modification* (pp. 253–281). New York: Guilford Press.

Markman, H.J. and Notarius, C.I. (1987). Coding marital and family interaction: current status. In T. Jacob (ed.), *Family Interaction and Psychopathology: Theories, Methods, and Findings* (pp. 329–390). New York: Plenum Press.

Marshall, P. and Palmer, R. (1988). Pregnancy without menstruation on recovery from anorexia nervosa: a case description and a warning. *British Review of Bulimia and Anorexia Nervosa*, 3, 13–15.

Marshall, W.L. (1989). Intimacy, loneliness and sexual offenders. *Behaviour Research and Therapy*, 27, 491–503.

Meadow, R.M. and Weiss, L. (1992). *Women's Conflicts about Eating and Sexuality: The Relationship between Food and Sex*. New York: Haworth Press.

Merikangas, K. (1982). Assortative mating for psychiatric disorders and psychological traits. *Archives of General Psychiatry*, 39, 1173–1180.

Methorst, G.J. (1984). Partners of psychiatric outpatients: the difference between husbands and wives on psychological well-being and its implications for marital therapy. In K. Hahlweg and N.S. Jacobson (eds), *Marital Interaction: Analysis and Modification* (pp. 375–386). New York: Guilford Press.

Mettetal, G. and Gottman, J.M. (1980). Reciprocity and dominance. In J.P. Vincent (ed.), *Advances in Family Intervention, Assessment, and Theory, Volume I* (pp. 181–228). Greenwich, CT: JAI Press.

Milton, F. and Hafner R.J. (1979). The outcome of behavior therapy for agoraphobia in relation to marital adjustment. *Archives of General Psychiatry*, 36, 807–811.

Minuchin, S., Rosman, B.L. and Baker, L. (1978). *Psychosomatic Families: Anorexia Nervosa in Context.* Cambridge, MA: Harvard University Press.

Mitchell, J.E., Boutacoff, L. and Wilson, D. (1986). Absence of early feeding problems among bulimic women: observations from parental interviews. *American Journal of Orthopsychiatry*, 56, 313–316.

Mitchell, J.E., Specker, S.M. and de Zwaan, M. (1991). Comorbidity and medical complications of bulimia nervosa. *Journal of Clinical Psychology*, 52 (Suppl. 10), 13–20.

Miyake, A. (1986). Gynecological hormone therapy for the reproductive disorder in women with anorexia nervosa. *Japanese Journal of Psychosomatic Medicine*, 26, 119–124.

Monsour, M. (1992). Meanings of intimacy in cross- and same-sex friendships. *Journal of Social and Personal Relationships*, 9, 277–295.

Monteiro, W., Marks, I.M. and Ramm, E. (1985). Marital adjustment and treatment outcome in agoraphobia. *British Journal of Psychiatry*, 157, 383–390.

Moore, B.J. and Greenwood, M.R.C. (1995). Pregnancy and weight gain. In K.D. Brownell and C.G. Fairburn (eds), *Eating Disorders and Obesity* (pp. 51–55). New York/London: Guilford Press.

Moos, R.H., Finney, J.W. and Cronkite, R.C. (1990). *Alcoholism Treatment: Process and Outcome.* New York: Oxford University Press.

Nachtigall, R.D., Becker, G. and Wozny, M. (1992). The effects of gender-specific diagnosis on men's and women's response to infertility. *Fertility and Sterility*, 57, 113–121.

Namir, S., Melman, K.N. and Yager, J. (1986). Pregnancy in restricter-type anorexia nervosa: a study of six women. *International Journal of Eating Disorders*, 5, 837–845.

Navran, L. (1967). Communication and adjustment in marriage. *Family Process*, 6, 173–184.

Newman, H. and Langer, E.J. (1981). Investigating the development and courses of intimate relationships. In L.Y. Abramson (ed.), *Social Cognition and Clinical Psychology: A Synthesis* (pp. 148–173). New York: Guilford Press.

Newman, N.E. and Zouves, C.G. (1991). Emotional experiences of in vitro fertilization participants. *Journal of In Vitro Fertilization and Embryo Transfer*, 8, 322–328.

Norré, J. and Vandereycken, W. (1991). The limits of out-patient treatment for bulimic disorders. *British Review of Bulimia and Anorexia Nervosa*, 5(2), 55–63.

Notarius, C.I. and Johnson, J.S. (1982). Emotional expression in husbands and wives. *Journal of Marriage and the Family*, 44, 483–489.

Notarius, C.I. and Markman, H.J. (1989). Coding marital interaction: a sampling and discussion of current issues. *Behavioral Assessment*, 11, 1–11.

Oatley, K. and Hodgson, D. (1987). Influence of husbands on the outcome of their agoraphobic wives' therapy. *British Journal of Psychiatry*, 150, 380–386.

O'Farrell, T. (1994). Marital therapy and spouse-involved treatment with alcoholic patients. *Behavior Therapy*, 25, 391–406.

O'Farrell, T. and Birchler, G.R. (1987). Marital relationships of alcoholic, conflicted and nonconflicted couples. *Journal of Marriage and Family Therapy*, 13, 259–274.

Olin, G.V. and Fenell, D.L. (1989). The relationship between depression and marital adjustment in a general population. *Family Therapy*, 16, 11–20.

Olson, D.H., Bell, R.Q. and Portner, J. (1978). *FACES: Family Adaptability and Cohesion Evaluation Scales*. St Paul: University of Minnesota, Family Social Science.

Olson, D.H., Portner, J. and Lavee, Y. (1985). *FACES III: Family Adaptability and Cohesion Evaluation Scales*. St Paul: University of Minnesota, Family Social Science.

Orford, J. (1990). Alcohol and the family: an international review of the literature with implications for research and practice. In L.T. Kozlowski *et al.* (eds), *Research Advances in Alcohol and Drug Problems, Volume 10* (pp. 81–155). New York: Plenum Press.

Ovenstone, I.M.K. (1973). The development of neurosis in wives of neurotic men: I. Symptomatology. *British Journal of Psychiatry*, 122, 35–45.

Parelman, A. (1983). *Emotional Intimacy in Marriage: A Sex Roles Perspective*. Ann Arbor: University of Michigan Research Press.

Pasini, W. (1995). *Nourriture et Amour: Deux Passions Dévorantes* [Food and Love. Two Devouring Passions]. Paris: Payot.

Patterson, G.R. and Reid, J.B. (1970). Reciprocity and coercion: two facets of social systems. In C. Nueringer and J. Michael (eds), *Behavior Modification in Clinical Psychology* (pp. 133–177). New York: Appleton-Century-Crofts.

Patton, D. and Waring, E.M. (1985). Sex and marital intimacy. *Journal of Sex and Marital Therapy*, 11, 176–184.

Penman, R. (1980). *Communication Processes and Relationships*. London/New York: Academic Press.

Perednia, C. and Vandereycken, W. (1989). An explorative study on parenting in eating disorder families. In W. Vandereycken, E. Kog and J. Vanderlinden (eds), *The Family Approach to Eating Disorders* (pp. 119–146). New York: PMA.

Perlman, D. and Fehr, B. (1987). The development of intimate relationships. In D. Perlman and S.W. Duck (eds), *Intimate Relationships: Development, Dynamics, and Deterioration* (pp. 13–42). Beverly Hills: Sage Publications.

Peterson, D.R. (1983). Conflict. In H.H. Kelley, E. Berscheid, A. Christensen, J.J. Harvey, T.L. Huston, G. Levinger, E. McClintock, L.A. Peplau and D.R. Peterson (eds), *Close Relationships* (pp. 360–396). New York: Freeman.

Pond, D.A., Ryle, A. and Hamilton, M. (1963). Marriage and neurosis in a working-class population. *British Journal of Psychiatry*, 109, 592–598.

Probst, M., Vandereycken, W., Van Coppenolle, H. and Vanderlinden, J. (1995). The Body Attitude Test for patients with an eating disorder: psychometric characteristics of a new questionnaire. *Eating Disorders*, 3, 133–144.

Raboch, J. and Faltus, F. (1991). Sexuality of women with anorexia nervosa *Acta Psychiatrica Scandinavica*, 84, 9–11.

Rand, C.S., Willis, DC and Kuldau, J.M. (1987). Pregnancy after anorexia nervosa. *International Journal of Eating Disorders*, 6, 671–674.

Raush, H.L., Barry, W.A., Hertel, R.K. and Swain, M.A. (1974). *Communication, Conflict, and Marriage*. San Francisco: Jossey-Bass.

Reis, H.T. (1990). The role of intimacy in interpersonal relations. *Journal of Social and Clinical Psychology*, 9, 15–30.

Reis, H.T. and Shaver, P. (1988). Intimacy as an interpersonal process. In S.W. Duck (ed.), *Handbook of Personal Relationships: Theory, Research and Interventions* (pp. 367–389). New York: John Wiley.

Reis, H.T., Wheeler, L., Kernis, M.H., Spiegel, N. and Nezlek, J. (1985). On specificity in the impact of social participation on physical and psychological health. *Journal of Personality and Social Psychology*, 48, 456–471.

Reiss, D. and Johnson-Sabine, E. (1995). Bulimia nervosa: five-year social outcome and relationship to eating pathology. *International Journal of Eating Disorders*, 18, 127–133.

Renshaw, D.C. (1990). Sex and eating disorders. *Medical Aspects of Human Sexuality*, 24(4), 68–77.

Revenstorf, D., Vogel, B., Wegener, C., Hahlweg, K. and Schindler, L. (1980). Escalation phenomena in interaction sequences: an empirical comparison of distressed and nondistressed couples. *Behavior Analysis and Modification*, 2, 97–116.

Revenstorf, D., Hahlweg, K., Schindler, L. and Vogel, B. (1984). Interaction analysis of marital conflict. In K. Hahlweg and N.S. Jacobson (eds), *Marital Interaction: Analysis and Modification* (pp. 159–181). New York: Guilford Press.

Richardson, H. (1939). Studies of mental resemblance between husbands and wives and between friends. *Psychological Bulletin*, 36, 104–142.

Riggs, D.S., Hiss, H. and Foa, E.B. (1992). Marital distress and the treatment of obsessive-compulsive disorder. *Behavior Therapy*, 23, 585–597.

Roberto, L.G. (1991). Impasses in the family treatment of bulimia. In D.B. Woodside and L. Shekter-Wolfson (eds), *Family Approaches in Treatment of Eating Disorders* (pp. 67–85). Washington, DC: American Psychiatric Press.

Robinson, E.A. and Jacobson, N.S. (1987). Social learning theory and family psychopathology: a Kantian model in behaviorism? In T. Jacob (ed.), *Family Psychopathology: Theories, Methods, and Findings* (pp. 117–162). New York: Plenum Press.

Roloff, M.E. (1976). Communication strategies, relationships, and relational change. In G.R. Miller (ed.), *Explorations in Interpersonal Communication* (pp. 173–195). Beverly Hills: Sage Publications.

Root, M.P., Fallon, P. and Friedrich, W.N. (1986). *Bulimia: A Systems Approach to Treatment*. New York: W.W. Norton.

Russell, G.F.M. (1979). Bulimia nervosa: an ominous variant of anorexia nervosa. *Psychological Medicine*, 9, 429–448.

Sarason, I.G. and Sarason, B.R. (eds) (1985). *Social Support: Theory, Research and Applications*. Dordrecht: Martinus Nijhoff.

Schaap, C. (1982). *Communication and Adjustment in Marriage*. Amsterdam: Swets and Zeitlinger.

——(1984). A comparison of the interaction of distressed and nondistressed married couples in a laboratory situation: literature survey, methodological issues, and an empirical investigation. In K. Hahlweg and N.S. Jacobson (eds), *Marital Interaction: Analysis and Modification* (pp. 133–158). New York: Guilford Press.

Schaap, C., Buunk, B. and Kerkstra, A. (1987). Marital conflict resolution. In P. Noller and M.A. Fitzpatrick (eds), *Perspectives on Marital Interaction* (pp. 253–295). Philadelphia: Multilingual Matters.

Schaefer, M.T. and Olson, D.H. (1981). Assessing intimacy: the PAIR inventory. *Journal of Marital and Family Therapy*, 7, 47–60.

Schaper, W.W.F. (1973). Some aspects of the interaction between phobics and their partners. In J.C. Brengelmann and W. Tunner (eds), *Verhaltenstherapie: Praktische und Theoretische Aspekte* [Behaviour Therapy: Practical and Theoretical Aspects] (pp. 92–97). Munich: Urban and Schwarzenberg.

Schwartz, M.F., and Cohn, L. (eds) (1996). *Sexual Abuse and Eating Disorders.* New York: Brunner/Mazel.

Schweiger, U., Laessle, R.G. and Pirke, K.M. (1988). Essverhalten und Fertilitätstörungen: Perspektiven für eine verhaltensmedizinisch orientierte Therapie von Störungen reproduktiver endokriner Funktionen [Eating behaviour and fertility disorders: perspectives for a behavioural medicine oriented treatment of disturbances in reproductive endocrine functions]. *Verhaltensmodifikation und Verhaltensmedizin*, 9, 3–10.

Scott, D.W. (1987). The involvement of psychosexual factors in the causation of eating disorders: time for a reappraisal. *International Journal of Eating Disorders*, 6, 199–213.

Scourfield, J. (1995). Anorexia by proxy: are the children of anorexic mothers an at-risk group? *International Journal of Eating Disorders*, 18, 371–374.

Selvini-Palazzoli, M. (1974). *Self-starvation: From the Intrapsychic to the Transpersonal Approach to Anorexia Nervosa.* London: Chaucer/Human Context Books.

Sillars, A.L., Colletti, S.F., Parry, D. and Rogers, M.A. (1982). Coding verbal conflict tactics: nonverbal and perceptual correlates of the 'avoidance-distributive-integrative' distinction. *Human Communication Research*, 9, 83–95.

Simpson, W.S. and Ramberg, J.A. (1992). Sexual dysfunction in married female patients with anorexia and bulimia nervosa. *Journal of Sex and Marital Therapy*, 18, 44–54.

Smith, D.E., Lewis, C.E., Caveny, J.L., Perkins, L.L., Burke, G.L. and Bild, D.E. (1994). Longitudinal changes in adiposity associated with pregnancy: the CARDIA study. *Journal of the American Medical Association*, 271, 1741–1751.

Snyder, D.K. (1981). *Marital Satisfaction Inventory (MSI) Manual.* Los Angeles, CA: Western Psychological Services.

Spanier, G.B. (1976). Measuring dyadic adjustment: new scales for assessing the quality of marriage and similar dyads. *Journal of Marriage and the Family*, 38, 15–30.

Stein, A. (1995). Eating disorders and childrearing. In K.D. Brownell and C.G. Fairburn (eds), *Eating Disorders and Obesity* (pp. 188–190). New York/London: Guilford Press.

Stein, A. and Fairburn C.G. (1989). Children of mothers with bulimia nervosa. *British Medical Journal*, 299, 777–778.

Stein, A. and Woolley, H. (1996). The influence of parental eating disorders on young children: implications of recent research for some clinical interventions. *Eating Disorders*, 4, 139–146.

Stein, A., Woolley, H., Cooper, S.D. and Fairburn, C.G. (1994). An observational study of mothers with eating disorders and their infants. *Journal of Child Psychology and Psychiatry*, 35, 733–748.

Stein, A., Murray, L., Cooper, P. and Fairburn, C.G. (1996). Infant growth in the context of maternal eating disorders and maternal depression: a comparative study. *Psychological Medicine*, 26, 569–574.

Steinglass, P., Bennett, L., Wolin, S. and Reiss, D. (1987). *The Alcoholic Family*. New York: Basic Books.

Sternberg, R.J. (1988). Triangulating love. In R.J. Sternberg and M.L. Barnes (eds), *The Psychology of Love* (pp. 119–138). New Haven: Yale University Press.

Stewart, A.J. and Salt, P. (1981). Life stress, life styles, depression, and illness. *Journal of Personality and Social Psychology*, 40, 1063–1069.

Stewart, D.E. (1992). Reproductive functions in eating disorders. *Annals of Medicine*, 24, 287–291.

Stewart, D.E. and Robinson, G.E. (1993). Eating disorders and reproduction. In D.E. Stewart and N.L. Stotland (eds), *Psychological Aspects of Women's Health Care: The Interface between Psychiatry and Obstetrics and Gynecology* (pp. 411–424). Washington, DC: American Psychiatric Press.

Stewart, D.E., Raskin, J., Garfinkel, P.E., MacDonald, O.L. and Robinson, G.E. (1987). Anorexia nervosa, bulimia and pregnancy. *American Journal of Obstetrics and Gynecology*, 157, 627–630.

Stewart, D.E., Robinson, G.E., Goldbloom, D.S. and Wright C. (1990). Infertility and eating disorders. *American Journal of Obstetrics and Gynecology*, 163, 1196–1199.

Strang, V.R. and Sullivan, P.L. (1985). Body image attitudes during pregnancy and the postpartum period. *Journal of Obstetrics and Gynecology*, 14, 332–337.

Stuart, R.B. (1969). Operant interpersonal treatment for marital discord. *Journal of Consulting and Clinical Psychology*, 33, 675–682.

Stuart, R.B. and Jacobson, B. (1987). *Weight, Sex, and Marriage: A Delicate Balance*. New York/London: W.W. Norton.

Straus, M.A. (1979). Measuring intrafamily conflict and violence: the Conflict Tactics Scale (CTS). *Journal of Marriage and the Family*, 41, 75–88.

Sullivan, P.F. (1996). Personal communication. Christchurch School of Medicine, Department of Psychology, Christchurch, New Zealand.

Szmuckler, G. (1985). The epidemiology of anorexia nervosa and bulimia. *Journal of Psychiatric Research*, 19, 143–153.

Thibaut, J.W. and Kelley, H.H. (1959). *The Social Psychology of Groups*. New York: John Wiley.

Thommen, M., Valach, L. and Kiencke, S. (1995). Prevalence of eating disorders in a Swiss family planning clinic. *Eating Disorders*, 3, 324–331.

Thompson, J.M., Whiffen, V. and Blain, M.D. (1995). Depressive symptoms, sex and perceptions of intimate relationships. *Journal of Social and Personal Relationships*, 12, 49–66.

Treasure, L., Wheeler, M., King, E.A., Gordon, P.A.L. and Russell, G.F.M. (1988). Weight gain and reproductive function: ultrasonographic and endocrine features in anorexia nervosa. *Journal of Clinical Endocrinology*, 29, 607–616.

Tuiten, A., Panhuysen, G., Everaerd, W., Koppeschaar, H., Krabbe, P. and Zelissen, P. (1993). The paradoxical nature of sexuality in anorexia nervosa. *Journal of Sex and Marital Therapy*, 19, 259–275.

Van Buren, D.J. and Williamson, D.A. (1988). Marital relationships and conflict resolution skills of bulimics. *International Journal of Eating Disorders*, 7, 735–741.

Vandenberg, S.G. (1972). Assortative mating, or who marries whom? *Behavior Genetics*, 2, 127–157.

Van den Broucke, S. and Vandereycken, W. (1988). Anorexia nervosa and bulimia in married patients: a review. *Comprehensive Psychiatry*, 29, 165–173.

——(1989a). Eating disorders in married patients: theory and therapy. In W. Vandereycken, E. Kog and J. Vanderlinden (eds), *The Family Approach to Eating Disorders: Assessment and Treatment of Anorexia Nervosa and Bulimia* (pp. 333–345). New York/London: PMA Publishing.

——(1989b). Eating disorders in married patients: a comparison with unmarried anorexics and an exploration of the marital relationship. In W. Vandereycken, E. Kog and J. Vanderlinden (eds), *The Family Approach to Eating Disorders: Assessment and Treatment of Anorexia Nervosa and Bulimia* (pp. 173–188). New York/London: PMA Publishing.

——(1989c). The marital relationship of patients with an eating disorder: a questionnaire study. *International Journal of Eating Disorders*, 8, 541–556.

Van den Broucke, S., Vandereycken, W. and Vertommen, H. (1994). Psychological distress in husbands of eating disorder patients. *American Journal of Orthopsychiatry*, 64, 270–279.

——(1995a). Marital intimacy: conceptualization and assessment. *Clinical Psychology Review*, 15, 217–233.

——(1995b). Marital intimacy in patients with an eating disorder: a controlled self-report study. *British Journal of Clinical Psychology*, 34, 67–78.

——(1995c). Marital communication in eating disorder patients: a controlled observational study. *International Journal of Eating Disorders*, 17, 1–21.

——(1995d). Conflict management in married eating disorder patients: a controlled observational study. *Journal of Social and Personal Relationships*, 12, 27–48.

Van den Broucke, S., Vertommen, H. and Vandereycken, W. (1995e). Construction and validation of a marital intimacy questionnaire. *Family Relations*, 44, 285–290.

Vandereycken, W. (1982). Uncommon eating/weight disorders related to amenorrhea, infertility and problematic pregnancy. In H.J. Prill and M. Stauber (eds), *Advances in Psychosomatic Obstetrics and Gynecology* (pp. 124–128). Berlin/New York: Springer-Verlag.

——(1983). Agoraphobia and marital relationship: theory, treatment, and research. *Clinical Psychology Review*, 3, 317–338.

——(1992). Validity and reliability of the Anorectic Behavior Observation Scale for parents. *Acta Psychiatrica Scandinavica*, 85, 163–166.

——(1993). The Eating Disorder Evaluation Scale. *Eating Disorders*, 1, 115–122.

——(1994). Parental rearing behaviour and eating disorders. In C. Perris, W.A.

Arrindell and M. Eisemann (eds), *Parenting and Psychopathology* (pp. 218–234). Chichester: John Wiley.

——(1995a). The families of patients with an eating disorder. In K.D. Brownell and C.G. Fairburn (eds), *Eating Disorders and Obesity: A Comprehensive Handbook* (pp. 219–223). New York/London: Guilford Press.

——(1995b). Family and marital therapy. In G.O. Gabbard (ed.), *Treatments of Psychiatric Disorders, Volume 2* (pp. 2163–2177). Washington, DC: American Psychiatric Press.

Vandereycken, W. and Meermann, R. (1987). *Anorexia Nervosa: A Clinician's Guide to Treatment.* Berlin/New York: Walter de Gruyter.

Vandereycken, W. and Van den Broucke, S. (1984). Anorexia nervosa in males: a comparative study of 107 cases reported in the literature (1970–1980). *Acta Psychiatrica Scandinavica,* 70, 447–454.

Vandereycken, W. and Vanderlinden, J. (1983). Denial of illness and the use of self-reporting measures in anorexia nervosa patients. *International Journal of Eating Disorders,* 2, 101–107.

Vandereycken, W., Kog, E. and Vanderlinden, J. (eds) (1989), *The Family Approach to Eating Disorders: Assessment and Treatment of Anorexia Nervosa and Bulimia.* New York/London: PMA Publishing.

Vanderlinden, J. and Vandereycken, W. (1997). *Trauma, Dissociation, and Impulse Dyscontrol in Eating Disorders.* New York: Brunner/Mazel.

Vanderlinden, J., Norré, J. and Vandereycken, W. (1992). *A Practical Guide to the Treatment of Bulimia Nervosa.* New York: Brunner/Mazel.

Van Vreckem, E. and Vandereycken, W. (1994). A sexual education programme for women with eating disorders. In B. Dolan and I. Gitzinger (eds), *Why Women? Gender Issues and Eating Disorders* (pp. 110–116). London: Athlone Press.

Vincent, J.P., Weis, R.L. and Birchler, G.R. (1975). A behavioral analysis of problem solving in distressed and nondistressed married and stranger dyads. *Behavior Therapy,* 6, 475–487.

Vogel, A.C. and Andersen, A.E. (1994). The treatment of bulimia nervosa: which regimen is most efficacious? An analysis of the evidence for physician assistants and primary care providers treating eating disorders. *Eating Disorders,* 2, 237–250.

Wampold, B. (1984). Tests of dominance in sequential categorical data. *Psychological Bulletin,* 96, 424–429.

Waring, E.M. (1983). Marriages of patients with psychosomatic illness. *General Hospital Psychiatry,* 5, 49–53.

——(1988). *Enhancing Marital Intimacy through Facilitating Cognitive Self-disclosure.* New York: Brunner/Mazel.

Waring, E.M. and Chelune, G.J. (1983). Marital intimacy and self-disclosure. *Journal of Clinical Psychology,* 39, 183–190.

Waring, E.M. and Patton, D. (1984). Marital intimacy and depression. *British Journal of Psychiatry,* 145, 641–644.

Waring, E.M. and Reddon, J.R. (1983). The measurement of intimacy in marriage: the Waring intimacy questionnaire. *Journal of Clinical Psychology,* 39, 53–57.

Waring, E.M., McElrath, D., Mitchell, P. and Derry, M.E. (1981). Intimacy and emotional illness in the general population. *Canadian Journal of Psychiatry*, 26, 167–172.

Watzlawick, P., Beavin, J.H. and Jackson, D.D. (1967). *Pragmatics of Human Communication*. New York: W.W. Norton.

Weiss, R.L. (1980). Strategic behavioral marital therapy: toward a model for assessment and intervention. In J.P. Vincent (ed.), *Advances in Family Intervention, Assessment, and Theory, Volume 1* (pp. 229–271). Greenwich, CT: JAI Press.

Weiss, R.L. and Perry, B.A. (1979). *Assessment and Treatment of Marital Dysfunction*. Eugene, OR: Oregon Marital Studies Program.

Weiss, R.L. and Summers, K. (1983). Marital interaction coding system –III. In E. Filsinger (ed.), *Marriage and Family Assessment* (pp. 85–115). Beverly Hills: Sage.

Weissman, M.M. (1987). Advances in psychiatric epidemiology: rates and risks for major depression. *American Journal of Public Health*, 7, 445–451.

Woodside, D.B. and Shekter-Wolfson, L.F. (1990). Parenting by patients with anorexia nervosa and bulimia nervosa. *International Journal of Eating Disorders*, 9, 303–309.

Woodside, D.B., Shekter-Wolfson, L.F., Brandes, J.S. and Lackstrom, J.B. (1993). *Eating Disorders and Marriage: The Couple in Focus*. New York: Brunner/Mazel.

Zerbe, K.J. (1992). Why eating-disordered patients resist sex therapy. *Journal of Sex and Marital Therapy*, 18, 55–64.

——(1995). The emerging self of the patient with an eating disorder: implications for treatment. *Eating Disorders*, 3, 197–215.

Name index

Subject index

Abbreviations used: AN – anorexia nervosa; BN – bulimia nervosa;
ED – eating disorders